EMIGRATING FROM CHINA
TO THE UNITED STATES

Second Edition

EMIGRATING FROM CHINA TO THE UNITED STATES

A Comparison of Different Social Experiences

By

YUSHI (BONI) LI, Ph.D.

Department of Sociology, Anthropology, and Philosophy
Northern Kentucky University
Highland Heights, Kentucky

CHARLES C THOMAS • PUBLISHER, LTD.
Springfield • Illinois • U.S.A.

Published and Distributed Throughout the World by

CHARLES C THOMAS • PUBLISHER, LTD.
2600 South First Street
Springfield, Illinois 62704

© 2017 by CHARLES C THOMAS • PUBLISHER, LTD.

ISBN 978-0-398-09167-5 (paper)
ISBN 978-0-398-98168-2 (ebook)

First Edition, 2010
Second Edition, 2017

With THOMAS BOOKS *careful attention is given to all details of manufacturing
and design. It is the Publisher's desire to present books that are satisfactory as to their
physical qualities and artistic possibilities and appropriate for their particular use.*
THOMAS BOOKS *will be true to those laws of quality that assure a good name
and good will.*

Printed in the United States of America
MM-C-1

Library of Congress Cataloging-in-Publication Data

Names: Li, Yushi (Boni), author.
Title: Emigrating from China to the United States : a comparison of
    different social experiences / by Yushi (Boni) Li, Ph.D., Department
    of Sociology, Anthropology and Philosophy, Northern Kentucky
    University, Highland Heights, Kentucky.
Description: Second Edition. | Springfield, IL: Charles C Thomas
    Publisher, Ltd., [2017] | Revised edition of the author's Emigrating
    from China to the United States, c2010. | Includes bibliographical
    references and index.
Identifiers: LCCN 2017009178 (print) | LCCN 2017019282 (ebook) |
    ISBN 9780398091682 (ebook) | ISBN 9780398091675 (pbk.)
Subjects: LCSH: United States--Social conditions--1980- | China--Social
    conditions--1976-2000. | United States--Emigration and immigration. |
    China--Emigration and immigration.
Classification: LCC HN59.2 (ebook) | LCC HN59.2 .L5 2017 (print) |
    DDC 306.0973--dc23
LC record available at https://lccn.loc.gov/2017009178

PREFACE

This is a supplementary textbook and its fundamental purpose is to facilitate students in associating the understandings in their personal daily lives with larger social forces. It will focus on my social experiences living in the United States and China and how those experiences have impacteded and changed my social values, attitudes, and behaviors. The main discussion of this book is how I was socialized in China and assimilated to and influenced by the American society.

As a professor of sociology, I feel that the real challenge of teaching, specifically my introduction to sociology courses, involves finding methods to make the discipline relevant to students' lives and aid their comprehendings of our society. However, this is not an easy task because students, like many other people, normally do not connect their own individual experiences with their learning process. A lot of sociological issues, which are considered to have close relationships with everyone in the society, however, are sometimes thought to be unrelated or uninteresting by some students. They may have different social opinions, they may not comprehend the whole scope of the situation, or they may feel that those social issues are irrelevant to their personal lives. Therefore, encouraging my students' involvement in studying sociological perspectives is always my primary goal. Throughout the years of teaching, I have found that students engage more when learning new views and ways to connect the world around them and their personal lives.

My cross-cultural international experiences have had profound connections to sociological concepts and theories. When teaching I have realized by pulling on my social life experiences, and using them in the classroom, my students become more engaged. My real life examples affect my students in such a way that the lessons behind the stories stay with them. When learning new concepts, a student who is able to connect those concepts with memorable examples can understand and retain the information more readily. It also makes the class more interesting because students are able to associate their personal lives with sociological theories and concepts. Furthermore, the connection between the class teaching and my experiences in Chinese and American societies helps students see a world beyond the borders of the United States. Sharing my experiences based on sociological concepts and theories lays a foundation on the subject of globalization and offers a comprehensive perspective by which to view other societies. These teaching methods will give students unique information about other societies besides America, which are considered essential for younger American generations living in the twenty-first century and beyond. These teaching methods also help students connect their personal life to the changing world.

In my classes when introducing students the connections between them and their society, I also use a famous American sociologist, C. Wright Mills' work, *Sociological Imagination* (1959). He proposes the proper connections between biography and history from sociological perspectives. Mills (1959) explains that sociology permits individuals to see how their personal experiences and the changes within society are interrelated. Mills (1959:2) also points out that "Neither the life of an individual nor the history of the society can be understood without understanding both." The basic meaning of this sentence is that for one to comprehend the complexities of their personal life, they have to understand the context of our society, culture, and world. Mills (1959:2) indicates that people are:

> Seldom aware of the intricate connection between the patterns of their own lives and the course of world history, ordinary people do not usually know what this connection means for the kinds of people they are becoming and for the kinds of history-making in which they might take part. They do not possess the quality of mind essential to grasp the interplay of man and society, of biography and history, of self and world. They cannot cope with their personal troubles in such ways as to control the structural transformations that usually lie behind them.

Therefore, we need to understand that time, society, and culture will always influence people's everyday lives. We also need to recognize that individuals' life experiences are reflections of social changes. These have taken place on the larger level in any society. Understanding sociological perspectives is crucial for all individuals when relating their lives with the changes in the world around them. They will gain in-depth knowledge about how the impacts of social changes affect their lives. A sociology professor's task involves assisting students in building a solid foundation for their future growth. The teaching materials comprised in this book will aid students to reach this objective.

The following book chapters will be included:

Chapter 1: Sociological Theories

This chapter draws upon my personal experiences with two different social systems: The socialist system, with its rapid economic development in China, and the capitalist system, with an advanced economy in the United States. The chapter will compare the sociological theories between these two systems. The major point of this chapter will be to concentrate on how different political and economic systems influence people's ways of thinking, their everyday life, and their social interaction with others.

Chapter 2: Research Methods

This chapter will incorporate some of my personal stories as a researcher and as a participant in research conducted in both America and China. These stories will help students recognize the importance of doing research projects, collecting data, and how to avoid common mistakes when doing a research project.

Chapter 3: Culture

This chapter will emphasize the comparison between the Chinese and American cultures. I will describe the cultural shock I had upon arrival to the United States and when traveling to other states within America. I will also discuss my efforts to "fit in" with the American culture. The emphasis in this chapter will be how I have assimilated into the American traditions as well as how immigrants' cultures have impacted American society.

Chapter 4: Socialization

This chapter will emphasize how new immigrants assimilate themselves into American society and how they have to recall or resocialize, once again, when going back to visit the country in which they were born and emigrated from. I will use personal experiences from my visits to China to describe the changes of values and norms in the Chinese society and how I had to readjust to unfamiliar situations in my home country. Socialization is not automatic; it is a lifelong process.

Chapter 5: Social Interaction

Learning a new culture involves interaction with other people. Most of the time, the interactions are different from society to society. This chapter will include why Chinese immigrants in America expect their children, while learning English as the language to survive, to also learn Chinese, and to keep their Chinese culture. This chapter will also include information on how Chinese immigrants interact with their children to teach them about American and Chinese cultures.

Chapter 6: Deviant Behavior

Some deviant or abnormal behaviors can be considered universal, but some directly connect with each culture in different societies. Some cultures may identify certain behaviors as deviant. However, some other societies may feel that these behaviors are acceptable. This chapter will concentrate on the relative and universal nature of deviance.

Chapter 7: Social Stratification

Since I have experienced living in both socialist and capitalist societies, I am in a good position to compare the two systems. In this chapter, the social stratification systems in China and the United States are discussed. China's current social classes—the rich and poor—will be illustrated. I will also discuss my experiences with the structure of an equal pay system in China in the past. The comparison between the two countries will also display how the political and social stratification systems work for capitalism in the American society.

Chapter 8: Racial Group

This chapter will delve into how I came to learn about American racial issues in China before I came to America. I will also discuss how I view myself as part of a minority group in America as well as describe my personal experiences and thoughts about racial issues after years of residing in America.

Chapter 9: Sex and Gender

Different cultures as well as individuals have various degrees of understanding regarding the behavior of sex and gender, especially on the roles of males and females in their family and within society. This chapter will mainly discuss how sex and gender are viewed similarly and differently in both American and Chinese cultures.

Chapter 10: Family

Family is the basic unit of society. This chapter will emphasize the different viewpoints on the importance of family according to Chinese and

American values. I will share the findings from a comparison study I did, which focused on the attitudes of American and Chinese college students toward family care and living arrangements for their elderly parents in the future. A comparison of different family's socialization processes and expectations on younger generations will also be discussed.

Chapter 11: Religion

I will discuss the differences between Chinese and American societies, regarding the religious beliefs as well as the influence of Confucius and Christianity. Also, this chapter will document my experiences in learning religious beliefs within American society as well as my understanding of religious beliefs.

Chapter 12: Population

This chapter will discuss how the one-child policy in the past and the new policy of one family with two children influence Chinese families. This chapter will discuss how these policies impacted the sex ratio and the increase in the number of elderly people in China, and how the traditional family care values have been abandoned because of the difficulties of offering care, as a result of having only one child in the family. I will also explain the different social values on abortion in American and Chinese societies as well as my personal viewpoint on the topic.

Chapter 13: Social Change and Urbanization

This chapter will discuss social changes in both American and Chinese societies. Examples include my state of confusion upon arriving in the United States and when I first returned to China in 1992. It will also include how social changes have impacted my life. This chapter will also discuss some key points of modernization, such as urbanization.

PROLOGUE

When I was a little girl, sometimes in order to burn my energy, my mother would give me a small shovel and told me that I could dig a hole at the backyard. "So, what will happen if I dug a very deep hole in the ground?" This was usually my question. My mother always answered, "You would reach a beautiful country on the other side. This country is called the United States of America." At that time, China and America were enemies. When I was young, I was always taught that the United States represented American imperialism. I never dreamed that in my life I would be able to step foot on this land. After the former President Nixon visited China in February of 1972, many Chinese people's curiosity about America flourished at an unprecedented rate. Soon after that, many American tourists began to come to China to visit the Great Wall, the Forbidden City, and other world famous tourist attractions.

Years later, as an English major in college, I did my co-op in the International Tourist Agency, Beijing Branch. One day, an American gentleman in a tour group, who fought in the Korean War, asked me to describe America from my perspective. I felt embarrassed because I really did not know much about the country. I remember I started my sentence with, "my mom told me that if I dug a hole . . ." and to my surprise, a lot of Americans in that tour group told me that they had heard the same story. I still remember when this group of American tourists left Beijing to go to Shanghai, many of them said, "Boni, please continue to dig as hard as you can. We will meet you on the other side of the hole." At that moment I started to dream that someday I would visit America.

Three years later my dream came true. I became a graduate student at Iowa State University. Of course, I did not arrive through a hole; I flew to the United States instead. When I was looking down from the airplane to enjoy this beautiful land, I was full of joy. The day I came to the United States was May 31, 1986. I can still remember the night before I left home; my mother told me that after I received my Master's degree, I should come back to China immediately. When I asked why, she said, "You are an unwed girl, and you do not want to get a Ph.D.; it will be difficult for you to find an ideal husband with the same level of education." I remember I raised my right hand and swore to her that I would be home after two years. Ultimately, I failed to keep my promise to my mother because I received a Ph.D., and I also decided to settle down in America permanently.

I have been living in the American society for about 30 years now and throughout this time I have experienced: culture shock, culture conflict, socialization, assimilation, and many learning processes. During my many years in this "melting pot," I have changed my status from a graduate student to a professor and from a young girl to a wife. Furthermore, I have changed from a Chinese citizen to an American citizen and from a person in a majority group in China to a minority member in America. Recalling the experiences I have had in this country has allowed me to accumulate many different perceptions that I would like to share with everyone, including my family, friends, students, and anyone who is interested in gaining a multifaceted perspective of my two homelands.

CONTENTS

EMIGRATING FROM CHINA TO THE UNITED STATES

Chapter 1

SOCIOLOGICAL THEORIES:
THE GUIDELINES FOR UNDERSTANDING
HUMAN SOCIETIES

**Key words: sociology; founding fathers of sociology:
August Comte, and Karl Marx; theory; theoretical perspectives; macro level; micro level; structural-functional perspective; social structure; social function; manifest
functions; latent functions; social dysfunctions; social
conflict perspective; symbolic interaction perspective;
dramaturgical analysis**

After finishing my four-year college degree, I was offered a position as a researcher at my alma mater. From this stemmed my role as a teacher in their English Department. At that time, most Chinese universities did not require a Master's degree or a Ph.D. in order to be qualified to teach college students. Regardless, I felt strongly that I needed more knowledge in order to fulfill my responsibilities as a teacher as well as a researcher. Thus, I began to study as an auditor in the Sociology Department at Beijing University, where I started my journey as a sociologist. I decided to study sociology because I wanted to learn sociological research methods for the purpose of enhancing my research ability. This was also the first time I learned the term **sociology**, which is defined as the logical study of human society and people's social activities, their interactions, and relationships with others.

The field of sociological studies started in the late nineteenth century introducing many brilliant minds that became known as the founding fathers of sociology. Widely regarded as the "father of sociology," **August Comte** (1798–1857) was the individual to coin the word "sociology" in the 1800s.

3

"Sociology" comes from the Latin and Greek words meaning companion and knowledge. August Comte was born and raised in southern France. He experienced rapid social changes in his time and became interested in studying society.

Karl Marx (1818–1883) is considered another important founding father of sociology. After I entered graduate school in the United States, I was surprised to learn that Karl Marx was categorized as a sociologist by the Western world. I recognized the reason that Karl Marx was not widely known as a sociologist in China was because three to four decades ago, sociology was not taught in many universities. In China, Marx is known as a communist, and is widely considered to be a fighter for the proletarians. Due to this fact, he is very familiar to many Chinese people. He is acknowledged as a philosopher, political economist, political theorist, and a revolutionary. He is also credited as the primary founding father of socialism and communism. During Chinese holidays in the past, such as International Labor Day and National Day, giant portraits of him and three other people, Engels, Lenin, and Stalin, would be displayed in Tiananmen Square, the center of Beijing, China. The portraits were no longer displayed there after 1989, because the Chinese government recognized that during holidays most countries in the world would only exhibit the portraits of their national heroes (see Fig. 1.1).

Sociology, known as the study of human interactions, emphasizes broad patterns and recurring events. When I say "broad patterns" I am talking about the study of social issues and problems that happen often at societal levels (a large scale). Sociology also studies small-scale patterns, such as groups with a few members, which will be discussed later in this chapter. One reason that sociologists study social issues is to help people see how their lives are connected to social changes in both their society and the world. This will open their mind to new ways of thinking and enables them to ask new questions about things people take for granted.

This can be illustrated by the following example. According to the statistics in 2014 (American Foundation of Suicide Prevention, 2014), the highest suicide rate was among those aged 85 years and older, which was 19.3 for every 100,000 people. Those between 45 and 64 years of age had the second highest suicide rate, which accounted for 19.2 out of every 100,000 people. Compared to the younger generations, especially adolescents and young adults aged 15–24, the suicide rate was 11.6 for every 100,000 people. The people who were 85 years of age maintained a much higher suicide rate. When comparing the suicides of older men with older women, we find that the number of suicides is increasing rapidly among the group of older men than it is with any other age groups (Nugent, 2012). These statistics indicate

Figure 1.1. Beijing is the capital city of China, and is the 23rd largest city in the world with over 8.6 million people. Built in 1415, Tiananmen, which translates to "Gate of Heavenly Peace" is the center of Beijing as well as China. There are many special events that take place here such as the National Day parade and other political parades. The center photo above the entrance is of Mao Zedong, who is one of the founders of the People's Republic of China. I was born and raised in Beijing, and have been to Tiananmen Square many times.

a general trend of suicide in contemporary American society, but it does not include a variety of individual cases or reasons.

The major factors in the suicides of those 65 and over include: depression, physical pain, multiple losses, downward social mobility, alcohol dependency issues, loss of a loved one, isolation, and/or loneliness, along with other possible reasons. However, learning about sociology will help people see different social situations and factors that affect society as a whole, rather than using a personal reason to explain a particular situation. It means that sociologists study many individuals as a group or on a larger scale. For instance, the older people feeling lonely can be categorized into two issues, social and individual. A social issue in this situation is the rapid technological advances; with this development older people are often left behind causing a strain on the social interaction between elderly people and the rest of society. An example of this is the rapid development of cell phones. When cell phones first came out they were only capable of making phone calls, now cell phones are basically a mini-computer. Today, much of the older generations struggle to learn how to use them causing a communication strain on elders and other people. Therefore, difficulties like technological change can become a social issue that affects the quality of life with the majority of the elderly population. However, not adapting to the new technological change can be seen as the specific seniors' problem as well. These problems not only affect the older generations as a group, but they are also the concerns that influence society as a whole.

Sociologists seek to develop new questions and to explore the unfamiliarity in their effort to show that things are not always what they seem. There are many situations that we take for granted in our everyday life, but may truly represent serious social issues. For instance, people haphazardly say "policemen" or "congressmen," completely disregarding the possibility of "policewomen" and "congresswomen." This happens because the United States is a patriarchal society, which means that it is male-dominated. Within the American political system, most of the Senators and House Representatives are male.

This raises the question: Why are there more men than women in American political power? To answer this question, certain issues need to be addressed, such as the late arrival of women's voting rights and the social values and expectations placed on women in American society. A few years ago while driving through my neighborhood and I saw an orange-colored sign that said "men working" signaling I was going to need to take a detour to get to work. As soon as I walked into class I told my students what I had seen on the way, which sparked the following discussion.

"It is unbelievable that the sign there said 'men working', but I saw female workers there too. Could anyone explain this situation to me?" I asked.

"The word 'men' is shorter than the word 'women'. The sign is very small and you can only put a few letters there," a male student tried to explain.

"You might be right, but I do not think that your answer is 100 percent correct. Are there any other answers?" I asked.

"Why should they put females on the sign? That is not correct either," another student said.

"It should say something like 'team working'," I tried to suggest.

"No, look at the work load between a male and a female. It should say 'men working'," another male student said.

"What do you mean by the term 'work load'?" a female student asked.

"Actually, I meant that more men are working," the previous male student said.

"What do you mean 'men are working'? I saw females working there too," I said.

"Yes, females are working too, but you can tell men do the *real* work. They are the ones repairing the road. The females are working, too, but all they do is turn the stop and slow signs around. So, those females are saying men are working on the road," he explained further more.

"Turning the stop and slow signs is a job, too. If the signs were not turned, there would be a traffic jam," I said, disagreeing with this male student.

"Yes, I know, but you should agree that men are working . . .," the student said.

I really disagreed with his ideas, and then I stopped him and said. "You should also see that women are working, too. They just have different responsibilities within this team."

The social outlooks on females have been altered with rapid social change, but sometimes we still hear the above opinion: males are doing the job and females are not doing as much; women just have the role of an assistant. The previous situation is only a small indicator of the larger social issue and most people do not question it at all. However, from the viewpoint of sociologists, these small indicators cannot be ignored because they echo a serious social issue. This social issue reflects the differences between current social expectations of males and females. The study of sociology will help people become more alert to many social issues, which are seldom noticed in our everyday life.

Studying sociology will help people see how their personal life experiences are intertwined with social changes in their society (Mills, 1959). Here is an example from CNN Money (Gillespie, 2015) stating that on August 21 (Friday), 2015, Dow (The Dow Jones Industrial Average–DJIA) fell 531 points. The Dow is a price-weighted average of 30 noteworthy stocks, which are traded on the New York Stock Exchange as well as Nasdaq. The Dow was established by Charles Dow in 1896. Nasdaq was invented by the National Association of Securities Dealers (NASD) in 1971. Nasdaq exchange includes many world famous giant companies, such as Microsoft, Amazon, Apple, and Google.

On August 24 (the following Monday), the stock market dropped again (Long 2015) in the first few minutes of trading. That's more than 16 percent lower than its all-time high set in May 2015, which put it into a market correction but not a bear market yet. A bear market means it is a general decline in prices and encouragement of selling in the stock market. So the falling of the market had influenced many people's investments. Therefore, an individual's personal life has a close connection with the things going on in society.

Another example that shows this connection is the fact that many college students' grandparents did not need a college diploma to find a decent job. Today, if a young person wants to have a job similar to what their grandparents had, they need to have at least some type of college degree, such as from a technical school or university. This is because of rapid social development that has changed the job requirements for many positions; meaning individuals are to obtain higher education to meet the new job qualifications.

An individual person reasoning for attending college has also changed because of the rapid social development. In the late 1980s, a few of my female students gave me their reasons for coming to college, one of which was, "My mother said that if I have to divorce in the future, my college diploma will guarantee that I can support myself." Today, many of my female students tell me that their parents never discuss whether they need to go to college or not after high school, one of my students said, "I knew that their expectation was for me to go college."

"Do you think that they wanted you to go to college so that you could support yourself, if you have to divorce in the future?" I was curious as to why their parents expected them to go to college.

"I am sure there is much more behind their desire for me to attend college than the simple reason of divorce." I received almost the same answers from most of my female students.

From their answers, we can see that women today think of themselves as more independent than how most women saw themselves in the late 1980s. They also view their education in light of their own career and benefits, rather than as a backup for their marriage. During the last thirty years there have been many great social changes that have taken place. These changes include advanced technological development, emphasis on the importance of education, and many other factors, such as women's movements, which increased independence and self-esteem among women. All of these changes have significantly influenced individuals and caused them to put more thought into their daily lives than before. With these developments, many individuals, including females, decided that changes were needed in their lives. For instance, many young women deciding to go to college results in changes that affect society as a whole. These social changes consist of more women in the work field and more dual income families. Clearly, society not only impacts individuals, but individuals' actions also generate social changes. Therefore, we cannot only think about our own lives without connecting to what is happening in the society, and vice versa.

To study sociology, we need to initially understand a few terms. The first term is **theory** and is defined as a statement describing the relationships among different concepts, and is confirmed modified or rejected through research methods, which will be discussed in the next chapter. The second term is **theoretical perspectives** and is defined as a basic rationalization of society and what should be emphasized and used to explain a certain social phenomenon. Due to the different viewpoints of the founding fathers of sociology, people have many different ways to explain the same social phenomenon. Years ago my husband and I, along with two other graduate students that had just arrived from China, went to a grocery store. On the way home, we stopped at a major intersection. A man stood there with a big poster that said, "I am willing to work for food."

"My God, I thought America was a rich country. Why do some people still have no food to eat?" one student inquired. He could not believe that someone was willing to work just to eat food.

"This is not fair. I think everybody should have food to eat," the other student said.

"They are homeless people. You will see more of them in downtown areas," my husband told them.

These two graduate students' statement, "This is not fair" represented the basic viewpoint of a society, which is based on Karl Marx's fundamental ideology of socialist and communist societies. That is, everyone should have food to eat, shelter to live in, and a job to be able to support him or herself. China was founded as a socialist society in 1949, and many Chinese have grown up with the equal-pay system until the 1990s. The equal-pay system means that everyone makes a little bit of money, and each person at working age has a job to support themselves and their family.

Due to the large population and rapid social change in the 1990s many Chinese lost or could not find jobs. This is due to many social factors, such as the Chinese government ending assignment of jobs to high school and college graduates, which resulted in competition for better paying jobs. Also, many government businesses went bankrupt. Today, there are still large numbers of Chinese people who are unemployed, which clearly indicates that the equal-pay system is ineffective. The two graduate students came to the United States in 1989 while China still had an equal pay system. Obviously, their ideas about homeless people were different from Americans. Many of whom feel that homelessness is just another one of America's social issues. Therefore, there are more than one theoretical perspective that can be used to explain even the same social issue, as just discussed with homelessness.

In any introductory-level sociology course, there are three major theories that are used: structural-functional perspective, conflict perspective, and symbolic interaction perspective. These theoretical perspectives of viewing human society can come from both macro and micro levels. The **macro**

level is defined as an analysis of society on large-scale societal levels. The **micro level** is an analysis of society from small-scale social patterns. Most people studying sociology easily understand macro level analysis of society, but micro-level also needs to be emphasized because without individuals' continuous interactions, there would be no social activities. By viewing groups as a whole consisting of individual units, people can further analyze different levels of social behavior.

The first major theory is the **structural-functional perspective** and it is studied at the macro level. In this theory, society is viewed as a system of many different parts that work together to generate stability. An example of this is the three branches of government and the practice of checks and balances to keep the government power equal. Each branch checks on each other and balances out the power to keep one person or group of people from becoming too powerful. The president may veto a law passed by congress but congress can override the veto with a two-thirds vote of both houses. I always have a difficult time explaining this theory because my students do not seem to understand words like system, subsystem, or function as a whole. This theory and these concepts are actually not very difficult to understand. An example would be that a cell phone includes different parts. We can call these parts the fragments/subsystems of the entire cellphone system, such as the hardware, software, and a battery. They are all different and have to work together to create a functioning cell phone which can make a call, send a text message, take a picture, or browse online. If one of these parts stops working, such as the battery, then the whole cellphone will not work.

This is similar to our social systems, which include education, economic, and political systems. They are supposed to work together to move society forward. The major limitation of the structural-functional theory is that changes are not emphasized. As for the cellphone, what will happen if the battery is defective, or if the software has a bug? By the same token, what if, due to a recession, the economic system does not work together with the education system? What will happen if a college student cannot find a job and cannot use the knowledge gained from his or her college experience in their careers? Will they agree that the economic system and education system work together to generate stability in the society?

Many various functional systems that students know of today are those that govern their own nation in America. I learned about American history and political systems when I was a college student in China. Like many other students, I studied hard, learned what I needed to for the course, and then proceeded to forget most of what I had learned. After I settled in the United States, I read a book to prepare for the examination I had to take to obtain my citizenship. While reading this book, I started to better understand the

American political system and its three different political branches: legislative, judicial, and executive. Together with other systems, including the education system and economic system, they are considered to be America's **social structure**, which is defined as the framework of a social system. The definition for **social function** is the result of the usage of the social system. An example of these two terms in action is the education system.

The education system is a part of the social structure, and the function of it is to provide people with opportunities to learn. However, American and Chinese education systems are different in many ways including a person's opportunity to further their education. Years ago, when I wanted to go to graduate school in China, I first had to get permission from my employer and also a letter of introduction to be able to take my entrance exams. Since there were many people who wanted to go to graduate school, it was competitive. Even if I passed the entrance exams, I still needed to pass the oral exam in order to be on the final list. Today, the Chinese education system has changed dramatically, but the written and oral exams still remain, due to the competitiveness of the admission process.

In contrast, if a person wants to apply to graduate school in America, there is no entrance exam other than the Graduate Record Examination (GRE). Foreign applicants need to take the Test of English as a Foreign Language (TOEFL) as well. The TOEFL is a test designed to assess a foreign student's ability to speak, understand, and write using English. Basically, admission of a student to graduate school will depend on the individual's qualifications along with their research interests and that individual's potential career development.

China and America both have education systems as a part of their social system. The functions of education in these two societies are the same, which is to offer learning opportunities for people in order to add a more qualified labor force to the economic system. However, the opportunities within the education system are different for these two societies, which are shown by the differences in the graduate schools' admission procedures and rules. Due to China's large population, admittance into universities is still limited because it is more competitive. This results in China not being able to fully maximize the benefits of their education system. In contrast, America gives everyone the opportunity to go to graduate school, as long as a person can meet the admission requirements, such as an appropriate undergraduate grade point average (GPA), a qualified GRE score, and positive recommendation letters. This is one of the reasons the American education system attracts students from all over the world.

When discussing social functions, there are three different types: manifest functions, latent functions, and social dysfunctions (Merton, 1967). The concept of **manifest functions** (official functions) is defined as the consequences that are intended for people to carry out within the society. **Latent functions** are the consequences that are not planned or intended by people in the society. **Social dysfunctions** are the negative consequences that affect society as a whole. An example of these concepts would be owning a car. The manifest function of having a car is to get from place to place including work, school, and home. The latent function is a person's car representing that person's social status, if you were to see someone driving a Lexus you would assume they have a high social status but if you see someone driving a 1968 Station Wagon you would assume they have a low to middle class social status. The dysfunction would be the air pollution caused by the motor vehicle emissions (see Fig. 1.2).

Having a television at home can also demonstrate social functions. Television provides us with entertainment, news, and information. For example,

Figure 1.2. Due to limited parking space in Beijing, limousines are rarely seen on the street. Limousines in China, like other expensive imported cars, such as Porsche, represent the car owner's social and economic status.

on September 11, 2001, terrorists hijacked passenger aircrafts and carried out suicide attacks against places, such as the World Trade Center in New York and the Pentagon in Washington, DC. The attacks not only killed all the passengers on the hijacked aircrafts, but also killed nearly 3,000 other people. People, including myself, received information from TV, Internet, newspapers, and also other communication channels. At that time TV, the popular mass media outlet, played an important role in relaying news to a large audience.

A possible social dysfunction of television, or Internet, is that people, especially children, may learn violent or deviant behavior. For instance, while in graduate school, I did not watch a lot of TV because I did not have time. Now, because I have more time to watch TV, I have become familiar with many English "dirty words" by watching movies. Similar to my experience, media influences many individual's values, lifestyles, and behavior. A large proponent of this influence comes from commercials. As previously discussed, Karl Marx was a very familiar name to me while I was in China. Not only did I know his ideology, but also how he looked due to the prevalence of his photos. Now I also know that he is the founding father of social conflict theory. This theory came about during a time when there was major conflict between the capitalist class and the working class over limited social resources. The **social conflict perspective** focuses on the unequal relationships between social groups that cause tension or conflict between the groups and eventually leads to a social change. The example I used most often in classes was Martin Luther King, Jr. and the Civil Rights Movement. Before Martin Luther King, Jr. stood up and asked for civil rights, the dominant values dictated that one racial group was better than all other racial groups.

Because of their skin color, some people were forced to have separate facilities, such as hospital waiting rooms, restrooms, and school buses. This type of behavior was discrimination, and it was the unequal treatment of people based on their different racial group and resulted in social conflict. As a result, the Civil Rights Movement was born causing social changes to be gradually put into place. Today, people are no longer required to use separate school buses, hospital waiting rooms, or restrooms based on the color of skin. The Civil Rights Movement is a good application of Marx's conflict theory and clearly shows that the racial inequality during that time resulted in social conflict, which motivated people to bring about social change.

As a person coming from a socialist country, I grew up in a so-called "equal" environment, especially with the equal pay system. For this reason, we had a low standard of living. Even though the quality of life was poor, we knew we had a guaranteed job with a limited income every month. People also knew that they would have a pension after their retirement, even though not enough money was assured. The Chinese government *guaranteed* each college student a job after graduation (after the mid-1990s, all the college graduates had to apply for a job themselves because the Chinese government no longer provided a job for them). I had never thought about becoming rich because there was no possibility for any Chinese person to make any changes to their income.

However, upon my first week arriving in the United States, I noticed many differences, especially about the quality of life in America and China. My first night I stayed in my professor's house because of the late hour of my arrival. In the early morning the singing birds woke me up. Looking outside in front of each house, I saw beautiful flowers, green bushes, trees, and grass. I was so amazed. When standing on the deck at my professor's house and looking at the colorful woods, birds, and squirrels, I had never imagined that people could have such a comfortable life. I strongly realized the immensity of differences between America and China.

The major factor that caused social conflict within Marx's two social classes (the capitalist class and the working class) was the limited access to social resources. The conflict and tension resulted from the unequal treatment of the working class and exploitation of the poor by the capitalist class. In modern American society, the majority of people are considered middle class, which did not exist when Karl Marx studied social classes. Therefore, the social conflict in Karl Marx's time and our time is different. However, conflict still exists, including competitions, disagreements, and contradictory social interests.

One of the limitations of this theory is that because we have a large middle class in today's society; many people, like myself, disagree that we are exploited, which means to derive benefits from the people who work for low pay. I have to work for food and shelter for myself. However, I cannot say I am exploited because others are not profiting from my work and becoming richer based upon my efforts. Due to the fact that I grew up in China, and was strongly influenced by Karl Marx, I am often confused about my feelings regarding the idea of exploitation. I think that because I have lived in the United States for so long, I have gradually assimilated America's values into my value system and therefore do not feel exploited. As I mentioned earlier, today there is a large middle class, which was not present in Karl Marx's time. Due to this, the concern of exploitation is not as great as it was during the time that Marx's theory was put forth.

The third theory is the only one that is studied at the micro level. The **symbolic interaction perspective** addresses the view of society stemming from individuals' everyday interactions with other people in various environments. In sociology, even at the micro level, at least two or more people are considered a group, and their interactions are studied. This includes how they interact with different people in different settings. For instance, a student told me that one day he was preparing to leave his house. It was raining outside and his mother said, "You need to drive carefully."

"Yes, I will," he answered.

He rushed to his car, which was in the driveway. His younger brother followed him into the rain.

"You need to drive carefully," the brother pointed at his face.

"Shut up. Go back to the house," my student said loudly. At ten o'clock in the evening, when he prepared to leave work and go home, his boss looked outside and said, "It is still raining. You drive carefully."

"Thanks. You do the same," my student replied.

These are three different settings. When his mother said that he should drive carefully, he took the advice and made sure that he did. When his boss said that he should drive carefully, he thanked his boss as well as shared the sentiment with him/her. When his younger brother told him to drive carefully, my student told him to shut up. Of course, he was very rude, but at the same time he showed his authority over his brother, and he also demonstrated that he knew more than him. Therefore, according to different settings, people will behave and interact differently. They may even think that certain behavior is appropriate; depending on the person they are interacting with as well as different environments.

When I was little, my mother taught me about appropriate behavior in certain types of situations. I often asked why things were the way they were. For instance, I was allowed to get drinking water from a kettle at home by myself, as long as it was on the breakfast table. However, I was reprimanded for getting drinking water that had not been boiled. This is because in China, even today, people cannot drink the tap water for sanitation reasons. In my day care center, there were many iron kettles that were not on the tables, which meant it was not boiled water. My teacher always told us to make sure what we drank was from a kettle with boiled water. Unfortunately, one day at day care, I drank water that was not boiled while feeling thirsty. I was punished not only by the teacher, but also by my mother. Gradually, I learned to behave according to the different situations and settings that I found myself in.

The symbolic interaction perspective studies how people go about their daily lives, and how they interact with each other. It also studies how people comprehend the meaning of interaction and how people are influenced by each other during their social contacts. I used to have a projection TV, until it broke one day, and I had a repairperson come and fix it. I spent about $500. The repairperson told me that it would be costly to buy an LCD (liquid-crystal display) TV, and if it were to ever break, it would be expensive to get it repaired.

After two years in 2007, my projection TV broke again and I did not want to spend another $500 or more to repair it. So I talked to a salesperson in an electronics store. He gave me a different perspective on LCD televisions saying that it is new technology and the price is now low enough for purchasing and repairing. After talking to the salesperson, my ideas about LCD have completely changed. I decided to buy a LCD TV. I would not have purchased it had it not been for the influence and interaction with that salesperson. Therefore, this example demonstrates how symbolic interaction theory focuses on how people interact with each other and how the interaction influences people's thinking and change their attitudes and behavior.

As illustrated earlier, people behave differently based on different situations. A sociologist named Erving Goffman (1922–1982), conducted a study called **dramaturgical analysis** (Goffman, 1959). He focused on how people change their behavior based on the situation they are in and that they try to exhibit certain behaviors to make a positive impression. A good example is to look at behavior when people have an interview after submitting a resume for a job. After I received my Ph.D., my dream was to find a job as a professor. I was called for an interview by the university I am working for now. I was extremely nervous because before my graduation I was unsuccessful in an interview. I applied for a few different jobs and one of them was a matchmaker position. At that time, I was looking for a topic for my Ph.D. dissertation. I thought that it would be interesting to study American attitudes in choosing a boyfriend or girlfriend. I also wanted to determine any differences between Americans and Chinese on this particular issue.

After submitting my application, I called repeatedly for ten days because I was sure that I was qualified for the job with a Master's degree in sociology. After finally talking to the person who was hiring by telephone, she said that she felt I could not be taken into consideration for the position. I asked why and she said that for this particular job, the company needed to hire a person with an American cultural background. She also said that with my ABD (all but dissertation), I was overqualified for the role as a matchmaker.

After I failed with the matchmaker job, I received a phone call for my upcoming interview to become a professor. Internet service was not available in 1994, so I went to the bookstore to find a few books on how to prepare for an interview. I not only read about the many possible questions that I might be asked, but I sought advice on the best professional attire to wear for the interview.

As part of the interview process, I was asked to prepare a short lecture for a class. I had a few options such as discussing my research, or giving a normal lecture. I finally chose to discuss my recent international comparison study on the younger generations' attitude with regard to caring for their parents in the future. The reason I chose this topic was because I could engage my students in my discussion during the lecture. It also allowed them the chance to implement hands-on learning and introduce them to the Chinese culture, which I believed would impress them. The interview was successful and a week later I received a phone call from my department chair asking me if I was still interested in the job. At that point, according to Goffman's dramaturgical analysis, I was fulfilling my role at that stage of my life successfully.

Symbolic interaction perspective explores people's motivations, their goals, and their observations of the world. According to this theory, the meaning we give to things is the result of social interaction. For instance, when I asked my students the meaning of a yellow traffic light, most of them answered with a laugh, "faster!"

"Faster? You all know that from the driver's manual, it says that you need to slow down and prepare to stop," I replied.

"Yes, we know it does, but it depends on the situation. If I can drive faster to pass, why shouldn't I?"

They all know the meaning of the yellow traffic light. They all go through an internal process of interpretation to attach a meaning to the situation. They then take action according to the meaning they give to the environment. As symbolic interaction theory has a micro-level orientation, focusing on how people go about their everyday life, studying such a small group of people with very culturally bound interactions can have many limitations.

One example of the limitations comes to mind. When counting in Chinese, I can use one hand with different combinations of my five fingers to tell people the numbers from one to ten. In America, people use two hands to count from one to ten. Since I have lived in America for years, I seldom use Chinese language or gestures when I talk to people anymore. However, I do occasionally slip into old habits and use Chinese symbols instead of American numbers.

One day, I went to a grocery store and planned to buy some small fish. The fish I wanted was difficult to count in pounds. When the shop assistant asked me how many fish I wanted, I showed him the number by using my thumb and first finger, which is the number eight in Chinese, but in America, the meaning is a gun.

"I want eight," I said.

At the same time, I wanted to make sure they were fresh, so I stooped down. I suddenly heard the shopkeeper say, "What do you want to do?"

I raised my head and found myself using my fingers but not pointed at him directly.

He raised his two hands up and asked again, "What do you want to do?"

He laughed loudly when he saw me frozen there, still using my two fingers.

"Oh my God," I said to myself, while at the same time I quickly moved back my hand and put my fingers into a fist, and said, "I meant that I would like to have eight fish. The thumb and the first finger in my country, by the way I come from China, means eight. I did not mean to make a gesture like a gun. You can see that I did not pointed at you, which makes the different gestures between the number eight and a gun." I did not know how to explain it to him. I started to feel very embarrassed.

"I did not know what you meant, but I do know that it must have something to do with numbers. Do not worry. I just wanted to make a joke because I did not understand it," he answered.

People with different cultures from all over the world have different methods of expression. Their gestures and ways of thinking are different. Sometimes this can create confusion.

Another example of symbolic interaction would be, when answering a question such as, "Are you not an engineer?"

"No, I am not," is an American way to answer the question. The word "no" is telling the fact that the person is not an engineer.

"Yes, I am not," is a Chinese way to reply. The first part of the answer "yes" means an agreement with the person who asked question and the second part of the sentence is the answer to the question.

In order to avoid such confusion, many Chinese people in America now try to express themselves by saying, "You are right. I am not an engineer."

There are many different sociological theories to explain human society and social interaction and activities, which are divided into classical and contemporary theories. There will be more theories developed due to continuing social change. However, for an introductory sociology student, structural-functional, social conflict, and symbolic interaction theories are normally introduced. The understanding of these theories will help people use these different perspectives to have a basic overview of human society. Either they can interpret the society as different parts that work together to produce stability (Structural-functional theory), or consider that the society has conflict among social classes, power, and other factors because of social inequality and change (Social conflict theory). We may also think of society as continuing social interactions among people and view how people relate with, and among each other (Symbolic interaction theory). These perspectives/theories will guide people's interpretation of human society and also direct their understanding of many social issues and problems.

Chapter 2

RESEARCH METHODS

Key words: variable; correlation; independent variable; dependent variable; hypothesis; four research methods: experiment, survey, participant observation, and secondary analysis; sample; population; value free

Many of us have experienced answering a telephone survey, a face-to-face interview, or a mail questionnaire, as well as an online questionnaire covering a variety of social topics. The purpose of social research done by sociologists and other researchers is to seek people's opinions and attitudes toward certain social issues or problems. This may include questions pertaining to their levels of satisfaction with a product, the quality of some services, or their attitude toward certain public opinions. All of these social research projects are led by sociological theories in order to determine a person's reaction regarding a social issue. For instance, Americans' attitudes towards the opinion of gun control. Researchers will also provide suggestions to improve a certain situation based on the results they have found through their research. When a researcher defines or starts a research project, a questionnaire that includes a range of questions will be created. In sociological terms, each question listed in the questionnaire is called a variable. A **variable** is defined as any concept that is valued differently in different situations.

When I was in graduate school I had a Chinese friend named David, who was also a graduate student. One day, David worked in his department laboratory until midnight. He was so tired that he almost fell asleep while driving back home. A police officer stopped him because he was driving erratically. The first thing the police officer asked David was, "Sir, have you been drinking?"

"No, sir, I have not been drinking," David replied truthfully. The police officer started to ask him to count numbers and walk in a straight line. Afterwards, the police officer decided that David was not drunk. In this situation, drinking was the most important question (variable) that the police officer asked the driver. In other circumstances, drinking as a variable may be included but may not be the only or the first question to ask. In another case, if an eighty-five-year-old lady had a heart attack at midnight, her family would call an ambulance and send her immediately to the hospital for emergency treatment. The first few questions that a doctor would ask the elderly lady or the family members could include: "what are the symptoms? is there any history of heart problems? do you drink or smoke?" Drinking, as a variable, in this case, is not valued the same as in the first example. In the first case, the variable of drinking had a greater value compared to the second case. In the first case, the variable of drinking was directly associated with the way David drove and the reason the police officer stopped him. In the second case, the variable does not connect closely to the emergency of the elderly woman's heart problem, even though it is known that lifestyle is correlated with health problems.

When variables are related, they are considered to have correlations. **Correlation** is defined as the variables that are associated with each other and show meaningful relationships. A correlation can be illustrated by the relationship of eating junk food and gaining weight, which are highly associated. Usually, for most people, their weight is dependent on whether or not they eat a lot of junk food. In another case, driving a long distance will cause the use of more gas. In this case, the number of gallons of gas used will correlate to how many miles a person will drive.

In social science, when studying real life subjects, there will likely be relationships between a few variables, instead of just one-on-one relationships. For instance, the variable of stress those family members experienced as a result of caring for a patient who suffers with Alzheimer's disease, can be attributed to many factors. These factors include witnessing the deterioration of a loved one, the repeated questions by their patient, lack of time for other social activities, or conflicts with their jobs and family members.

The correlations among variables are divided into independent variables and dependent variables. An **independent variable** is defined as the variable that causes any changes. A **dependent variable** is the variable that is affected and then changed. In the previous examples, "junk food" is the independent variable, which is the cause for the "weight gain." In the second case, "the amount of gas used" is the dependent variable and the "miles that can be driven" is the independent variable, because how much gas is left in the tank will depend on how many miles a person drives. Describing the relationships between independent and dependent variables is the definition of **hypothesis**.

A statement, "the more I read, the more knowledge I will gain" is a hypothesis. In this case, "the more I read" is the independent variable, which will influence the dependent variable, "the more knowledge I will gain." Hypotheses are critical when doing a research project. It directs researchers to define the relationship between dependent and independent variables, which connects to the solution of a research topic. In our everyday life, it is easy to talk about a relationship between an independent variable and a dependent variable because they are easily identified. However, when doing a social research project, we must observe many social aspects and study how these social factors impact each other. The following is an example.

Since the early 1990s, China experienced rapid social change and economic development. With the addition of new highways, skyscrapers, offices, and residential buildings, many cities have grown and changed dramatically. The evidence shows that the standard of living in China has also greatly improved, which has significantly affected Chinese people's way of life. I have visited China many times in the past. Every time I visit I am amazed with the rapid development and changes that have happened since I was last there. These changes, especially the rapid economic development, which is represented by the Gross Domestic Product (GDP) and improved domestic goods for daily necessities, could be the independent variables. They have significantly influenced the dependent variables: the life styles and the standard of living for Chinese people. However, the attributes of the Chinese people's standard of living could also be an independent variable, which accelerates and impacts further economic advancement and social development, such as language and cultural shifts in China. Now there are more new Chinese words and phrases that I have to learn.

In 2006, I visited China for the fourth time after living in the United States for many years. One day I went out with my brother and my niece. While my brother was sitting in the passenger's seat and talking to the taxi driver, I could not understand what they were saying, even after I moved close to the front seat. The problem was that I could not understand the meaning of their discussion. This was due to rapid social change, which brought about many new terms into people's daily life. An example of this is when I left China, computers were not popular. So I am not familiar with computer terms in Chinese language. Therefore, the entire time I was listening to the conversation between my brother and the taxi driver. I kept asking, "I beg your pardon?" My brother would try to explain the meaning to me. My niece kept saying, "You do not know that word, do you?" and she started to laugh loudly, which made me feel embarrassed.

Later, as we came to a stop at the traffic light, the taxi driver turned to me and asked, "You can speak very fluent Chinese but do not understand our conversation. Where are you from?"

"My aunt comes from a rural area, far away from here. That is why she could not understand you," my niece answered the driver's question for me. She knew that I did not want to tell any strangers that I was visiting from a foreign country because at that time I would be charged more for the taxi ride (this is no longer true today in China).

"Oh I see." The driver suddenly understood why I kept asking questions.

When the driver stopped again at another traffic light, he turned back to me and asked kindly, "Do you know how to read and write?"

"What?" I heard exactly what he said, but could not believe he had asked me that.

"I mean; can you write your name?" The driver had obviously changed his expectations on me by only asking me if I could write my name.

"Of course, I can write my name," I answered uncomfortably. Since he asked me if I knew how to write my name, I had to give a "yes" or "no" answer to his question. I had received a Ph.D. and it was ridiculous to answer his question. Knowing that my answer could further mislead him, I felt hesitant to explain my years of education, my background, and my years of living in another country.

However, I decided to make it clearer to him by saying, "I can read Chinese, but I do not write it very often."

The answer I gave to the taxi driver was true at that time. I frequently read online from many Chinese websites, but I did not write in Chinese often. I sometimes even forgot how to write certain words in Chinese due to lack of practice. After the embarrassing experience I had with the taxi driver, I started to pay more attention to the Chinese language on the Internet. In recent years, due to the language options by Microsoft, I have been able to write Chinese by using my computer or iPad/iPhone. Since I have been back to China many times, I feel I have learned many new terms from other Chinese people. I feel this is a way for me to continue to connect with China and the Chinese culture. I also feel that with current economic development in China, the country has experienced rapid social changes not only on the creation of many new terms but also on different impacts of the traditional Chinese culture. In the past, most Chinese would think they should pay in full for something they buy, meaning that they should not buy anything if they do not have the money. Now many people have already accepted a new idea, which is, to borrow money from banks in order to purchase a house/apartment and pay back mortgage monthly. Borrowing a loan to purchase a product has greatly impacted Chinese traditions (see Fig. 2.1).

Figure 2.1. China has the largest population in the world. Because of housing issues, many new residential homes were built in recent years. Between the new residential buildings in this photo, you can see the remaining older buildings, which will be under construction soon.

My personal experience can be used to explain the relationship between independent and dependent variables. The rapid social development in China is the independent variable, which is the catalyst for me to make changes. The dependent variable is that I started to learn new terms and concepts. This really helps me stay connected to Chinese values and traditions. Therefore, my hypothesis could be stated as, "The more social change and development China has experienced, the more terms and concepts will be created, either developed by the Chinese or adopted from other cultures." My hypothesis could also be stated as, "The more rapid social development is in China, the more people will have to learn or adopt new terms or concepts." This hypothesis describes the relationship between social change and people's action to learn or to adopt new concepts, meaning that with rapid economic development people have to learn new knowledge to fit into society. The rapid growth and development is an independent variable, and the learning of new concepts is the dependent variable. The hypothesis also indi-

Figure 2.2. These are office buildings. Beijing is now an internationally famous metro-politan city. American companies in the past two decades or so have established many branch offices in Beijing and other cities within China. Globalization has greatly impact-ed the Chinese people's social values and way of life.

cates that researchers are interested in how the social issues at the societal level impact individuals' lives (see Fig. 2.2).

Traditionally there are four research methods when collecting data for the study of sociology: experiment, survey, participant observation, and sec-ondary resources. Due to technological advancement, now we also have online surveys and email questionnaires. The benefit of online surveys or email questionnaires is that they can reach more people. However, some people argue that online surveys can only be reached by those people who read that particular website or by those who are interested in a particular issue. It is also important to note that, if people do not know how to use a computer, do not have one, or do not read this particular website, they would be completely excluded from the online survey. Those who are not interested in the survey will not answer the questions, either.

In addition, people argue that there is no control over how many times they answered the website questionnaires if someone is extremely interested in the issue. We have to understand that the online survey is a relatively new procedure and improvements may be needed. I also have received email questionnaires from different organizations and researchers. The benefit is that it saves expenses and is faster. However, there is a limitation of the functionality of the email questionnaires, because email addresses are not public. The method highly depends on if a researcher can obtain enough respondents' email addresses. Email questionnaires can be used by individual institutions but are not popular for a larger population or on a societal level as a survey of public opinions.

When I started to learn sociology, I questioned why there are four research methods instead of only one. These methods are designed for different research purposes depending on what kind of data is needed and the appropriate method by which the data can be collected. As mentioned earlier, the first method is the **experiment**, defined as a research method that tests the logic or correlations between cause and effect variables. We all know that eating more junk food will result in people gaining weight. Eating junk food is the cause and weight gain is the effect. This method, compared with other social research methods, is a less widely used technique in sociology. It is often used in scientific studies, such as biology or chemistry.

The experiment method has advantages and limitations. One advantage of using the experiment method is that the cause and effect relationship may be identified clearly. In addition, the research may be done repeatedly with ease. However, there are limitations. If the research environment is not carefully controlled, the results may not represent the cause and effect relationship due to the influence of external factors. As a sociologist, I often design questionnaires to collect data for different research projects. Therefore, when I receive a questionnaire by mail or through a telephone interview, if I can, I take the time to answer it. The first time I refused to answer a mail questionnaire was because it asked about a married couple's sexual relationship. I felt that the researcher was looking for too much detailed information about the respondents' private life. This made me uncomfortable, so I did not take the survey. When a respondent feels that his/her privacy has been intruded, the person may refuse to answer the questions, which will result in a low return of the survey. In addition, when designing a questionnaire, the major investigator should not only have the knowledge to develop questions, but also have ethics and values in mind. The latter is especially important. By doing so, we are able to design a qualified questionnaire and not intrude on other's privacy. This is the reason many American colleges require that professors and students who are involved in a research project need to complete some Collaborative Institutional Training Initiative (CITI) in order to understand how to do a survey.

As a graduate student, I learned that a researcher must design questions for a questionnaire carefully; otherwise, it will bring a low return rate. Any personal questions, such as age and income, must be placed at the end of the questionnaire. The most effective way is to show income and age as a range, such as categorizing the income question into: $25,000–$34,999, $35,000–$44,999, and so on. Age can be ranged from, such as 40–49 years old, or 50–59 years old, instead of asking the respondents to give specific numbers. People feel more reluctant to answer personal questions. Once during a telephone interview, I was asked my exact age as the first question.

I said, "Why did you ask my age first?"

"We have different questionnaires for different age groups. You have to answer this question first, and then I can use the correct questionnaire for you," the interviewer explained.

Due to the design of the questionnaire that I did not like, I refused to participate. We can use this example to explain the experiment method discussed earlier. My rejection to answer the questionnaire is the effect, and the cause is the design of the questionnaire, which asked a respondent too much private information.

After I became a professor, I was able to do a small experiment to test a cause and effect relationship. I designed one questionnaire, but placed the age and income questions at different locations in the survey. In one questionnaire, age and income questions were placed at the beginning and in another questionnaire the age and income questions were at the end. All the questions in the two questionnaires were identical, which means they were all asked in the same manner. The only difference was that the age and income questions were placed in different positions in the questionnaire.

When the questionnaires were returned, I received only a few responses to the one which had the age and income questions at the beginning, but I received many more responses from the questionnaire that placed the age and income questions at the end. I felt that the respondents that had to provide their personal information first would feel uncomfortable without understanding what else a researcher wanted to ask in the survey. After answering all the questions, people would understand the purpose of the survey and they would feel better in answering certain personal questions. Therefore, where the sensitive issue questions are placed might be the cause that results in a negative effect.

The second method is a **survey**, which is defined as a research method designed to collect data from individual respondents by using questionnaires. Surveying is a widely used method in today's society. Traditionally, surveys include three ways of collecting data: telephone interview, face-to-face interview, and mail questionnaire. As discussed earlier, people also use email and the Internet to post questionnaires for specific topics. As a sociologist, I have done many different surveys. The first survey I conducted, after becoming a professor, was a study on community development and social attachment in the Northern Kentucky area in 1996. The research project was entitled, *Influences of rapid growth on residential satisfaction and community attachment: A case study in the Northern Kentucky community.* This was a research project to gather a statistically representative and comprehensive data set concerning the factors that have influences on the local people's community attachment. The data from the survey was from a sample of community residents. Both mail questionnaires and telephone follow-ups were used in the process of survey research. I used mail questionnaires as the major method of collecting data because sampling can help survey a large population.

The definition of **sample** is a small proportion selected to represent the population of the study. **Population** is defined as the entire population which shares the same research interests. The sample for this survey was a random sample, chosen from the Northern Kentucky area. When doing a survey, it is important to select a random sample because it will cover a variety of people's opinions and reduce the possibility of biased results. A total of 4,000 questionnaires were mailed to a random sample of residents found in the county telephone books. As a result, the return rate was approximately 27 percent (1,074 out of 4,000 questionnaires). Some residents wrote comments on the survey, both positive and/or negative, reflecting their views on the issues, problems and growth facing their communities.

Even though I defined that sample as a representative part of the population in the study, it is important to know that a sample only includes a small part of the population. A sample cannot be used as the population. When doing data analysis, the actual results of the study is the sample but not the population. The results can be used to estimate the population, but they are not the actual population. For instance, many people shopping in grocery stores have experienced sampling food products, such as a small piece of pizza. For taster A, this small piece might have everything, such as pepperoni, cheese, and tomato sauce. Taster B was not as lucky as he/she might get the edge of the pizza, which did not have the pepperoni, cheese, or tomato sauce. It was still a sample, but it was completely different for taster A than taster B. The point here is that a sample is only a sample; it will never represent the population as a whole.

A student asked me this question: "We will never know the result of the population if we study a sample. Then, what is the purpose of studying statistics?"

"Well, statistics will help us to better estimate our population," I answered.

"Can we study the population?" a student asked.

I answered, "Most likely it is impossible for us to study the population, although it depends on how big your population is. If your population is the whole class, you do not need to choose a sample, just go ahead and ask everyone. For social science, we need to study a large group and sometimes it is impossible to collect information from the whole population. When studying Americans' attitudes toward a certain social issue, it is impracticable to survey every American. Therefore, a sample should be used in the research."

When drawing a sample for a research project, it needs to involve people who can represent the population. For instance, in the late 1990s, American people talked about whether oral sex should be considered sex or not due to former President Bill Clinton's affair with a White House intern. One day, my husband and I had breakfast while watching TV. The program we watched was an interview of three young people, about twenty years of age, discussing how they felt about this issue. When the interviewer asked, "Do you think oral sex is sex or not?"

The three young people immediately answered, "No, it is not."

"What?" I suddenly found my husband so surprised that he opened his mouth and spit out his food.

"My God, how can they say that? Are you going to say that oral sex is not sex?" He could not believe what he heard. Then he turned to me and asked, "How could you be so calm?"

"Well, this is not the first time I have heard that oral sex is not sex. I have been educated by my students on their views of this issue," I answered.

I did not watch the program from the beginning, so I did not know what the interviewer's intentions were for only asking about young Americans' ideas. If it was true, the interview had done nothing wrong. However, these three young adults' attitudes toward oral sex did not represent all Americans' thoughts. If doing a social research project to find people's opinions about whether oral sex is considered sex or not, the sample should include different people from different age groups.

Age may become an important variable that tells why people have different opinions on some issues. There are many research projects studying a specific age group of people, but other representative factors of the respondents should be taken into consideration, such as sex, social classes, locations, education levels, and many others. All of these elements will help researchers have a more accurate result, which could be used to characterize the population.

Performing follow-ups is a good way to ensure a high percentage rate of return on surveys and is critical when doing a mail questionnaire. After receiving a questionnaire, people may or may not be willing to answer it. Even if they are willing to answer the questionnaire, they may not do it immediately. Follow-ups are an important reminder for people. Follow-ups can be a small postcard or a simple phone call. The questionnaire for my survey of the Northern Kentucky community was the second time I designed survey questions. After sending out the questionnaire, I also did telephone follow-ups. It proved to help increase the percentage of the return rate. This research laid a good foundation for my professional career.

After receiving my Ph.D., I have designed and completed many other surveys. One of my research projects included an international comparison study between Americans and Chinese on the topic of Alzheimer's patients' home caregivers and the pressure involved in the process of caring for their loved ones. At that time, I had just started to do research on issues connecting to the elderly population. In November 1994, our former President Ronald Reagan announced that he was diagnosed with Alzheimer's disease. That was the first time that I heard the phrase "Alzheimer's disease."

I clearly remember two years later, when I looked for a Chinese research partner, a person responded to me and used the term "old timer's disease." At that time in China, research had not been conducted in regard to Alzheimer's disease or memory impairment. Most Chinese thought that Alzheimer's was caused by old age. At that point, surveying Alzheimer's home caregivers would still be an educational process, which would at least bring people's attention to the survey questions and related issues. I successfully completed this comparison study in China and the United States and I have attended conferences and been published in different journals, based upon this survey.

The method of mail questionnaires, compared with telephone or face-to-face interviews, can reach a large sample of respondents. Mail questionnaires have limitations though, such as, not being able to dig out in-depth information. As a graduate student, I took a class which focused on telephone interview skills. I interviewed twenty undergraduate students to ask them a variety of questions about many things from their attitudes toward higher education to their sexual relationships in the past three months. If it were a mail questionnaire, the respondents would probably skip the sex-related questions. With a telephone interview, they were more likely to give an answer in the process of conversation.

"I do not know why you ask these questions," a female student replied when I asked her about her sexual relationships in the past three months.

"We would like to study college students' actual sexual behavior before marriage and their attitudes toward sexual relationships," I explained.

"Oh my God, my mom is going to kill me," she felt reluctant to answer.

"So, can I understand that the answer is 'yes'?" I tried to ask.

"No, I do not want to answer this question. It is too private. How about you put down 'I do not know', " she said.

"Sorry, there is no such category. By the way, this questionnaire is 100 percent confidential. Your answer will be grouped with other respondents' answers to be analyzed. Your name will never be shown in the database," I was happy to have a chance to explain the nature of the survey.

At this point, if using a mail questionnaire, I would not have had an opportunity to talk to respondents, even though mail questionnaires can reach more people. In other words, face-to-face and telephone interviews would not be able to involve a large population compared to mail questionnaires. One of the limitations of mail questionnaires is that researchers have no control on the return rate. People might receive the questionnaire and throw it away immediately. Sometimes face-to-face and telephone interviews enable a direct conversation with the respondents, which may generate higher response rates.

Once I did my dissertation research project in Alabama and a respondent mailed back the questionnaire five months later. She apologized that she did not answer the questionnaire as soon as possible, even with my follow-up phone call. She had found it while cleaning her desk one day and immediately answered the questionnaire. She also said that she hoped it was not too late for my research. Therefore, in order to have a higher return rate, a few follow-ups may be needed when it is possible.

There are also advantages and disadvantages to using surveys. An advantage to surveys is the ability to use sampling to reach a large number of participants. Also, face-to-face or telephone interviews will help researchers to study further. A disadvantage of this method is that researchers have no control of the return rate. Although in depth responses may be produced, the interviews are often time consuming and costly. Furthermore, the questionnaires must be carefully designed to prevent unintended consequences.

The third research method is **participant observation**, defined as a relatively long-term, planned, intensive observation of a particular group of people, an individual person, or event that happens in the natural world. The meaning of participant observation is that the researcher will be among the people in the study and observe people's behavior naturally. As for the natural environment, the behavior observed needs to be informal and unbiased. Participant observation is always a case study that can only represent what the observer has observed and cannot be applied to other cases.

In the past, I had an assignment for students in my Introduction to Sociology classes requiring them to do a participant observation in a church with which they were not familiar. I gave this assignment because when I was a teaching assistant in graduate school, my professor did a similar assignment. I think it is a helpful exercise for students to experience a research method such as this. I usually have eight questions on the survey and asked the students to observe: (1) how the church looked, (2) how many people were there, including the sex ratio, (3) different age groups, (4) what they were wearing, (5) what the music was like, (6) what the topic of the sermon was, (7) how the people responded to the sermon, and (8) how people in the church reacted toward the appearance of the student. After the observation, my students would submit a paper to me summarizing their observations.

Many students felt that this was a significant opportunity for them to study something new. This is because when people attend their own church, they seldom visit and observe other churches. I remember one student wrote to me that she really disliked the church she went to because people carried on too much side conversation during the whole process and children ran around. I wrote back to her and asked if she still remembered an important concept I taught in class: **value free**, which is defined as the nonappearance of any personal values while doing research. The meaning of this perception is when researchers do a project, they should report the results of the research as it is, not what they think it ought to be.

This is the basic research ethic a researcher should possess when doing a project; otherwise, the results of the research might be biased. Sometimes it is not easy for a researcher to be value free when doing a research project, especially for face-to-face or telephone interviews. Due to interviewer's attitudes, the results of the survey might be biased. If the interviewer asks a question and when giving the answer options makes a certain facial gesture or voice tone, then the respondent may react to the question differently based upon the interviewer's actions or attitudes. Therefore, it is important to train interviewers to behave correctly before doing a project in order to reduce any possible factors which might alter the final results.

One advantage of participant observation is that natural behavior will be studied. Although this method is time consuming, it is not usually costly. It is difficult for researchers to reproduce the behaviors observed. Most Americans have seen reality TV shows, such as *The Bachelor* or *The Real World* that record people's natural behavior. Individuals differ in their responses to the presented situations, signifying their natural behavior, and those are not always replicable.

Secondary analysis is the final research method and it uses existing sources for the data collection, which means that the data was collected by other people. I did a secondary study on the Hong Kong population in 1996. Hong Kong was handed back to the Chinese authorities on July 1, 1997, which ended more than 150 years of British control. Before Hong Kong was handed over to China, a journal editor invited me to write an article about

Hong Kong's population. I have never been to Hong Kong myself, nor did I know too much about this area, but I thought it was an opportunity for me to study the population in this particular region and to introduce what I knew to other people. I started my secondary study from my university's library and found many different useful books with important information. I also called an office, located in the United States, which had been established by the Hong Kong government. After reading these books and journals, I selected a lot of important information on Hong Kong's population and related social issues, such as young people's attitudes toward marriage and pregnancy. Due to researching current social issues, I also interviewed students on campus from Hong Kong to obtain more information and verify the accuracy of the data.

By collecting the existing sources, I felt that I had learned a lot. In my personal experience, I believe that the method of a secondary study with the existing sources has advantages and limitations. When other research methods cannot be used to collect certain data, such as historical data or my study of Hong Kong, the existing sources could be a more efficient way to acquire the information. The problems I encountered were that I read many books and journals, but often still found limited information that I could use, because the original author's research purpose was different from mine. Occasionally, the data might have some mistakes that I may not be able to correct, especially some of the historical data. An advantage of secondary analysis is that it is not as expensive as surveys, or as time consuming as participant observations. In addition, historical data may be studied for certain research purposes. A limitation is that possible errors in the original data collection may create biased results.

At this point, you might say I am ready to do research now. What will be the initial step and what will be the next? There are different steps that a researcher normally follows in order to do a project. The initial step is to have a detailed research topic, meaning that this research project has to have an exact focus. Therefore, I cannot just say that I would like to do a research on college students, because there are a variety of topics with which one could cover, such as underage drinking issues, campus activities, study habits, or dating issues.

Therefore, once you decide to study college students, the research topic is the narrowed down area of focus. I could say that I would like to study American college students' political preference for an upcoming election. After the research topic is decided, the next step is to do a literature review. This step will help people understand other researchers' work on this research topic, methodology, and also their study results. This step is important because a literature review is the major portion of the research, the role which functions as the leading point for the whole project. The third step is to formulate a hypothesis, which shows the relationships between independent and dependent variables.

After the hypothesis is designed, a decision must be made on which research methods will be used: mail questionnaire, telephone interview, secondary analysis, or any other methods. Since I am going to study college students' political preferences for a particular election, I would like to have a telephone interview with 500 college students, from a region representing a diverse sample of universities, such as public, private, and community colleges. Political preferences may change at a rapid pace based on different events. Therefore, a mail questionnaire may not be an appropriate method due to the slow return rate. A telephone interview allows for a faster response about their current beliefs. The next three steps are collecting data, analyzing the data, and drawing a conclusion. From the conclusion, a new research idea will be generated and a new project can start.

Research methods are important in conducting sociological research and choosing the correct method of design is also critical. Each method has its strengths and limitations. Where one method fails another might work. Different methods can be utilized for different types of social research and sometimes two methods can be used together thus providing more information on the research subject. For instance, when doing a survey, since many questions in a mail questionnaire are designed in a scale ranging from "strongly agree" to "strongly disagree," This can make it difficult to gage the varying attitudes about a subject. Therefore, a face-to-face interview can also be used, to help researchers better understand people's opinions and behaviors.

Chapter 3

CULTURE

Key words: culture; culture shock; ethnocentrism; cultural relativism; material culture; nonmaterial culture; symbols; language; values; norms; folkways; mores; subculture; counterculture; cultural lag; cultural integration

America is one of the most affluent countries in the world with well-developed industrialization and urbanization. From the Mayflower to today's immigrants, people have had the experience of learning a new culture as well as "fitting into" society. **Culture** is defined as people's values, norms, beliefs, social activities, and material life. The melting pot is a place where different elements melt together to create a harmonious and shared culture, when we relate this back to America most would focus on how immigrants should "fit into" this society and culture. However, few people think about the ways in which immigrants' different culture also helps shape American society and culture. To a certain extent, American society are also changing in order to "fit in" along with the combinations of other cultures which are brought in from different societies (see Fig. 3.1).

When I was about 6 years old, my family moved to Beijing from a city in the northeast of China. Along with my young age, moving within the same country never brought out a significant feeling of change for me. In 1986, I moved from China to America. When I arrived, I did not have anywhere prearranged living so I ended up staying with my professor's family the first night until I could rent a small apartment near my school the following morning. After registering for my two summer classes in the afternoon, I went back to my apartment. During my walk back, I was not in any rush so I was looking around enjoying the green trees and beautiful flowers in the street. Suddenly, I smelled something that was different from the enjoyable

Figure 3.1. China's culture has a history of more than 4,000 years. This country's culture originated from two rivers, the Yellow River and Yangtze River. China has developed a rich culture throughout its history. China has 56 nationalities with diversified subcultures. China's culture has also influenced the nearby countries of Japan and Korea. This photo shows the Forbidden City which was constructed from 1406 to 1420. Twenty-four emperors lived there during the Ming and Qing dynasties. The Forbidden City is about 178 acres, and is in the center of Beijing.

environment, which instantly changed my mood. It took me a few minutes to realize that what I was smelling was food, especially peppers, onions, meat, and something that I was not familiar with. I was wondering where the strange smell was coming from. Then I started to use my nose to search around. I continued breathing deeply until I was 100 percent sure that the smell was coming from a fast food restaurant.

"Wow! How does that happen?" I felt extremely surprised from negative feeling about the smell. "Oh! I cannot believe American people eat such food."

Culture shock is the shock and confusion that accompanies a person's experiences in new surroundings. This food disorientation was my first culture shock in America. I eventually accepted different kinds of American foods such as pizza, hamburgers, salad, and many others which I never had in China, but I always refused to eat at this particular fast food chain due to the smell of its food. In the summer of 1990, after my husband found a job in Alabama, we decided to travel to Atlanta, Georgia to visit the CNN headquarters. It was noon and we wanted to have lunch at the CNN food court. When I saw my husband returning with the food from the restaurant I had smelled on my first day in the United States, I immediately said, "No. I do not like it. Can you buy me something else?"

"I know. But how can you refuse food that you have never tasted before?" he replied.

"I do not like the smell," I answered.

"How about having a small piece? If you really do not like it after tasting it, you can buy something you like. Okay?" my husband suggested.

"Okay." I answered reluctantly.

After tasting a small piece, I could not help myself from saying, "Oh, it tastes so good!"

Prior to coming to America, I had never had any foreign cuisine. Nowadays in China, there are many "foreign food" restaurants, such as KFC, McDonald's, Pizza Hut, Korean, Japanese and also other countries' cuisine. Most people have different experiences other than culinary, when visiting an unfamiliar place. An unfamiliar place does not necessarily have to be a foreign country; it can just be a different region in the same country. In the summer of 1991, my husband and I decided to drive from Huntsville, Alabama to Houston, Texas. During our trip we decided to stop in New Orleans. It was a Saturday night and we had heard that it was a popular party city, we decided to join. We arrived in New Orleans in the early evening. After dinner, we were told about a famous party establishment.

When we finally found the "party street", my husband looked around and said, "Oh my God! Is this America?"

We walked for about fifty meters, and then I stopped, turned to my husband, and said, "Honey, close your eyes. Let's leave here right now."

At that time, we had been in the United States for about four or five years. We had never seen any photos of women wearing little to nothing in magazines or on posters. We had never been to a topless show, which was completely forbidden in China. So, when we saw posters of women wearing almost nothing, we felt shocked and embarrassed.

When traveling or moving to an unfamiliar place, most people will encounter different cultures and lifestyles. It is easy for people to create certain comparisons between their own culture and the new culture in which they have been exposed. People tend to think that their own culture is better than those they are not familiar with. This is because people have already become well adapted to the culture into which they were born; making it difficult to accept a new culture. People usually refer to this unfamiliar experience or disorientation as culture shock, which is not, of course, only limited to unfamiliar food or going to a foreign country. It may also accompany people when visiting different geographic areas in the same country, where there may be different subcultures.

Everyone has a culture to which they are accustomed. When I lived in China, most people did not take a bath every day due to the large population, limited living spaces, low living standards, and a lack of bath service facilities. Instead, they only washed their face after getting up and they also washed their face and feet before going to bed. Also, a majority of the families did not have a private bathroom, meaning that people had to walk, on average, twenty to thirty minutes to a public bathroom and had to share one showerhead with three or four other strangers. With rapid economic development, Chinese people's living standards have changed and most families have their own bathrooms at home, so their lifestyle has been changed too.

After years of living in America, I grew accustomed to the American way of life, including bathing daily. I told my American students about the living standards I had endured while living in China. Most of them opened their eyes widely and one student asked me if I took a bath every day now.

"Oh yeah, I take two baths per day now. So you don't need to drop my class because of that," I joked.

Yes, I take two baths per day now. I cannot imagine how bad I would feel if I only took a bath every two weeks. This is a typical example of **ethnocentrism**, which means thinking that one's own culture is better than other's. Ethnocentrism happens when people judge other cultures based on their own cultural standards. For instance, after years of living in America, I feel that I am very familiar and comfortable with this culture now. So, when I visited China, I often felt guilty for not tipping after eating in restaurants, because tipping is not a tradition in China. The feeling of being uncomfortable comes from the American tradition that I have learned for years. There was this one time where an American friend visited China and tipped the server. After finishing his food, he left cash, which was about 20 percent of the expense of the dishes on the dining table. As soon as he walked outside, he heard a voice from a running waitress, "Sir, is this your money? You forgot it on the table." My friend felt very embarrassed at the situation, he did not know that in China it is not custom to tip.

Today, with our exposure to many different cultures, we need to practice the idea of **cultural relativism**. Cultural relativism can be defined as respecting other cultures and not using one's own culture as a reference when judging other cultures, acknowledging that other cultures are worthy in their own right, without comparing it with your own.

Culture can be categorized into two terms: nonmaterial and material. **Nonmaterial culture** is comprised of beliefs, values, and behavior. These are insubstantial elements of culture, created by members of the society and cannot be directly identified through the senses. The Supreme Court legalized same sex marriage, in a 5–4 decision, in 2015. This constitutional right is an example of nonmaterial culture. In our everyday life, the guidance, such as speed limits, food and drinks being forbidden inside of libraries, or having to wear shoes inside stores, is nonmaterial culture. **Material culture** is defined as the substantial objects that people may use for daily life, such as a cell phone or television. Human society needs laws, rules, values, and beliefs, but it also needs a material culture. American society has a high standard of living that supports people with a high quality of life and a large quantity of materials. As an immigrant coming from a less developed country, it was easy for me to love and accept the high quality of living; but I also felt that it was important to not become a materialistic person. The reason for this is if I am only concentrating on materialistic lifestyle, I feel that I will not have enough attention and energy for my important goals, such as working hard to be successful for my career.

Human beings cannot live comfortably without basic material goods. However, many people now are seeking to have high quality products. Initially, my husband used to buy only name brand products after he moved to America. Years ago, he told me that he needed a new pair of glasses. He asked not only for the extra services for the lenses, but he also wanted expensive frames. Like many others, he believed that the more expensive items are, the better quality they will be. On the first day of work with his new glasses, he came home looking very disappointed.

"What's up with you today?" I asked.

"Nothing." He answered.

"You do not look very happy today. Is there a problem with your new glasses?" I continued.

"No, there isn't a problem with my glasses, but. . . ." I had a feeling that he was trying to tell me something.

"What?" I asked.

"My colleagues told me that the money I spent on the frames is worthless," he started to say.

"Why?" I asked.

"They told me that all of the frames are actually from the same manufacturer. The frame store puts different labels on the frames with different prices."

"Oh my lord, I cannot believe that. Your colleagues are just trying to make fun of you. You should not worry about that," I tried to persuade him.

He replied. "I do not believe that either, but . . ."

"Next time you shouldn't buy anything so expensive and then you would not worry about whether or not it is worth the money," I answered, even though I truly believed that what my husband's colleague said was a joke. I also believe that the more you pay for a product is because you are getting a better quality item.

Material culture is emphasized not only in America, but also in other parts of the world. In recent years, when visiting China, I found that many young Chinese people want to buy American name brands, especially Apple products like the iPhone. They also admire Japanese or German cars, such as the BMW. On one hand, their behavior indicates their needs for high quality products, although sometimes the quality of these name brands may be overexaggerated. On the other hand, purchasing foreign goods is also a process of learning and recognizing other cultures (see Fig. 3.2).

Figure 3.2. In 1978, the Chinese government established a new policy of opening its doors to the world. Since then, great changes, especially economic development, have taken place in China. Many foreign companies, products, and cultural elements, as well as Western influences, have transformed China. The above photo shows one of the Apple stores in Beijing.

In addition to material culture, nonmaterial culture is also important for human societies. As mentioned earlier, nonmaterial culture includes rules, beliefs, and behaviors, all of these are created by human beings. However, rules, beliefs, and human behaviors differ in different societies. An illustration of nonmaterial culture is China's establishment of the "one-child" policy, which was an important part of the family planning policy from 1979 to 2015. This policy, promoted by the Chinese government, strongly encouraged people to delay having a child and to have sterilizations or abortions after their first child. This policy has helped slow the population growth rate. During this period, Chinese people gradually accepted the idea that abortion was an effective method to help change the increasing population in the country. Before the one-child policy, the Chinese total fertility rate was 6.5 in 1952 and 2.75 in 1979 (Potts, 2006). After years of practicing this policy, the Chinese population growth maintains a slow increase now.

When my American students debated the issue of pro-choice and pro-life, I always felt that abortion, as an individual's choice, was acceptable. This opinion was based upon the Chinese Family Planning Policy that I learned before I came here. My thoughts changed after eight years of living in American society due to the learning of American values on this issue.

One day, I was stopped at a traffic light and happened to read a bumper sticker on a minivan in front of me. It said, "You even save a deer's life. Why don't you save your dear baby's life?"

A few months later, I saw another car sticker. It said, "Abortion only means you are a dead baby's mom!"

These two stickers made me reflect for a long time, contemplating different beliefs about abortion and how it may apply in different cultures. China, with the pressures of low economic development in the 1970s and a high unemployment rate in the 1990s, wanted to slow down the population growth rate. In addition, China, compared to America, has a different cultural background and different religious beliefs. When I teach the course on population, I always introduce China's one-child policy and the pressures of rapid population growth. I also point out that the policy is momentary, because it is only a temporary strategy to limit the rapid growth of the population for a number of years and it cannot last forever. This policy has already been adjusted now due to the current Chinese population and the rate of economic development. The policy now encourages a young couple to have two children starting from 2016. If the one-child policy is not adjusted, China will have a shortage of working people contributing to the future development of the society.

As a matter of fact, China is facing an elderly issue due to the one-child policy and a longer life expectancy. In 2025, the total population in China will reach its peak at 1.41 billion. After that, it is projected to decline to 1.3 billion in 2050 (Fu, 2015). By 2030, it is expected that China will become the most aged society in the world (Huang, 2013). The total number of the people aged 65 and over was 137 million in 2014, which was 10.1 percent of the Chinese population. In 1982, the Chinese senior citizens were only 4.9 percent of the total population. In the year of 2050, it is projected the elderly population 60 years and older (60 years older is defined as senior citizen in China now) will be 35 percent of the total population (Wang, 2016). According to the current number, China has the largest group of the elderly in the world. The government has realized the issue. However, population policies can be decided over one night, but any changes in the structure of a population would take years to achieve it. This is because to add new people to a society, especially to add those people to the labor force would take years for them to reach working age.

Culture also includes five components: symbols, language, values, norms, and material culture. **Symbols** are gestures, words, or signs that have had meaning attached to them by members of a society (see Fig. 3.3). Traffic lights are symbols which tell you to stop, go, or slow down and prepare to stop. The traffic lights are just different colors until we, as human beings, prescribe different meanings to them. For instance, I have to drive about a fifty-mile roundtrip to work. One day on the way to school, I was driving about seventy miles per hour. While driving, I had to change to the left lane to avoid a slow moving semi-truck.

I continued to drive the same speed after changing the lane, and suddenly I saw a red car behind me driving extremely fast, it almost rear-ended my car before it slowed down. After I passed the semi-truck, I changed back to the right lane. The red car passed me and switched to the right lane as well. As soon as the car passed and was in front of my car, the driver slammed on the brakes and slowed down to about forty miles per hour. The driver rolled down the window, stretched his left arm out and showed his middle finger. This was the first and only time in America that I have ever seen a person behave like this. As soon as I saw that gesture, I laughed and said loudly in my car, "You should recognize that I am Chinese and I have no idea what that gesture means. Sorry."

Truthfully, I understand the meaning of this gesture. The middle finger probably has the same meaning in many countries. As a symbol, the middle finger had no implication until human beings used it as a gesture and assigned a meaning to it. The gesture, depending on different cultures, has different connotations. These are known as symbols. Putting together the letters "ABC" can have different meanings for different people. To the Chinese families in America, ABC means American Born Chinese. This is more compli-

Figure 3.3a and 3.3b Historically, marble lions, normally two of them, are decorations often located to the left and right side of front doors in places such as palaces, temples, and tombs. Lions symbolize the idea of "avoiding evil spirits and accepting auspicious." The male lion often has a ball underneath his right paw, and the female lion often has a baby lion within her left paw.

cated than a gesture, it is a language. **Language** is comprised of a group of symbols, which allows the members of a society to communicate. When I came to America, I confronted a lot of language problems, even though I graduated from a Chinese college with a major in English.

One day when I went to class I saw a notice that said, "White collar crime has moved to the next office." I was absolutely confused by this, but I later learned that it meant that the group of law professors who studied "white-collar crime" had moved. I could understand the sentence only after I understood the situation. In my personal experiences of learning English, if a person can understand the situation and the context as well as the culture in a society, he/she will better comprehend the language. Even if I know English terms, without understanding the American culture I will not be able to understand part of the English language. For instance, when my husband took the road examination for his driver's license in the United States. He drove the car carefully and desperately wanted to pass the test.

Suddenly he heard the examination officer say, "Turn left." Following the instruction, he changed to the left lane. Before he actually turned to the left, he tried to make sure and asked, "Turn left?" The examination officer answered, "Right."

"Right?" he was thinking the officer might test his ability to deal with an emergency situation. Then he immediately drove to the right lane and prepared to turn right.

"Why are you turning right when I am asking you to turn left?" the officer exclaimed with an irritated voice.

"I asked you if I should turn left or not. You said to turn right. I am following your instruction, sir," my husband felt confused.

"I meant you were right to turn left," the officer explained.

"Then, you should say 'correct' instead of 'right'. It is very confusing," my husband argued.

My husband did not pass this road test but he did take it again the next day and passed.

Another story has something to do with a "party." My friend and her husband came to the United States years ago. She could not understand any English at that time. She started her English class in a church and learned a limited vocabulary. She opened a home day care for young kids; most of them were from other graduate students' families. One day, a three-year-old girl came in and said, "I want to go to the party."

My friend said, "There is no party outside. It is snowing and cold."

"No, I need to go to the party. I went there before." The girl looked like she could not wait another second.

She kept asking to go to the party a few times and my friend felt annoyed. Then she said, "If you want to go, you go yourself. I will not go with you."

The girl quickly ran into the bathroom. After a couple of minutes, she walked out with a look of relief on her face.

"I think American families are very interesting," my friend began a conversation with me. "They call going to the bathroom 'going to a party.' What will happen if they go to a real party? Do they call that going to a bathroom? English is a very difficult language to study," she summarized.

"Really? I have never heard about it. Do you mean PARTY? Don't you think the word is POTTY?" I was puzzled.

"How do you spell it? What's the meaning of that?" she wanted to know.

In America, people never confuse the meanings of going to a party with going to a potty. It is difficult for people who are learning English as their second language because they are not able to pick up some subtle variances in pronunciations, or the different meanings of ordinary English words versus how Americans actually use them.

As a professor from a foreign country, I have experienced using my second language to teach American students. I feel that most difficulties come not from the words, but rather, the cultural background. To me, I feel the process of teaching is also a process of learning. I remember back in the 1990s when I first began teaching, the most popular classroom tool was an overhead projector. Since I could only write limited words on a transparency, I always had to read aloud important points to my students. At the end of each sentence, I would say "full stop," which means the end of the sentence in British English.

During my lecture one day, a student wrote down, "Values are not explanatory public statements full stop. They are basic social concepts full stop. Norms are guidance for people to behave in different situations full stop." She read and reread the sentences, but could not understand them. At the end of the class she raised her hand and said, "Could you explain the sentences you just asked us to write down?"

"Yes, no problem," I said.

"I do not understand. What do you mean by 'Norms are guidance for people to behave in different situations full stop?" she asked.

"You do not understand 'full stop'?" I was surprised by what she asked.

"No," she answered.

"It is a punctuation, which tells you that this is the end of the sentence," I replied.

"Oh my God! It is a PERIOD!!! Sorry." She felt a little embarrassed. "Oh, do you call it a period? I have learned a word today. Thank you." I was excited because I did not know it should be called a PERIOD. As a result of teaching, I also learn from my students and I never feel embarrassed when I make a mistake in English. It does not matter whether I make a pronunciation or spelling mistake; I always feel excited when I am corrected because I have learned something new.

Language is a tool that allows human beings to communicate with each other. It also represents a society's culture, which includes people's beliefs, values, and social rules as well. Different societies have different values. **Values** can be defined as social standards which members of a society use as a framework for their daily lives. For instance, Americans and Chinese view sexual behaviors differently. China used to be a traditional conservative society in which sexual behavior was not a public topic. In the past, only when a daughter was going to be a bride, would her mother explain to her what sexual intercourse was to prepare her for the night of her wedding. Chinese people believed sexual behavior to be an undesirable and uncomfortable topic, but today, due to the rapid social development, many younger generations, who are mainly born into the Internet Age, have different thoughts about sexual behavior compared with the older generations.

I used to have two Chinese friends in graduate school. After they got married in the United States, they decided that they were too busy with their schoolwork to have a child. They planned to wait on having a baby until they both graduated. My female friend, Jenny did not want to take birth control pills because she heard that sometimes the pill was not 100 percent effective in preventing pregnancy. As a result, the dilemma of who would go to a grocery store to buy condoms arose. Both the newly married husband and wife felt embarrassed to do so. If they were in China, the Family Planning

Committee members would deliver the pills or condoms to them. They felt uncomfortable purchasing condoms in an American store. Their embarrassment reflected the values they learned in Chinese tradition, which continues to influence their thoughts and behaviors in America.

Later on, Jenny asked her mother to mail some condoms to her from China. In this case, she would be completely relieved of the pressures of purchasing the condoms, which are free of charge from the Family Planning Committee in China. Her mother mailed her condoms only once and then told the daughter that this was the first and last time she would do this for her. There was a reason for this, when the mother asked the Family Planning Committee members for condoms after several visits in a short period, they told her, "You are already over fifty years old. Take it easy." The bride's mother said she was too embarrassed to ask for more condoms because she did not want to be considered sexually active.

Sex in China was an unspoken topic. This was quite different from American values. In America, sex is viewed as a natural part of human life. From a young age, generally speaking, students are usually taught to know their body and are given correct information about sex and the results of sexual behavior. A student told me that "The town where I am from taught us in middle school about sex. We were also taught not to be ashamed for wanting sex because it is just human instinct to want to reproduce." They are also encouraged to use many kinds of birth control facilities to protect themselves from undesirable consequences.

Compared to values, **norms** are guidelines that govern people's actions within a given culture. For instance, everyone knows that the question, "How are you?" essentially means "Hello." In my first winter in America, I was in graduate school. During final exam week, I caught a cold and had a fever, but I still needed to take the final exam. As I was walking to the classroom on a snowy and windy morning, I heard a voice.

"How are you, Boni?" It was a professor I had met several times.

"I do not feel well. I am running a fever, I could not sleep well last night, and I have been coughing a lot," I stopped walking and answered him with my stuffy nose.

"Oh, what can I do for you?" he asked.

"Nothing, I am just answering your question, since you asked me how I am," I answered.

Years later, of course, I understand the meaning of "How are you?" Now, when people ask me this, I always say, "I am fine." It does not matter whether I am fine or not. My behavior demonstrates the guidelines mirrored in the American meaning of the phrase: "How are you?" This is because my answer to this question is now reflective of the reply given by any other

American. I now understand the cultural norms and know how to answer this question according to the American standard.

My students used to tell me that the difference between values and norms was that values were an individual's thoughts and judgments, but norms were society's creations. I disagreed with them because both values and norms are society's products. People live within a particular culture and learn particular values and norms. Values are nonrepresentational concepts and evaluations of what is right or wrong. Norms are the social rules for people to follow. Norms apply to different social standards, such as "no food or drinks in the library" or "you cannot drink if you are under twenty-one years old." Values are judgments, such as "it is bad if you eat food in the library" or "it is bad if you are drinking underage."

Within the concept of norms, there are two sociological terms: folkways and mores. **Folkways** are norms that may be considered abnormal, but may be accepted. **Mores** are norms that will be considered abnormal and cannot be accepted. If one wears a prom dress to a casual BBQ restaurant, it may not be sanctioned by any social penalty. However, if a person wears nothing but a tie to a BBQ restaurant, it would be unacceptable. The former example represents a folkway and the latter is an instance of a more.

American society is called a melting pot because it has immigrants from countries all over the world. People coming into this society must learn American dominant values and culture, but at the same time, they want to keep their own traditions and identity. This process has made the meaning of the melting pot even more significant because it includes many different subcultures. **Subculture** is defined as a group of people, whom even though they may have different lifestyles, all follow aspects of the dominant culture in a society. Subcultures include people of different racial groups or different ways of life. I frequently see examples of subcultures when I go to the big international market in my city to buy groceries, especially fish.

Each time after weighing the fish, the shop assistants always ask, "Do you want me to gut the fish and leave the head on?"

"How do you know that?" I responded the first time I was there, surprised by his question.

"I just know it," he smiled as he answered.

Later on, I realized that when they see people's faces, if a person looks Asian, they will ask the same question as he asked me. Why? Many Asian people like to cook the fish with the head on and with the fish bones. Even after years in this country, my husband still refuses to eat a fish filet because he thinks that a fish filet does not taste like real fish.

A few years back, my husband and I used to travel to Atlanta, Georgia for Chinese groceries and we often stopped at a Chinese restaurant for dinner after going to the market. The restaurant had at least three different menus. One menu was for Americans, which was printed in English and had stars by the spicy food. Another menu was for Chinese people and was printed in Chinese. The third menu was on many red pieces of paper on the wall using Chinese blush and Chinese black ink and was, of course, written in Chinese. This menu included the kinds of food they believed no Americans would dare to try, because it is authentic Chinese food. Unlike the Chinese, most Americans just eat the meat of pork, beef, chicken, or turkey. Chinese people eat every part of the chicken and the pig including the head, feet and some of the internal parts (see Fig. 3.4).

I used to have a student whose father was a farmer. One day, he came to me and said, "Happy Chinese New Year!"

"Thank you," I said. "How do you know it is the Chinese New Year?" I felt surprised.

"A lot of people from Chinese restaurants in town came to my dad's farm to buy chickens. They told us that it would soon be the Chinese New Year.

Figure 3.4. Chinese cuisine has a long history, and focuses on the color, flavor, taste, shape, and meaning of the food cooked. People can find restaurants everywhere in Beijing. The restaurant in this photo is a chain restaurant that offers 24-hour service.

They said the reason they came to my dad's farm was because they must buy chickens with the head and feet on. Do you know why?"

"Of course I know why." Even though I did not want to tell him, I asked if he wanted to know why.

"Yes, I do want to know; it will help me to understand another culture," he answered.

"Good, I am very glad that you realize that Chinese culture is different." I felt more secure in discussing this topic with him.

I continued, "It is very simple. Chinese people like to eat the whole chicken. A chicken without the head and feet is not a whole chicken."

"I do not understand how much meat you can get from the head or feet," the student replied.

"Not too much, but this is the way Chinese people eat chicken," I said.

With rapid social development today, grocery stores in China have changed the traditional way of selling chickens. Now, similar to American grocery stores, Chinese grocery stores also cut the chickens into different parts, including wings, legs, or breasts. The stores also sell chicken feet packages. People call it "phoenix feet," and many considered it a delicious snack. Many older Chinese people still prefer to cook a chicken with the head and feet attached. In America, it is almost impossible for Chinese immigrants to buy chicken with the head and feet still attached. However, I observed in an international market that the majority of Chinese buyers, when purchasing fish, will still keep the head on. Second generation Chinese immigrants that are born in the United States, will be more than likely to keep some of these Chinese traditions.

American society is also in a process of accepting foreign traditions. The international store I used to visit now sells pig heads. I saw many children often go there to touch the pigs' nose, eyes, or ears. During a visit to China, I ate some grilled salmon heads and thought they were delicious, so I went to an American grocery store after coming back to look for some.

"Do you sell Salmon heads?" I asked the seafood sale person.

"Why do you want salmon heads?" he questioned.

"I want to grill salmon heads. I think they are delicious," I answered.

"Okay. I will save the heads for you next time. We normally throw the heads away," he promised.

A few days later, I grilled my first marinated salmon head in my backyard.

Compared to subculture, **counterculture** is defined as a group of people who may share some aspects of the lifestyle but reject or disagree with part of the dominant culture in a society. The Ku Klux Klan is an example of this term. Counterculture can sometimes be bad and can sometimes be good.

When Martin Luther King Jr. asked for civil rights, he was considered a counterculture figure at that time, due to his opposing view compared to the views held by the dominant culture at that time. It is because of his Civil Rights Movement that American society changed dramatically.

In 1990, when my mother-in-law visited Hong Kong, she asked my husband what she should buy as a gift for my father-in-law. We suggested that she should buy a microwave with a turntable function. Two years later, we went back to China to visit our families. I held a mug with water in it and asked, "Mom, where is your microwave?"

"Did you say microwave? It is over there in the corner," she replied as she pointed to the corner of the room.

"I don't see anything but a bed over there." I thought I was looking in the wrong direction.

"Yes, it is under the bed in a box," she answered.

"So, Mom, you do not use it?"

"No, I do not use it," she said, much to my surprise.

"Why do you not use it?"

"I do not think it cooks good food," she answered.

This is an example of incompatibility with technological advancements and people's attitudes or reactions with the use of the technology. The "incompatibility" is called **cultural lag**, which is defined as an inconsistency between different social components due to different rates of cultural development. Cultural lag occurs everywhere, but especially where a society experiences a rapid technological and social change.

Contrasting the concept of cultural lag is **cultural integration**, which can be defined as the compatibility between different social elements in the process of cultural development. Cultural integration represents a situation that the different aspects/elements of a culture system are expected to work together. So people's acceptance and the technological development should always be compatible with each other. For instance, with the development of a series of robot vacuums, people should always accept and use the newest products. We know this is not always true in our real life. Instead, we may often be found incompatible between the above two elements.

Another personal experience regarding cultural lag is a story about an American gentleman. In 2002, I stopped at a gas station of a big wholesale warehouse when I saw a man in his mid-seventies, standing on the other side of the gas pump I was using. He was trying to use his warehouse club membership card at the pump. After moving his card from front to back several times against the bar code reader, he expected the machine to recognize his card, but it did not. Then he put the backside of the card up with his photo facing the device. He kept saying "Hi, it is me." "Hello, here is your buddy."

Knowing that he was having trouble getting gas, I walked toward him and asked, "Hi, sir, do you need any help?"

"Oh, thank you. I think there is something wrong with my card. The machine will not recognize me," he said.

I said, "Oh, I see. I think you might want to try the bar code instead of your photo." I then showed him how to do that. Finally, he lifted the nozzle and got gas. He told me that he did not know how to use any electronic cards with bar code readers and, saying that his wife knew how to use those fancy cards.

After talking to this gentleman, I began wondering how many elderly American people have difficulties dealing with such advanced technology. How do the current technological advancements, including computers, email, Internet, smart phones, and other electronic devices, influence elderly people's daily lives in America and other countries? With the rapid technological development in human society throughout the past three decades, it can be assumed that elderly people's daily lives have been highly impacted. This issue is important for researchers in any society to explore. This is especially important when a country has become an aging society, which, is when a society has 10 percent or more of their total population over the age of sixty-five.

Culture is created by people. At the same time, people are significantly influenced by their culture. These influences are most likely not recognized. For example, having lived in American society for about thirty years, I have learned a lot of American values, norms, beliefs, and lifestyles. The only times I am able to recognize what I have learned are when I go back to China.

When visiting China, I still take two baths and change my clothes every day, which Chinese people usually do not do. When talking with my family and friends, I always use American values and norms to evaluate Chinese social issues and problems. I am even sometimes unable to find an exact word in Chinese to best express myself for something. Instead, an English word often automatically comes out of my mouth. At that moment, I am shocked at realizing how much I have been Americanized.

At the very beginning when I settled down in the United States, I often compared the two cultures of America and China. Now that I am comfortable with the American culture. I feel that the majority of the culture is the way it ought to be. On the contrary, I often feel that since I came from a foreign country, I am still in the process of learning American culture and trying to "fit in" with this society.

The process of "fitting in" with American society is not one sided. For immigrants, this process means survival and respect of the dominant culture.

However, for Americans, this process means accepting or allowing room for new cultures that newcomers bring in. This process has greatly changed and will continue to affect American society. To a certain extent, American society has to change in order to "fit in" with the combination of other cultures. If a cook makes a pot of soup, the taste of the soup will depend on what kinds of ingredients that he/she puts into it. The taste differs depending on whether the cook puts in more sugar, salt, or pepper. Many new "ingredients" have changed American culture as well.

In recent decades, with more and more Asian immigrants moving into America, many Asian grocery stores and restaurants had opened to meet the needs of these individuals. An important thing to note is that many Americans also shop at these grocery stores and restaurants. Not only have they tasted some Chinese, Korean, or Japanese food, but some have also learned how to use chopsticks. This example has reflected how American people are influenced by other cultures. It is important to study the foundation of American culture that has existed for hundreds of years; however, it is also important to study the influences of other cultures on American society.

Chapter 4

SOCIALIZATION

Key words: socialization; nature; nurture; Jean Piaget's four stages of cognitive development: the sensorimotor stage, the preoperational stage, the concrete operational stage, and the formal operational stage; looking-glass self; generalized other; peer group; anticipatory socialization; public opinion; mass media

After living in the United States for six years, I went back to China for the first time in 1992. I never realized that I had been socialized by the American culture until my husband and I visited our families. The second day after our arrival in Beijing, we invited my best friend and her husband for dinner, which included eight different Chinese dishes. In China, when family members or friends eat together, it is a tradition to sit at a round dining table and place all of the dishes in the middle to share. Traditionally, people do not use public serving spoons; rather, they use their own chopsticks to pick up the food from these dishes. After the food arrived, my friends began to use their chopsticks to pick up food directly from the dishes, which caused me to feel uncomfortable and lose my appetite. This led me to realize that I had become assimilated to the American way of life.

In America, when people share meals with others they tend to use a separate plate and a clean fork, something vastly different than what I was experiencing during this dinner with my friends. I then realized that I had been in America for so long and had forgotten the custom way of traditional eating in China. I called for the waitress and asked her to bring us a few serving spoons, however my friends said they were fine without using them. Regardless of their comments I insisted on having a separate serving spoon for each dish while being selective, picking food I felt had not been touched by other's chopsticks.

Later, my friend remarked, "You said you really missed Chinese food. Why did you eat very little?" While she was talking to me, she picked up a piece of meat with her own chopsticks and put it onto my plate. What she did shocked me, but I thanked her anyway because I recognized this as a Chinese tradition signifying a close friendship. Throughout the meal, I carefully avoided touching the food that she had put on my plate. Before living in the United States, I had never questioned this type of sharing food with others in China. After having lived in the United States for several years, I knew that eating with my friends would be uncomfortable. It was true, I had assimilated into the American culture and way of life.

The process of assimilation is called **socialization**, a lifelong process based on the learning of social values, beliefs, norms, and other patterns of social behavior through individual interactions with others (see Fig. 4.1). In order for people to succeed in a society, they need to be socialized, it does not matter if they are born into a country or come from another culture. If

Figure 4.1. The Chinese government is now taking steps to solve issues with pollution. Since 2000, China has instituted the use of recycling cans in an effort to reuse natural materials. This is an example of a socialization process because Chinese people have to learn how to classify garbage and remember to make it a part of their daily behavior.

they are originally born into a culture they will be able to naturally learn the process of socialization by interacting with those around them. Everything they learned will continue to enhance their socialization. For those entering a new country, the challenge is more significant. They have to confront and grasp a completely new culture immediately; however, some cultural attributes of the new country may be similar to some of those that already exist within the newcomers. For instance, I was accustomed to eating popcorn in China when I was a child, therefore it was not a completely unfamiliar food when I came to the United States, although the taste was not the same. The difference is because butter is not put on popcorn in China; instead, just plain salt or sugar is used.

Oftentimes cultural heritage may follow immigrants to their new home. This was true to me, I grew up with rice and flour as main food staples and because of this, I often purchase 25 pounds of rice and 50 pounds of flour, the same amount hotels and restaurants use. After coming to the United States, I have since begun to purchase "all purpose" flour and now I have learned to use bread flour to make Chinese noodles. It is very seldom that I purchase nor make bread at home because bread is not a part of the everyday Chinese cuisine. It seems as though after years of living in America, I still follow the Chinese way of life; however, this is not completely true. I have adopted many American customs. To further illustrate this point, I would like to share a personal experience I had using washers and dryers when first coming to America. In China, washers are used more than dryers because traditionally, Chinese people tend to hang their wet clothes on a line outside, therefore, manufacturers, when making cotton clothes do not have to take shrinkage into consideration. Even today, most Chinese people, after using the washer, tend to hang their wet clothes to dry on a line outside and dryers are still not popular in Chinses families.

When I first came to America, the owner of the apartment I lived in told me that I had to use a washer and dryer if I needed to wash my clothes. I used it once and did not know how to operate the dryer, but the owner helped me turn it on. When I got all of the clothes out of it, I found that none of them could be worn again because they all had shrunk. Later on, I used the bathroom sink to wash my clothes, and secretly hung them in my room. The owner of the apartment warned me many times because he felt that I should use his washer and dryer. It was obviously he did not want me to hang my wet clothes and let the water drip on the floor. I soon realized it was inconvenient to continue living there because it was too different from my Chinese lifestyle.

After living in a few different places in America, I understand that this is the American way of doing laundry. If I had been born in America, this would not have been a problem because I would have learned how to use a dryer at a young age, and I would not have had to deal with the clothing issues that I mentioned above. This is similar to the way in which an American traveling to China would have felt. They may feel surprised to see wet clothes hanging everywhere, and would not understand why Chinese people do not use dryers. Now having lived in the United States for many years, I have become accustomed to using washers/dryers when cleaning my clothes. When I visited China after years of living here, I still accepted that hanging my jacket or jeans on a line outside was normal. However, I always felt very uncomfortable and embarrassed to hang my underwear up on a line. This example shows how people raised in different cultures are socialized in a different way. Once people have become accustomed to a culture it becomes difficult for them to change and accept another one.

Socialization is an active process in which a person has to initiate the learning. An example of this would be someone either born in America or immigrating here. It is not logical to assume they are able to speak fluent English and cook American food, but rather that everyone is expected to learn how to do these things in order to survive. Only through the process of learning can a person become socialized. However, the process of socialization has to be voluntary, based upon that individual's efforts or willingness to learn and practice.

When I started my first year of elementary school, I felt uncomfortable. Not only did I have to learn something new every day, but I also had to obey various school rules. Some of the rules included students not being allowed to use the restrooms, eat snacks, have side conversations with another classmates during class time, or be late for class.

After realizing I had to go to school every day, I kept asking, "Mom, when can I finish school and stay at home like before?"

"Oh dear, you have to be in school for years," my mother would reply.

"I do not like school. Can I stop going?" I begged my mother.

"No, you cannot do that. You need to learn and be useful for society when you grow up." She would answer, trying to persuade me to stay in school and to be a good student.

"Everyone needs to go to school to learn, you need to do the same." Usually by this point she would walk away and stop the conversation.

In an attempt to stay at home, I purposely failed both of my two midterm tests: math and Chinese. When the teacher talked to my mother she was disappointed and angry with me. Afterwards, I had to go with my mother to see my grandma in another district of the city. When we passed the window of a department store, I stopped because I saw a pretty dress.

"Mom, I like this beautiful dress. Can you buy it for me?" I asked, even though I knew she was not happy with my school performance and would not agree to buy it.

"No, I will not buy it for you," she refused, without hesitation.

"Why? It is very pretty. I like it," I exclaimed, trying to persuade her.

"It does not matter what you are wearing, you do not look pretty," she was growing impatient.

"I am not pretty? Mom, you said that I am not pretty?" I could not believe what she had said and I began crying loudly with tears running down my face.

Later that evening, my mother and I had a long conversation. I remember clearly that my mother said that if I wanted to be a pretty girl I would need to get an "A" in all of my courses in school. After that conversation, I tried to study as hard as I could and be successful in school. The reason was simple: I wanted to be a pretty girl. After years of education, I have come to understand the reason my mother connected the status of being a pretty girl with having a good school performance. This was because she wanted me to study hard for my education. Although, I still disagree with what she said to me, the idea of becoming a pretty girl did encourage me to work harder for the remaining years that I had in elementary school. The education I received at that time has no doubt laid a good foundation for my future. It shows that the process of being educated or socialized is not an automatic one, it is instead brought on by a person's voluntary hard work.

The process of socialization for a young person often happens based upon social interaction at home with parents or in school with teachers (see Fig. 4.2). It is important for parents and teachers to socialize younger generations with the social norms and values in their society. I felt my mother did that to me by linking my education with my desire to be pretty. She did not follow the normal social values to encourage me to learn, but went too far in forcing me to conform to standard social expectations. She should have realized that the process of learning for anyone was based upon an individual's self-effort with positive encouragements from others. Recently there has emerged a term "Tiger mother" in America, which is meant to describe a demanding mother who may use different strict rules to push her children hard into achieving certain goals which are admired and expected by the mother. The "Tiger mother" situation is more popular in China and some parts of East Asia, as well as some Chinese and Asian mothers in America. Another example of the learning process that I experienced when I came to the United States was learning how to cook pizza, something I had never had when in China. One day my husband and I went to a pizzeria, and while we were waiting I said to my husband, "I think next time if we want to have a pizza I will cook it at home."

"I really do not think you should try it. If you like pizza we can always order one," he said.

"I will prove to you that I have the cooking skills to do so," I replied defiantly.

Figure 4.2. Before the early 1990s, many Chinese families did not have a landline tele-phone at home. Since then, public telecommunication services have been developed. In addition, these public telephone services are now available to people on the street to allow them to communicate with other people when they are not at home. Now, with the development of cell phones, many Chinese no longer use public phone services, and instead use cell phones to interact with one another.

The following day, true to my word, I bought all the ingredients I thought I needed to cook my first pizza on my own. At 5:30 in the evening my husband arrived home from work. He walked into the house and said, "Oh, it smells good. What is for dinner tonight?"

"Take a guess," I replied, very proud of myself.

"My guess is that you made a pizza. Am I right?" he asked.

"Bingo," I replied, as I was taking the pizza out of the oven.

"Wait a minute. You call this pizza?" he questioned, hesitating to take a piece.

"Well, it may look like an ugly pizza, but it will taste fine. All the ingre-dients I used for the pizza are fresh. You are not going to be poisoned," I answered as I cut a small piece of pizza for him.

"Are you sure?" he took the pizza and studied it. "Do you have anything left over from yesterday in the refrigerator? I think going to a pizzeria will save you time and it will be easier than cooking a pizza yourself."

After this incident, I was discouraged from learning how to cook American food. As a result, now when I cook at home, it is usually Chinese food. If I want to have something different, we go to an American restaurant. Still after years of living in America I do not know how to cook typical American dishes, even a simple food like cookies. However, I can cook many different Chinese dishes, which were not taught by my mother. When I was in China, I never cooked any meals. I lived with my parents and my mother cooked for my family. Though when I came to the United States, I often missed authentic Chinese food. After I married my husband, I was pressured to learn how to be a good wife. I learned from Chinese cookbooks how to cook Chinese food. I often tried to recall what my mother did for a particular cuisine when I was a child. This example also indicates how important the impacts of the socialization process are in the period of childhood, which is gradually instilled into the life of a child. At the same time, the willingness to learn is also a key point.

To be socialized, people not only need to put in the time, but they also need to be active in their learning. This is also a lifelong process and anyone at any age needs to be able to adapt to new experiences in order to deal with different situations. Young children need to learn how to speak in order to express themselves so that they can have their basic needs met. An elderly person needs to learn how to handle life after retirement. An immigrant needs to learn almost everything about a new culture in order to fit in and survive in a new society.

When studying the process of socialization, the concepts of nature and nurture should be addressed. We often say that if someone has a talent for something with which they were born, such as a high IQ or a beautiful voice. This is a result of **nature**, which is defined as a human being's biological instinct. People claim that human behavior is based on biology. They attribute every pattern of human behavior to an instinct natural to the human species. Nurture is a different concept, and people who say that nurture plays a large role in socialization believe that the environment affects patterns of human behavior. **Nurture** declares people's behavior as a result of learning within a social environment.

When I was young, my mother began to teach me how to knit and sew, which was customary with Chinese tradition. My mother told me that if I learned these skills it would be beneficial to me in the future. I remember the first thing I tried to knit was a pair of winter socks for myself, but I was never able to knit them the right size. After many failed attempts and some embarrassment, my mother helped me finish. I tried hard to learn sewing skills, but I never completed any project without my mother's help.

After I married, my husband said, "I cannot believe that you didn't learn how to do housework when you were young."

"That is not true, I learned a lot of housework skills," I replied, trying to protect myself and prove to him that I was a good wife.

"What are they?" he asked, showing disbelief at what I said.

"I know how to knit," I said, without too much confidence.

"Really, you know how to knit?" he questioned, hesitantly.

"Of course, my mother taught me when I was twelve," I answered in a half-truth; not explaining my problems with making socks the right size.

"I really doubt it," he said in a laughing tone.

"How about I knit a sweater for you, to prove how good I am," I shot back.

"Go ahead and do it, I want proof that you know how to knit," he answered.

About a month later I finished the sweater. When my husband tried it on, he burst out laughing and refused to wear it again because the sweater was too loose and so short that I could see his belly button. After that, I began to believe that I was not born with the skills to knit. Despite lacking this ability, I have learned how to do many things over the years. For instance, before I came to the United States, I was not able to cook, but now I can make delicious Chinese food, which came from practicing every day and from reading Chinese cookbooks.

Although some skills are innate, most people have to learn the skills necessary for survival and comfort, especially children. Jean Piaget (1954) suggested that there are four stages of children's cognitive development. The first stage is the **sensorimotor stage**, which is defined as the stage of child development in which children through physical contact with others to experience the world. This stage of child development happens between birth and two years old and is acquired through physical contact with parents and other people.

The first newborn baby I took care of was my relative's daughter, Sarah. She was a healthy baby, but her mother, Barbra, had some health issues after delivering her. The day following Sarah's birth, the gynecologist decided Sarah's mother needed surgery, which resulted in my husband and I deciding to offer some help and flew out that morning. By the time we reached the hospital, Sarah's mother could open her eyes and nod her head at us. Her doctor said that her life was still in danger and she had to remain hospitalized for a few weeks. The nurses informed us that the baby was fine and would be released from the hospital the next day. The question of "who is going to take care of the baby?" soon became an issue. I felt my husband and Barbra's husband expected me to take care of Sarah because I am a woman. However, I had no knowledge in caring for a baby who was only twenty-four hours old. A few nurses tried to teach me how to undress the baby, how to change a diaper, and how to give the baby a bath. Even though I watched what the nurses were showing me and could hear what they were saying but none of it made sense in my head and I felt frustrated.

The next morning, we left the hospital with the baby and went to a children's clinic. When the nurse from the clinic said to me, "Undress the baby," I had assumed some other nurses would show up and do that for me. So I waited for about ten minutes, but no one showed up. The nurse came in and said again, "Undress the baby."

"I heard you, but I am waiting for someone to come in here and do that for me," I replied in a dissatisfied tone.

"You need to undress the baby yourself," she replied.

"Oh my God, I do not know how to undress the baby," I answered helplessly.

"Are you the mom?" The nurse asked.

"No, I am not," I replied.

"Well, I am sorry, I am very busy now. How about you try to do it first? I will check back to see if you need help," she said.

After the nurse left, I looked for the buttons on Sarah's clothing, but I could not find them. The diaper was so tight that I could not even pull it down until I realized I had to open it first. When I put Sarah on the scale to weigh her, she started crying loudly, which may have been because the scale was cold or because she did not feel comfortable with me, I was not sure. Many people who were walking by the room showed their sympathy for her, which embarrassed me. They made it seem as if I had done something wrong to hurt the baby. I understood they were concerned for the baby's well-being, and I tried saying soothing words to Sarah, even though she could not understand. She continued to cry very loudly; some doctors even opened their office doors and asked what happened. I felt so embarrassed and frustrated I started to plead with the baby.

"Sarah, stop crying, please, please."

Sarah ignored what I said to her. She stretched her arms and legs, and her skin turned red and her lips were shaking. When Sarah's father came in and asked why she was crying I almost burst into tears myself. I felt like I had no way of communicating with Sarah.

The first night with Sarah, I could not help myself from touching her nose and hands throughout the night to make sure she was still alive. A few days later, Sarah got a cold and she refused to let me put her back into bed.

I held her for the entire night, even when she was asleep. Whenever she woke up, I would say, "Sarah, I love you. You are a good baby. Everybody loves you." I even tried singing some songs to her to make her feel better.

After that night, Sarah developed a habit in which she used her small hand to grasp my collar tightly. It did not matter what kind of clothing I was wearing, whenever I held her, she would grab my collar and calm down. I believe she must have felt safe and comfortable when I had physical contact with her. This is one representation of the sensorimotor stage of cognitive development of a child.

The second stage of Jean Piaget's cognitive development is called the **preoperational stage**, which is defined as the stage of child development in which language is starting to be used. This stage occurs between the ages of two and seven. Many Chinese families, especially the first generation coming to America, would like their children to learn how to write and speak Chinese. To accomplish this, many parents will spend two hours every Saturday with their children in Chinese schools. In addition to wanting their children to be able to speak the language, many try to teach their children Chinese traditions.

I used to have a Chinese neighbor who had two lovely daughters. The first daughter, Michelle, was about five years older than the second daughter, Mindy. One day, the mother and two daughters visited my house and I remember Michelle's mother talking to me about how to make a particular Chinese dish. Later on, she asked me to take care of her children so that she could go back home to pick up the recipe. As soon as her mother left, Michelle, who was about six years old, asked me if I was willing to adopt her so that she could move to my house. I was surprised and asked, "Why do you want to move to my house?"

"Because I think you could be a good mommy," she said.

"Your mommy is a wonderful mommy, too," I replied.

I felt somewhat uncomfortable with this conversation, but I was afraid that something was wrong with Michelle, so I kept asking questions.

"Well, mommy used to be a good mommy, but she is not anymore," she answered reluctantly.

"Why do you think she is no longer a good mommy?" I continued to ask, because I feared something had happened to Michelle.

"Before mommy had my sister Mindy, she was nice. But now she always asks me to give up my toys so Mindy can play with them even if I just picked up that toy. This is not fair. My school teachers always tell me that everybody needs to learn to share. My mommy says that I have to let Mindy play with the toys first because she is younger than me. Why can't Mindy learn to share with me?"

Obviously, she was not happy with the new conditions set forth by her mother and teacher. I was surprised that a six--year-old girl could converse in such long sentences, and compare what her mother and teacher said. What little Michelle did not realize was that she was confused by different etiquette and expectations shown to her as a result of her two cultures. Americans typically teach their children to learn to share, but traditional Chinese culture usually teaches children to take care of the younger ones and learn to be modest.

There is a famous Chinese story about a boy learning to be humble. It has been passed down for hundreds of years. His name was Kong, Rong (Chinese names are structured last name first) and he lived in ancient China. Rong was the sixth child of seven in his family. When eating pears, Rong always picked up the smallest one and said, "I am one of the youngest in the family so I should take the smallest pear." Rong's parents were proud of his modesty. To this day, many parents use the story of Rong as an example to help educate their children. When this happens, a traditional Chinese value has been maintained and passed down, continuing to guide their behavior with this story. Simply stated, this tradition teaches Chinese people to respect their elders and take care of those younger than they are. It is under the guidelines set by these values that Michelle's mother tried to teach her to take care of her younger sister. Unfortunately, Michelle did not understand this. However, she was able to express her emotions using language at this stage of child development.

Jean Piaget's third stage of cognitive development, the **concrete operational stage**, is the stage of child development where children will begin to use logic, but remain focused only on what they see in their daily lives, and occurs between the ages of seven and eleven. Basically, children in this stage begin to develop logical thinking skills. Sarah, the girl I discussed earlier, at the age of eight received our Christmas gift in the mail and told us she wanted to be a mail carrier.

"Can you tell us why you want to be a mail carrier?" I asked.

"Every time the mail carrier brings a gift to me, I get very happy. I want to bring happiness to other kids too," she said.

"Oh, that is so wonderful! Sarah, you have a great idea. I am very proud of you," I replied.

I meant what I said, I was proud of this young girl. During this development stage, Sarah could distinguish between good and bad things logically, based only on what she could observe.

This also means that during this stage, Sarah had not yet reached the **formal operational stage**, which is the fourth stage of child development and is defined as the stage where children start to use conceptual thinking and alternatives to imagine issues surrounding them. This stage begins at about twelve years of age. By the year 2006, Sarah was twelve years old and starting junior high school. She qualified to be in an advanced math class after passing a pre-entry math exam. Her parents were so proud of her, and before she started her second year in junior high, we visited her and her family. When I asked her again what she would like to be in the future, she said, "I would like to be a lawyer or CEO, and after my retirement I would like to be a realtor."

"Why?" I asked.

"Because I will be rich and have a comfortable life that way," Sarah answered. "I will have a big office facing the sea. Inside I will have a big red leather sofa, where I can sit comfortably and drink coffee," she continued with a smile.

At the age of thirteen, Sarah was able to use her imagination to design her future, although she was not yet mature, and did not think of any possible problems that may arise while she worked toward her goals. She may change her mind when she receives more information about her career choice, or she may gain more knowledge in general, which will widen her thought process. However, this is the beginning of her logical thinking about the future. This is also the last stage for a child's cognitive development.

Mirrors are an important object for us to see ourselves and imagine how we look to other people. In sociology, a person derives their self-concept from a social mirror in order to observe how others react to them. This is known as the **looking-glass self**, which was coined by Cooley (1964; orig. 1902). He stated that the looking-glass self is a conception of self that is obtained from the response of others. For instance, one day, a department store was having a sale, so I went there to shop. I ended up finding a pretty dress, so I tried it on and liked how it looked on me. I did not purchase it immediately, but asked the shop assistant to hold it for me so that I could come back with my husband for his opinion. After dinner, we went back to the store together so he could see the dress. Before I picked up the dress in the store, I found a chair near the fitting room. I asked him to sit there and close his eyes. Then I secretly took the dress and went into the fitting room. I wanted to surprise him, so before I came out I told him once more to close his eyes.

"Honey, close your eyes."

"I never opened my eyes," he replied.

I quietly walked bare foot toward his chair and said, "Is it pretty?" I turned around and showed him the dress.

"Is this the dress you were talking about at the dinner table?" he replied.

"Yes, is it pretty?" I continued.

"Do you like it?" he asked.

"Yes, you do not like it?" I could tell by the tone of his voice that he did not like it.

"I did not say I did not like it," he answered vaguely. I had trouble understanding his exact feelings about the dress.

"Then, did you tell me that you like it?" I continued to try to get a straight answer.

"I did not say I did not like it," he repeated.

I walked back into the fitting room, took it off, and had the saleswoman put it back.

"Let's go home," I felt very disappointed.

"You do not want to buy it?" He questioned me with a puzzled expression.

"If you do not like it, why should I buy it?" I replied and felt completely disappointed.

"I did not say I did not like it!"

"Ni bu yao zai shuo le," I answered loudly in Chinese. Which means "stop talking about it."

The looking-glass self has three major points when developing the self, which are: (1) imagining how someone looks to other people, such as I thought it was a pretty dress, which is how I imagined the dress myself, (2) interpreting other people's attitudes toward them, such as my husband's attitudes toward the dress served as a social mirror by which I could observe his reaction, and (3) developing a self-concept based on others' attitudes/reactions, like how I developed a self-concept based on my husband's dislike of the dress.

Another story to help illustrate the concept of the looking-glass self takes place when I was in my second year of elementary school in China. I had a male teacher that all of the kids were in love with, especially because there were few male teachers in the school. One day, after he came into the classroom, several students in the front row started to laugh. Eventually, more and more students laughed and after several minutes the entire class slowly erupted into laughter, he then realized that his pants zipper was down. At the dinner table that evening, I could not help myself from laughing when I thought back to that incident. When my mother asked me why I was laughing, I could not get out a word because I was laughing too hard. My family sat there and waited for my story and I was finally able to get it out, but only in broken sentences because I was still laughing so hard. Much to my surprise and embarrassment, no one laughed.

To make the situation worse, one of my brothers even said, "You are so stupid to laugh so hard about that. Anyone could forget something like that."

After seeing the reaction of my family, I felt I was stupid and began crying. From then on, I always kept quiet in front of my family because I developed a self-concept and I was always afraid they would think I was stupid.

The concept of looking-glass self is important when studying the process of socialization. Many people have experienced the way in which their behavior, or the way they think about themselves has or has not been accepted by others. If they feel other people agree with them, they will continue that behavior. Otherwise, if they feel people do not agree with them, they may make changes to their behavior. Therefore, their behavior or thinking will follow the majority, which is considered accepting the social norms and values.

When people make this change it also means they would like to conform to the majority in society. An illustration of this point would be, after a few years of living in the United States, I feel that I have been socialized by American values and norms. American people never ask each other about their age, salary, or weight. In China, it was common to ask these things. So prior to being socialized by American norms I would have felt comfortable either asking or answering these questions. As a result of the development of individualism and privacy in recent years, younger Chinese people started to refuse to answer the above questions. This is especially true today about salaries. With rapid economic development in China, people seldom talk about how much they earn nowadays.

A few years ago, I met a Chinese person who was a graduate student from a nearby university. The student had married an American and quickly adopted American values and norms. I remember one day immediately following a general election, she said that her professor, who also came from a foreign country, had asked her what party she supported and for whom she had voted. As a result of her development of American norms and values, she told me that she felt uncomfortable telling other people her political affiliation. The changes in thoughts and behaviors of Chinese people, who have immigrated to the United States, including my friend, are examples of behavior modification because they have conformed to their new society's norms and values.

People may not realize the process of their conformation until they face some conflict situations with the values and norms they adapted gradually in their everyday life and kept in their mind until they use them. George Herbert Mead (1863-1931), an American philosopher, sociologist and psychologist, developed a concept called **generalized other** (1962; orig. 1934 edited by Charles W. Morris). Generalized other discusses keeping social cultural values and norms within the mind. Essentially, this means that people in any given culture need to remember all the rules that guide their behavior.

This is similar to when children learn how to play basketball or football. They maintain the rules in their mind in order to be successful. One example of the generalized other is when my student Michelle gave a speech with me about Asian cultures at our federal district court in downtown area. Michelle was born in America, but her mother came from Korea, and her dad is American. She discussed different expectations between her parents and cultural conflict at home. After we left the court we were in a hurry to catch the bus. Most Chinese people, when crossing a road, would cross if they see there is no traffic on the road, even though there are crosswalks. American people often use the crosswalks, regardless of traffic patterns. After I went across the road for the first time to see the map at the bus station, Michelle started to tell me, "You cannot go from here. . . ." Before she finished her sentence, I already crossed the road. The second time we both needed to go across another road, Michelle asked, "Can we use the zebra crossing?"

"Sure," I started to feel embarrassed. In China, teachers are considered a role model for students and are expected to watch their behaviors and try to be a positive example for their students. This Chinese value has been rooted in my mind and was the reason I felt so uncomfortable that I had not followed the rules.

The above story includes two examples of the generalized other. First, Michelle kept the rules in her mind that people should use the zebra crossing when passing a road. Second, I felt self-conscious when Michelle said that I should not cross the road even if there was no traffic, not only because I did something wrong in front of my student, but also because I felt I should have followed the rules as a role model.

For a lot of teenagers, socialization also happens within their peer groups. A **peer group** is a group of people with the same interests or who share some characteristics, such as age. A peer group is important for adolescents in their development by facilitating interactions and improving social skills. People seek help and social support from their peer groups that they may not receive from other social groups such as family.

When I was in fifth grade, my classmates and I started to understand the biological differences between boys and girls. It resulted in all the boys and girls in my class from talking to each other out of embarrassment. This period lasted between the ages eleven to fifteen. In my childhood, this was a special relationship among teenagers. Due to the impacts of rapid social change on the patterns of interaction among Chinese teenagers, boys and girls no longer keep such traditions today. As a result, I did not have any male peers throughout my childhood. I had only two female peers and I have kept a close relationship with to this day. Each time I visit China we meet and chat to talk about our teenage years and recall the good times we had in school. I cannot believe how deeply we influenced one another to this day.

Anticipatory socialization is defined as the advanced education people receive, in order to prepare for a future desired position in their careers. Anticipatory socialization usually occurs after people graduate from high school and prepare for their future jobs. A college education or vocational school education serve as examples of this term. After entering graduate school, I dreamed of having a career as a sociology professor. I had taken many classes, such as sociology theories, methodology, community studies, and human ecology, in order to satisfy my sociology major. My husband wanted to be an engineer, so he had to take many computer classes to learn about hardware and software. The process in which we obtained different knowledge, especially in college and graduate school for our future careers/jobs, is an example of anticipatory socialization. In the process of socialization, **public opinion** is a very influential concept, which can be defined as people's different attitudes toward social issues. America is a democratic country in which people have many rights, including freedom of speech. They can express their different attitudes and ideas about many different public issues, such as, gun control, pro-life and pro-choice, the death penalty, and many other issues.

The development of **mass media**, which is defined as channels of communication that can reach a large number of people, has allowed public opinion to spread more widely in American society than ever before.. The development of mass media has resulted in some of my students often arguing about certain social issues in classrooms. For instance, people recently discussed the issue of refugees from Syria. So far, I heard that many of them had entered into European countries, such as Germany, and in the past three years (2012–2014), America has accepted 70,000 refugees from all over the world. In one of my population classes, when discussing the chapter on migration, I presented different perspectives about refugees. This resulted in class debates, which was brought up by the students:

"Do you mean we should accept those refugees" a male student asked.

"I think the government is trying to accept more refugees from Syria now," I answered.

"Do you think the government can solve this problem? In my opinion this is a very hard problem to solve," a female student inquired.

"Refugees are still human beings. We should help them if we can," another student added.

"I think we have very limited resources. We need to take care of our own people first," one student argued.

Listening to all these comments, I knew I could not answer all of their questions, which have a lot to do with political policies, but I really enjoyed discussing with my students the current issues that the American society faces. I believed the more public issues the younger American generations pay attention to, the more likely those issues and problems will be addressed or perhaps solved in the future. As a professor, I have responsibilities to teach and lead them to comprehend global issues in order to understand the needs of our social as well as individual problems.

With the technological development of the world, the idea of a global community has been formed. Some of the processes of socialization might be the same around the globe. One example of this includes McDonald's food. A long time ago I heard a story about a Japanese boy who went to Disney World in Florida with his parents. As soon as he left the airport, he saw a McDonald's, and was excited and exclaimed, "America has McDonald's, too." Today, many countries around the world have McDonald's. Many younger generations may consider McDonald's to be exclusive to their native country. To me, McDonald's is not only a restaurant, but also a culture that impacts the life of Americans and people around the world. A sociologist, Rizer in his book *The McDonaldization of Society* (1993) points out that when a society adopts a fast-food restaurant, it also accepts the characteristics of the fast food culture. At this point, McDonaldization means a transition from traditional to rational thoughts, as well as scientific methods of management.

The process of socialization is important both for people and society. This is because all societies need to have social values and norms that guide people's social behavior (see Fig. 4.3). Without these social values and norms, a society will not be able to further develop. Socialization is also a process of interaction that helps individuals educate each other, learn, and communicate effectively. As a Chinese native, I feel that the socialization process in America has a particular meaning to me because this is a remarkable resocialization experience which happened after my college life. The process of socialization I went through is unforgettable due to the difficulties and different experiences prior to and after my immigration.

Figure 4.3. On June 1, 2015, Beijing City's government banned smoking in public areas. This has become another socialization process. According to a 2015 report, it is estimated that about 740 million people, including 182 million children, have been exposed to second-hand smoke daily. It's also estimated that each year 100,000 people die because of second-hand smoke and more than 1 million people die because of the use of tobacco (Schwartländer & Fong, 2015).

Chapter 5

SOCIETY AND SOCIAL INTERACTION

Key words: society; Gemeinschaft; Gesellschaft; mechanical solidarity; organic solidarity; primary group; secondary group; social group; instrumental leadership; expressive leadership; reference group; network; status; status set; master status; ascribed status; achieved status; role; role set; role strain; role conflict

While my true passion is sociology, if I were to decide that a career change was in order, I would very much enjoy teaching history. I believe that I can learn from the many experiences that have occurred throughout human history. As a student in China, classes like Chinese and World History were always required as general studies in junior and senior high, as well as college. I majored in English while I attended university and was required to study American history, a course which fostered a curiosity in history. This interest blossomed into a passion, which is still active today.

I still remember the discussion facilitated by my professor about the Founding Fathers and other influential people in the United States history including President Abraham Lincoln and Civil Rights leader Martin Luther King, Jr. There were many significant events in the United States history too, such as the American Revolution and the Civil War, that fundamentally altered American society. Years after graduating from college I would occasionally read history books so I decided to take a history class to learn the subject formally. I was able to take a course about American history from 1877 to the present at the university where I teach sociology. Through this class, I obtained additional information because I was able to get a wider sense of American culture and traditions than I did in China.

When students are learning sociology they must also focus on human history. When sociologists study history their concentration is highly based on

71

different social developments and social changes. According to sociology, human history is divided into two parts: preindustrial and industrialized societies. Tönnies, Durkheim, and Cooley have different descriptions in their comparisons of these two societies. Though they expressed different explanations, all agreed that industrialization should be a distinguishing characteristic in analyses of human societies.

Society is defined as a group of people who interact with one another and create a culture within a defined territory. There are four important factors in this definition: people, interaction, culture, and territory. Neither preindustrial nor industrial societies can continue without these factors. Additionally, there are three pairs of sociological terms to discuss the major differences between preindustrial and industrialized societies. The first pair is Gemeinschaft and Gesellschaft, the second pair is mechanical and organic solidarities, and the third pair is primary and secondary groups. For each pair of concepts, the first term is used to discuss preindustrial societies while the second is applicable to industrialized societies.

The first pair is called Gemeinschaft (preindustrial) and Gesellschaft (industrialized) coined by Ferdinand Tönnies (1963; orig. 1887). Tönnies, a German sociologist, observed that people's relationships/ties were different in preindustrial and industrialized societies and categorized these different social relationships/ties into two dichotomous types of sociological terms. **Gemeinschaft** (*guh*-mahyn-shahft) is defined as a community characterized by a well-built social cohesion and common identity, where people's interaction is based on personal relationships and traditions. **Gesellschaft** (guh-zel-shahft) is an association characterized by a fragile social cohesion, with people's interactions based on impersonal relationships that result from different cultures and a detachment from traditional concerns. It is a challenge to evaluate preindustrial societies and analyze people's relationships during that time because we cannot get a firsthand look at people's relationships/ties in a Gemeinschaft type of society. We can, however, assume that this is somewhat similar to today's rural areas, small towns, or even some traditional societies, where typically possess strong solidarity and maintain personal relationships. For instance, I used to have a Chinese friend named Molly who attended graduate school with me. She had been married for a while but had not gotten pregnant because she felt that her education should be her priority at the time. When she returned to China to visit her family, they posed the question why she did not have children yet, some even questioned the couple's ability to conceive.

Molly attempted to explain the personal decision she and her husband had made by saying, "It is difficult enough just taking care of my husband and myself. How can I take care of a baby as well while I am still in school?"

Her mother and mother-in-law immediately stated, "We can and would like to take care of your baby. All you need to do is to go ahead and deliver the baby and send the baby back to China."

"I cannot do that. It would be my baby. I have to take care of him/her myself," Molly answered.

"No, this is our grandchild, we will take good care of the baby," both her mother and mother-in-law emphasized.

Later on, Molly's best friend called her and said, "I have already made an appointment for you to see a gynecologist here in China, to see if you have any physical problems. The appointment is tomorrow at 9:00 a.m. You'd better show up on time."

After Molly came back from China, she met her husband at the airport. The first thing she said to her husband was, "Dear, could we have a child as soon as possible?"

"Why? What happened in China?" her husband was curious.

"I am not ready to take care of a child now, but I cannot bear the pressures from our families and friends. They asked me so many personal questions about my private life. I would like to have a baby because I just want to show them that I have no problem physically getting pregnant," Molly was saddened and discouraged.

As a Chinese native, I know how people behave in a Gemeinschaft way when interacting with each other. Several decades ago, people kept closer relationships than they do now. Back then, there was almost no privacy. This was especially true when most people lived in single-story homes in a courtyard. Most had to share a limited number of public restrooms. These kinds of close relationships do not exist in the urban areas of China today since the majority of families moved into apartments of 20–25 floor buildings. While the courtyard life may allow some people to be nosy and to be interested in someone else's business, I really miss the courtyard life, the closeness with others, the opportunity to receive more help., having a deeper connection with others, and more delegated relationships (see Fig. 5.1). Delegated relationships and ties are the kind of friendships where people share everything with others beside their family members. With rapid social change in China today and an increase in individualism and privacy, people now have relatively weak social solidarity. This is not only because people have moved into apartment buildings and seldom have contact with their neighbors, but also people's lifestyle has been changed due to the rapid development of urbanization. Another significant phenomenon I have observed was when people in China asked me how much money I earned as a professor in America. They used to share their income information with me but not anymore. This is because they started to build up values and norms they had never had before, including individualism and privacy.

Relationships similar to Gemeinschaft also exist in American society. These type of relationships are seen mostly in rural areas or small towns where everybody knows each other. One summer, I taught a five-week sociology class and the students and I met every day for two hours. One of my students, Jennifer, had just graduated from high school that same month. One day she told me that she needed to miss the next day's class for an overnight graduation party. When Jennifer came back, I asked her if she had a good time at the party.

Figure 5.1. Most of Beijing's courtyard houses are on one floor. This type of residential house has existed for over 1,000 years. The rooms are built from four directions in the main courtyard: the north, south, east, and west, and all are facing toward the central courtyard. The courtyard has one main entry door on the side to the street. The majority of the design of the courtyard has one or two sub-courtyards in the front and behind the main courtyard. After the establishment of the People's Republic of China, the government, in order to solve housing issues, assigned these rooms to different families within one courtyard. Even though it is very crowded, this design has greatly increased the social interactions among neighbors because most residents' outdoor activities are in the central courtyard. Since there are almost no family or individual's secrets among the neighbors in the courtyard, people experience a Gemeinschaft-like relationship.

Her response was, "Do not ask me that question. I am tired of answering it."

"Why? You did not have a good time?" I could not understand why Jennifer felt so annoyed by the question.

"Everybody has asked me the same question," she said.

"So? You just need to say yes or no," I replied.

"No, it is not that simple," she exuded a kind of anger.

"Is it complicated?" I did not understand.

"You really want to know? Okay, I had a good time at the party. I did not have a good time after the party. Before the party, my boyfriend picked me up from my house in the evening and he drove me back to my house the next morning. After I got back home, one of my neighbors showed up and asked me if I had a good time. I said yes. She asked me if I got drunk or not, if anybody had sex after they got drunk, if I stayed the night there, and with whom, and if I had done anything I did not realize. I have had enough! I am tired of answering these stupid questions," she replied.

I understood why she was so annoyed. This is a typical Gemeinschaft type of relationships. With this kind of interaction, people maintain close personal relationships and also voice traditional concerns. Their interactions are also based upon their common identity and certain standard values.

Compared to Gemeinschaft, a Gesellschaft type of society has a weak social solidarity and impersonal relationships due to a detachment of traditional values and social concerns. As mentioned above, Chinese people used to have a Gemeinschaft type of relationships. In the past two to three decades, due to rapid social change, not only people's relationships are transiting toward a Gesellschsft type of relationships, but they have also changed a great deal behaviorally. Traditionally in China, when buying expensive products, such as a car, people preferred to pay the price in full. If they did not have enough money, they would ask for help or borrow from their friends, family, or relatives. Today, more than likely, if their family cannot help them financially, they will go to a bank and take out a loan. This could be considered a transition from a type of Gemeinschaft relationship to a Gesellschaft type of relationship. Generally speaking, in most urban areas, people are strangers and the interactions between them are impersonal. People are known to each other by their names, positions, or occupations, rather than as individual persons.

A few years ago, I met a representative of a textbook publisher who was pregnant. After she delivered the baby she took time off from her job, but came back some time later. When she saw me, she asked if I remembered her.

"I remember you. You have a daughter. Is she about five years old?" I asked.

"Yes. My daughter is about five. Do you know that I am divorced? I finally kicked him out of our lives. It is a big relief to me," she continued.

I completely stopped talking because I did not know what I should say. Should I say "Yes" because divorce, in her opinion, is good for her, or should I say "No" because I think divorce may hurt not only the couple, but also her daughter? I did not give any comments because we are living in a Gesellschaft kind of society, and our relationships were not personal but business related. I felt that in my position I should not say anything or judge her status of marriage and divorce. As a matter of fact, after years of living in America, I learned to respect other people's privacy, which was not considered an issue when I was in China. As I discussed earlier, Chinese people started to pay attention to their privacy too in recent years with the further development of a Gesellschaft type of society (see Fig. 5.2).

Figure 5.2. An increase in Beijing's population has led the city to build high-rise residential buildings in the last two decades. People living in these types of residential buildings have few opportunities to interact with each other. This leads them to experience Gesellschaft-like relationships because of decreased social interaction.

The second pair of sociological terms discussing the differences between preindustrial and industrialized societies regarding how society is held together and was given by Émile Durkheim (1964; orig. 1893). The first concept is **mechanical solidarity** (preindustrial). This concept can be understood as social cohesion in preindustrial societies based on shared social activities, beliefs, and traditional values. Societies with mechanical solidarity are characterized by the similarity of its members, and are similar to Gemeinschaft societies. **Organic solidarity** (industrialized) is defined as social cohesion of industrialized societies based on interdependence among people with a specialized division of labor. Organic solidarity is characterized by the differences of social responsibility among members, which make them interdependent on each other. This type of social solidarity is similar to Gesellschaft societies.

When discussing these two concepts, Durkheim, a French sociologist, focuses on how a society can be organized. In mechanic solidarity, a preindustrial society is formed because people are alike, which means they do the same kinds of jobs and they belong together, such as farmers. A society is formed in accordance with the characteristics of the people. In organic solidarity, an industrialized society is formed because people have interdependent relationships. Due to the division of labor, people are doing specialized jobs, and they have to depend on each other to survive. I have an old story that happened in the mid-1990s that illustrates the interdependent relationships among people. On day, I asked my husband to buy a Walkman, which was very popular at that time. It used a tape to play music. People often used it while exercising. He asked me, "What is your budget?"

"$9.99," I answered.

"You do not need to ask me for such a small amount of money," he replied.

After work, I went to an electronics store. At the entrance I saw a student who was in my Introduction to Sociology class.

"Hi Boni, how are you? Do you remember me?" he said.

"Yes, you are in my 10:50 intro class." Even though this was the beginning of the semester and the class had seventy-five students, I immediately recognized him.

"Why are you here?" I asked.

"I work here. What can I do for you today?" he smiled.

"I would like to buy a Walkman," I replied.

"What is the budget?" he said.

"$9.99," I answered.

He abruptly stopped walking and said, "You should check another store. We do not carry cheap Walkman products," he replied.

"How about $19.99?" I immediately increased my budget.

"No, we do not have any in that price range either," he said impatiently, obviously not wanting to do business with me.

"How about $29.99? I only use it when I go out to walk. There is no need to buy an expensive one," I tried to explain.

"Yes. If you want to buy a cheaper one, $29.99 will work. But you should know that a cheaper Walkman will not last long . . .," he replied.

"I do not use it often. I . . . ," I interrupted.

"Listen. In your class I am very quiet. When you tell us to make a copy of something I do it because you are the expert. Here in this store, I am the expert. You have to depend on me for advice," he tried to persuade me to buy a better Walkman.

After a while, I walked out of the store with a box labeled "Sony." When I got back home, I placed the box with the Walkman inside on the dining table. When my husband came home from work, he said, "Oh my god! Did you only spend $9.99 for a 'Sony'? That is a super buy. Tell me where you bought it. I will get ten of them for my friends and family in China," I could tell he did not believe the Walkman was $9.99.

"Honey, I think when I told you my budget I mistakenly put the decimal point in the wrong place," I felt hesitant to tell him the truth.

"Where should the decimal point be?" He obviously was curious about what I said.

"Honey, I think it should be on the second nine but not the first nine," I was a little embarrassed.

"Wait a minute, you mean you spent $99 for this Walkman?" he asked.

"It was not $99 but very close after tax. This Walkman is $89.99. My student said it is very high quality and I will be able to use it for a very long time," I replied.

It has been more than twenty years since I bought that Walkman, which I have now stopped using because of the introduction of the CD player, MP3, and later on smart phones or iPod. The Walkman is still working well in the basement of my house, and still has many buttons for radio functions that I have never learned how to use.

The interactions between my student and I represented an interdependent relationship that only happens in industrialized societies. People perform different kinds of jobs in a society, but everyone must depend on one another in order to survive. For instance, when a construction worker is sick, he needs to see a doctor and go to a pharmacy to get medication. At the same time, the doctors and pharmacists need him or her to build their homes and offices. This is a simple example to describe the relationships between people in our society. In our everyday life, individuals have more complicated needs that require more sophistication in handling daily life and social activities, and it is rarely as simple as one-on-one interactions; instead, the interactions often include multiple people with many different roles.

The third pair of sociological concepts that represents preindustrial and industrialized societies is primary group (preindustrial) and secondary group (industrialized). The definition for **primary group** is the interaction of a group of people that is intimate, personal, and leads to long-lasting relationships. **Secondary group** is defined as the interaction of a group of people that is transitory, less personal, and leads to distant relationships. These two concepts were given by an American sociologist named Charles Cooley (1909) who discussed people's relationships. Primary group focuses on the traditional personal interactions that occurred in preindustrial societies. Today we can use contacts between family members to describe such social interactions, which are permanent personal relationships. The relationships in the secondary group are impersonal and temporary, such as classmates or coworkers.

In 2007, my husband and I went on a cruise to the Caribbean. We took a shore excursion and met a couple while climbing the waterfalls. We were hand in hand with this couple as well as other people while we walked together in the water for nearly an hour. After talking to them, we learned that we were all from the same hometown. The difference was that they flew to the island and we took the ship. They were there on their honeymoon and we were there to celebrate our wedding anniversary. We were so excited that the world was so small. Even though we both left our contact information and said that we would like to get together for a drink sometime when we arrived back home. After our short bonding experiences, we never did call each other. This is an example of a secondary group relationship.

We have mentioned social groups many times in this chapter. A **social group** is defined as two or more people sharing some bond or relations or common identity. The teaching position I have now with other colleagues is a social group. We are related by sharing the common identity that we all serve our students at the university. Our family is a social group, because members have a common identity and relationships. Parents take care of the children and they work together both as a family and a social group. Another example is that I am from China, so I belong to my Chinese social group. We are normally busy with our work; many of us do not have time to have parties together, however, we always share the tradition of celebrating Chinese Lunar New Year. Many Chinese people get together to have a party on that day. We cook traditional Chinese dishes and many of us wear traditional Chinese clothes. This is also in the scope of the definition of a social group, because even though we do not meet often, we still meet once a year based upon our common identity as Chinese.

There are two different types of leadership in a social group. The first one is called **instrumental leadership**, which is defined as a leadership of the group that focuses on getting the job completed. In my job as a professor, I must have instrumental leadership. I taught a class which only met once a week for a three-hour session. After voting on the time to take their tests, the majority of the class agreed to take the test at the beginning of the class. This meant that after the test, which only took an hour, I had to give a ninety-minute lecture. Even though I fully understood that my students were tired after the test, I had to continue my lecture because I had to follow my teaching schedule and get the job done.

Another example is that my husband has worked for a few companies since he finished graduate school. Although he really enjoyed the jobs he has done and the job he is doing now, he would feel tired if he had to work extra hours on the weekend. Sometimes I would say, "It is the weekend now. You'd better stay at home and rest. Family is also important for you."

"I know that it is a weekend, but I have to go to work because this job needs to be done. I have to follow the work schedule and my manager expects me to complete the project by next week," he tried to explain the importance of his completion of the job.

The second term is titled **expressive leadership**, which can be described as a leadership that focuses on the interests and benefits of the collective group. Expressive leadership is different from instrumental leadership because it is for the well-being of the group members. I used to work with an American professor who lived in a condominium with his Chinese wife. I often visited their family, and one evening he opened the door for me and prepared to walk out.

"Where are you going? You do not have time to talk with us?" I asked him.

"You can talk to my wife. I have to go door-to-door to collect signatures," he replied.

"What are you collecting signatures for?" I questioned.

"Do you know that some people suggested building a bar in front of our condominiums? This proposal will be discussed by the city council very soon. I have to stand up as our community leader to fight against this project. I guess I will collect the signatures first. If most people do not like the proposal, I will volunteer to take the leadership for the benefits of my community," he explained to me. What this professor did was expressive leadership because his volunteer work was for the well-being of the residents in his condominiums.

Later on, my husband and I bought a house and attended subdivision meetings. I realized many people voluntarily worked for their residential community, just to serve for the greater good. The difference between these two types of leadership is that instrumental leadership serves a purpose of ensuring the completion of tasks. Expressive leadership provides the function of organizing certain activities for the interests of others. Both leadership styles are important to ensure things are taken care of in a timely and productive manner and both contribute to the benefits of the group.

Reference group is a group that serves as the guiding principle for individuals to make decisions. My mother acted as a member of my reference group, while I was growing up because my father worked in a different city for years, so he had less influence on my upbringing. My first year in elementary school, I struggled to sit on a chair for forty-five minutes in the classroom. I was not interested in learning anything. After purposely failing my exams, my mother connected my school performance to whether or not I was a "pretty girl" (see Chapter 4).

Years later, working hard grew into a habit for me but the sense that "I am not pretty" became deeply rooted in my mind, even though I knew that being pretty had nothing to do with my school performance. So when a handsome young man, who was very popular in school, asked me to go out for a date, I refused him.

When I got home, I told my mother. "Mom, there was a handsome young man that asked me to go out on a date today."

"Really? Oh my girl is growing up. I am very proud of you," her eyes were full of tears.

I stopped her, "Wait, Mom, I told him no."

"Why? I do not mind if you go out with someone since you are in college now," she replied. She could not understand what I was saying nor my decision.

I started to feel embarrassed, "You know he is very handsome."

"So?" my mother continued.

"But I am not pretty!" I replied, spelling out every single word.

"What? Who said my girl was not pretty?" My mother started to pull up her sleeves and sounded like she was ready to fight.

"Mom, you said that when I was in elementary school. Remember? It was after I received two Fs for my math and Chinese midterms." I tried to recall her memory.

"I never said that! Are you crazy? I am your mom. How could I say that my dear daughter was not pretty?" she was shocked by what I said.

My mother later apologized to me many times, but I teased her that it was too late to apologize because she had already hurt my confidence. However, this was not true. I understood that she did not intend to hurt me, and the real reason I refused this young man was that I did not think he was the type of person my mother would like. I knew my mother did not like a young man who was so attractive to girls. She felt that a popular man could not fit into my personal characteristics. At this point, my mother served as a reference group for me. She would always answer my questions: was I pretty or not, if I wanted to be pretty, what kind of behavior should I have, and what kind of boyfriend should I have to receive positive feedback from other people around me? When growing up, gradually we find that we have many people in different reference groups. Advisors and professors are in our academic reference group, parents are the reference group in making important decisions, or peers function as an emotional support group. These groups are so important in our everyday life. Without them, we may have a difficult time understanding a situation or making an important judgement or decision.

If I ask you how many people you know, you would probably say that you do not know many people. In each person's life we have a much larger network of people that we have contact with than the people we truly know. A **network** is defined as people who have different interdependent relationships but may not have any direct social interaction. I used to like to eat a certain brand of ice cream. One day in class, I asked a student if he had a job or not. He said he worked in an ice cream factory. "What kind of ice cream do you make? Do you know that I love ice cream?" I asked.

"Really, what brand of ice cream do you like?" he asked.

I told him the brand of ice cream I really liked.

"You know I make that ice cream. Probably the one in your refrigerator is made by me," he laughed and he obviously felt proud of himself.

When I ate ice cream before, I never thought about who made it. All I knew was that I bought it from a grocery store. This thought is typical in our everyday life because we seldom realize that we are supported by many other people. We may not have the same identity or a strong connection, but we cannot go about our lives without others' support. A long time ago, I bought a clock. When I opened the box, there was a small piece of paper on the top of the clock with the printed words "Mary inspected." Later on, my husband and I called this clock Mary because we felt an attachment to the person who inspected our clock. This type of situation does not happen normally, because most of these workers are anonymous. Since we live in an industrialized society, machines make most of our products. They are not handmade, and the relationships between and among people have become impersonal.

In a society, everyone has his or her own personal status. **Status** is an individual's social standing in a society. American citizen, student, employee, child, parent, etc., all can be one person's social status. Combined, these statuses create what we call a **status set**, which are the statuses a person has in a given period of time. I am a professor and at the same time I am a daughter, and also a wife. These statuses comprise my status set.

Master status is a status that significantly influences a person's life. My best friend's husband had a dream to become a pilot. He had a physical examination and doctors determined that he was healthy, but he was color-blind. Because of this, he was refused admission to flight school. Color blindness has become a master status for him, and he had to redesign his career around this status.

An example of master status is that I loved to watch basketball games when I was young. I was one of the shortest students when I was in elementary school; however, one day I told my mother that I wanted to be a basketball player in the future. One of my older brothers, after hearing what I said, burst into laughter; he even fell down, rolled his body on the floor laughing, and said, "It is so funny."

"Why?" I felt so embarrassed.

"You are too short to be a basketball player," he answered.

"I still have time to grow up," I responded angrily.

"No, you will not be a basketball player even though you still have time to grow a little bit." What he said really hurt my feelings.

I gradually understood that it does not matter how much I dreamed of being a basketball player, I would never be tall enough. My height has become my master status, which decided that I would not be a basketball player.

Status also includes two different concepts: ascribed status and achieved status. **Ascribed status** is an involuntary social standing that is given at birth or later in life. I was an unexpected baby for my parents. My mother, after already delivering two boys who were nine and twelve at that time, felt that she was done having children. Therefore, after she got pregnant again, her first thought was to have an abortion, which was common practice for a married woman during this time in China. It was my dad who saved my life. He told my mother that it might be a girl and she would be my mother's best friend and take care of her when she was old. Today, because of advanced medical technology, people who are pregnant can know the sex of the baby if they would like. At the time my mother was pregnant, she, and other pregnant women, could only know the sex of the baby after the delivery. I was born as a girl, which is my ascribed status. Today, even with the availability of ultrasounds, hospital technicians in China are forbidden to identify the sex of the baby to the pregnant woman and her family due to a general preference of boy babies in China and a possible abortion. I doubt if this rule will be changed even with the two children policy starting at the end of 2015 because most Chinese families still prefer boys over girls today.

People can also obtain their ascribed status after they are born. For instance, people can develop cancer or get injured in a car accident, resulting in a disability, later in life. No one chooses to be a cancer patient or to be disabled. They involuntarily received the statuses that were given to them in their life later.

Years ago, a student of mine asked me a question, "Let's say a young girl, around eighteen years old, was raped, became pregnant, and became a mother because of her prolife beliefs. How would you explain this issue?"

"This is an interesting question. How about we have a class discussion?" I replied.

"I definitely think the rape is an ascribed status, because it was given involuntarily," a female student answered.

"How do you explain the part about being a mother," I asked.

"Can we say that being a mother is a voluntary status? To be a mother is her choice and she achieved this status," another student said.

Compared to an ascribed status, **achieved status** is a social standing that a person has to voluntarily work for and that represents the person's capability. Compared to the story above, since I was born as a female I was expected by my dad to be a good caregiver for my parents when they became elderly. Being the only daughter of my parents, I had no choice because this responsibility was given to me, as my ascribed status. However, becoming a professor, not a caregiver, is my achieved status.

Being educated in China until my graduation from college, I am strongly influenced by the Chinese culture, especially the traditional values of taking care of and being responsible for my elderly parents. To my knowledge, my Chinese friends here in America also have similar feelings, because we all received the same Chinese values. Even though we are far away from China, we often worry about our elderly parents. My feelings of responsibility for the care of my parents often bothered me, because I feel pulled in many different directions. This is because I also have other achieved statuses, such as my own family and job; my other social statuses also require me to take different roles which sometimes cause conflict.

Role is defined as an expected behavioral pattern related to a person's socially defined status. For instance, being a mother is one single status, and her roles are to take care of her child while also being responsible for educating and disciplining her child. A person's single social status, associated with several roles, is defined as a **role set**. Remember that a role set has a number of roles that have different functions. In the above example, both disciplining and caring for the child are roles of the mother. These roles function differently and sometimes contradictorily. Many teenagers do not want to tell their parents the truth about their everyday lives. On one hand, they understand that their parents love them, but on the other hand, their parents may criticize them if the parents may have different ideas about their children's behavior or attitudes toward certain things. At this point, parents' roles conflict with one another.

The term of role includes two different concepts: role strain and role conflict. **Role strain** is the conflict between roles with a single status. A professor like me is a single status, but I have to take on many different roles under this status. As a professor, I try to be a friend to my students and at the same time I have to discipline them by having different class rules, such as the requirement of submitting assignments on time. As a professor and an employee at a university, I not only have the responsibility to teach, but I also have to do research, publish my work, and apply for grant research funding. Besides that, I also need to have civil engagements, such as community services. I have limited time for all the roles I have to take on, with my single status as a professor, and the collective responsibilities attached to this single status often results in role strain.

Role conflict is an inconsistency between roles with two or more statuses. As discussed above, I am a daughter, so I should take care of my elderly parents, and I am a professor, so I should teach my classes and support my students. However, these two roles come into conflict. If I take care of my elderly parents, I have to be in China to stay with them because that is where they live. The issue is that I have my own family and job in the United States. Therefore, I am having a role conflict, which is based upon a few statuses with different roles.

In this chapter, we first discussed the ways in which, at societal levels, sociologists study human society and people's relationships, based on the historical changes in preindustrial and industrialized societies. We then analyzed group levels of relationships among people. Third, we focused on individuals' social statuses and the roles corresponding to the positions they occupied in a society. The reason for putting these three levels of analyses together is to emphasize that sociology concentrates on people's relationships at different layers of interactions and the way they relate and communicate to each other.

Chapter 6

DEVIANCE AND DEVIANT BEHAVIORS

Key words: deviance; crime; four theories of deviant behavior: cultural transmission theory, structural strain theory (five categories: conformity, innovation, ritualism, retreatism, and rebellion), control theory, and labeling theory; primary deviance; secondary deviance; stigma; four types of punishment: retribution, deterrence, incapacitation, and rehabilitation; three theories: structural-functional perspective, symbolic-interaction perspective, and social conflict perspective

Every society has its own values and norms that the majority of people will learn and follow. Some individuals do not want to obey these rules set by the culture they are often considered deviant behavior. **Deviance** in sociology is defined as some kind of behavior or attitude that differs from the social norms and values in a society. To decide if someone has certain deviant behaviors or attitudes, one must take into consideration the current values and norms in the society in which people live. In 2015, China banned smoking in restaurants. In the United States, it has been banned in most places for a long time. Therefore, smoking inside a public building in China was not deviant behavior before 2015. Ten years ago my husband and I were in a restaurant for dinner in China and I asked the waitress to change our seats. When I asked her a second time she wanted to know if there was a problem.

"We do not smoke. I do not want to inhale secondhand smoke." I felt a little embarrassed. Why did I feel uncomfortable? It was because I had asked the waitress twice to change our seats, due to the smoke filling the restaurant.

"I cannot find a table that is distant from someone smoking," I was not surprised by her answer. The thing that really made me uncomfortable was that she said, "If we forbid people to smoke, we will have no business."

"You should at least divide restaurant space into smoking and nonsmoking areas," I suggested.

"What are you talking about? I have never heard of a nonsmoking area. Where did you get this strange idea?" she asked.

I immediately stopped talking. I did not want to tell her that I live in America, where I learned about smoking and nonsmoking sections. This is how people avoided inhaling secondhand smoke in my state before a law went into effect that banned smoking in all restaurants. I truly understood that China had a different view regarding public smoking, because different societies have different rules. One society may think it is a normal behavior, and another might consider it abnormal. This all depends on the social values and norms at the time in that particular society (see Fig. 6.1).

Figure 6.1. This is a very famous walking street as well as a shopping center. In this popular "walking street," vehicles are not permitted. This not only helps prevent pollution, but also supports the improvement of people's health by making them walk. This is just one of the new regulations in China in recent years. Other regulations include no smoking in public areas and no jaywalking when crossing roads. These regulations have successfully limited many deviant behaviors.

Unlike social values and norms, deviance is considered a kind of non-conformity. People may ask if deviance is a crime or not. **Crime** is a violation of social norms that has a connection to criminal laws. Therefore, crime is deviance, but deviance is not necessarily crime. For instance, I was in a checkout line once at the store and I was standing in front of my cart about two feet away from a tall large man who did not have a cart. While I was waiting, he suddenly turned towards me, bent down, and started to talk to me. I could not catch everything he said, but I could smell strong liquor radiating from him and saw that his face was red.

"I beg your pardon, sir." I could not move my cart back because a lady behind me started to put her groceries on the counter. At that moment, I started to shake a little bit. The man straightened his back and slowly moved his body and then, to my surprise, he said, "I am talking to myself."

It is acceptable to think that he was talking to himself. I was shocked yet remained silent and did not say anything, I believed that this was a deviant behavior. If you talk to someone face to face, you are obviously talking to that person. He claimed that he was talking to himself, however, it was apparent that he was drunk. It is okay that he drank liquor because he looked much older than 21 years of age. What he was doing could have gotten him arrested due to public intoxication. It would become a crime if, after checking out his groceries, he got in his vehicle and drove. According to the laws of the United States, it is illegal to drive if you are intoxicated.

I had a female student who was arrested and put in jail for one night because she was intoxicated while driving. Later on, she and her three friends applied for a job, which required her to be able to drive to see customers. Her three friends applied and received job offers, but unfortunately, she did not due to her drunk driving incident being on her record.

A few years ago, I had dinner with my relatives at a restaurant in Beijing and some of them ordered beer. I suddenly heard a relative say, "I cannot drink today because I have to drive after dinner." This was the first time I had ever heard of people becoming aware of drunk driving in China.

"What will happen if you are drunk while driving?" I asked.

"I will be in trouble. I might be arrested or my driver's license will be suspended depending on how serious the problem is," my relative answered.

"Do you have any penalty in the U.S.? What happened if you are driving drunk? Is the penalty even more serious than here?" he asked.

"Yes, drunk driving is a very serious problem in America," I answered.

"I do not remember China having such laws before and I wondered how long have they been in effect," I continued.

"It has been a law for at least a few years. In the past, if a police officer stopped a drunk driver, the driver would be scolded and released. Now drunk driving will be severely penalized if you are caught. This is due to the increasing number of car accidents caused by drunk drivers."

My relative could not tell me exactly how many years the law had been in effect. The fact is that in the past, drunk driving was treated as deviance, but now it is a crime. In recent years, I heard a few times that some famous Chinese people, such as movie stars or singers were arrested due to drunk driving and were kept in jails for different periods of time. However, there is not a legal drinking age established yet.

Deviant behavior is based on social norms and values in each individual society; therefore, we will say it is a social product. To define what kind of behavior is norms or deviant, will highly depend on those people in social power. I used to live in a southern state which had a new freeway. We drove on this highway on the first day it was opened to the public. While driving, I saw many people who were stopped by the police and were receiving speeding tickets. I warned my husband while he was enjoying the new road, "The speed limit is only fifty-five miles per hour. Slow down please."

"How can that be? All of the highway speed limits are 65 miles per hour," he could not believe his eyes.

"That is the reason why so many people have been stopped by the police," I said.

Three weeks later, I drove on the same highway but something was different. The speed limit had changed to sixty-five miles per hour, and later the speed limit was changed to seventy miles per hour, which is the normal highway speed limit in some southern states. The people who made the decision to change the speed limit have the authority/power to do so, such as the police department. As an ordinary driver like me, I had no power to change the speed limit.

In 1998, I was invited to speak about China at a high school near my university I teach now. The instructor asked me to be in the classroom at 11:00 in the morning, and said that he would tell the front desk about this invitation. My understanding was that I would be allowed to go into the classroom directly without the instructor meeting me at the front desk of the school building. I was at the information desk near the school entrance at 10:35. When a receptionist asked me what she could help me with, I told her that an instructor had asked me to give a lecture.

"You can wait over there," she pointed to some seats on the other side of the room.

"He asked me to go in by myself. Did he tell you that?" I tried to explain.

"You cannot go in by yourself. You must wait there," she did not answer my question and treated me like I was a student in her school.

I sat down and waited until 10:55. Then I walked toward her and said, "I understand you do not want me to go in by myself, but the instructor told me that I have to be in his classroom at 11:00. Could you please go with me to the classroom?" I asked.

"I told you to sit there and wait. He should be out to meet you in a few minutes," she said.

"What will happen if he does not come to meet me? He told me to meet him in the classroom." I felt I had no power to control anything.

"You have to be patient. PLEASE sit there and wait." At that moment, I wanted to cry.

Twenty more minutes passed before I went to the desk and told the receptionist that I had to go to the classroom now because I was already fifteen minutes late. She looked at me for a moment and then asked a student to send me to the classroom. When I walked into the classroom the instructor and students all said they thought I was not going to come today. I briefly told the class what happened. A student said, "That is her job and she has the power to make you wait."

Power is important because people with authority will decide what conformity or deviant behavior is in a society. Deviant behavior is often considered to have a negative effect on a society, but people seldom concentrate on the positive functions of deviant behavior. For instance, most people may have the experience of seeing a police officer stopping a car that was speeding. This, in turn, reminds other drivers to obey the speed limit and avoid any negative consequences, such as a ticket or an accident. It is a positive effect on a society when people see a deviant behavior, which may help them recognize what the social values and norms are. The university I am working at now is a smoking-free campus. While I still occasionally see people hiding places on campus and smoking. This always helps other students recall the campus norms and also helps people identify the correct and acceptable behavior. Another positive function of deviant behavior is that it can result in unifying groups of people. The September 11th attack by terrorists was a tragic event, but it also had a positive function that united not only American people, but also the entire world together, which resulted in the fight against terrorism.

Up to this point, most of you will recognize that deviant behavior can sometimes have positive effects. An example of this is when Martin Luther King Jr. organized the Civil Rights Movement; he was considered a deviant due to the fact that his ideas did not conform to the social norms and values at that time. It was because of the ideas presented by Martin Luther King Jr. that the Civil Rights Movement began. Today, even though we are still working toward equality of different racial groups, we no longer have separate school buses, hospital waiting rooms, or restrooms based on one's skin color.

Deviance can often cause social change. When it occurs, it can lead to many different changes. A simple example of this is deviant lifestyles may result in changes of social values or norms. These lifestyles may be considered as disconformities in a society but may attribute to the acceptance of such changes. When jeans were first introduced in China, many people, who were my mother's age, felt jeans would only be worn by people who did heavy manual labor jobs, even though younger generations thought that they were fashionable. Now, in China, it is popular to wear jeans and it is no longer looked at as a symbol of manual labor. Chinese people have been greatly affected by the introduction of jeans and other aspects of material belongings, which resulted in changes in nonmaterial creations, such as alterations of lifestyles in China. People have recently changed the concept of beauty. I saw some young people now in China, wearing jeans with big or small holes. By the Chinese traditional ideas, it means that this person should purchase new jeans, or this person may come from a poor family and cannot afford new jeans. However, wearing jeans with holes in China, now, is fashionable and represents a different lifestyle, which goes far beyond the expectations of jeans.

There are four different theories explaining how and why people exhibit deviant behavior. The first theory is called **cultural transmission theory**, originally developed by Shaw and McKay (1942), which indicates that people have deviant behavior because they have learned it from other people through social interaction.

In China, other than public schools, there are also private schools. Most of the private school were established within the past twenty years and are expensive. My relative told me that it ranges from $30,000–$50,000 for a private junior or senior high schools in Beijing. When I was in school in China I had never heard of private schools because all of the schools were public at that time. The first time I heard that my student had graduated from a private high school in the United States, I was curious and asked, "Did your family need to pay for your private school?"

"Of course, it was pretty expensive for my parents," she answered.

"Why did your parents not send you to a public school?" I could not understand why her parents spent money to send her to a private school since there were many public schools.

"I guess they wanted me to get a better education. Plus, they also wanted me to learn about my religion," she said.

"Have you learned a lot about your religion?" I asked.

"Yes," she replied.

"Do you think you have received a better education?" I continued.

"That I do not know. You have to understand that I am still in the American society, even though I was in a private school. I think I have learned some good and bad values and behaviors like other kids of my age," she summarized.

What she said reminded me of my teenage years. My mother really expected me to be a good model citizen, so she kept an eye on me at all times to make sure that I behaved. She did not want me to talk to certain children because she believed that I would learn bad habits from them. When I was in my second year of junior high school all the students started to use dirty words when talking to each other. I admired them because they used profanity. However, due to the education from my family, I was not able to use those words in public. On one hand, I knew that my parents would not accept this kind of behavior. On the other hand, if I refused to use dirty words, I would not receive any respect from my peers. Therefore, I had to use dirty words to show that I was a part of the group. Later, I went to a public restroom located in my neighborhood because at that time in China, the majority of the people used public restrooms. I began to try some bad words by speaking out loud. Suddenly, I heard a voice.

"Is that my daughter inside?"

I immediately recognized that the voice was my mother's. I froze and kept silent.

"Is that my daughter inside?" she asked again.

I remained silent and expected that my mother would eventually leave the restroom.

"It is okay if you do not want to answer me. I will wait outside until you come out," she insisted.

Knowing that she would wait for me outside, I stayed inside of the stall for a while. After another couple of minutes, when I did not hear anything from outside the stall, I opened the door a little bit. I saw my mother with tears running down her face. I opened the door, lowered my head, kept quiet, and felt guilty. I could not remember ever seeing my mother cry this much.

"Mom, I am wrong. I am sorry; I learned these dirty words from my friends." I thought I had to say something to comfort my mother.

"Do you think that they are your friends? First, you should have good friends and learn good behaviors from them. Second, if you cannot learn good manners from them, you should cut off the relationship." My mother was sad and angry. I started to cry.

"Mom, I swear I will not continue to use dirty words, and I will not play with those kids again in the future." I felt ashamed that I tried to be cool with my peers and I was so stupid because I practiced those dirty words in a public restroom.

Today, I truly understand why my mother felt angry and was worried about me. This is because she did not want me to learn any bad behavior from other children. Cultural transmission theory focuses on how social interaction causes people to learn from each other, which results in either conformity or deviant behavior. In other words, no one is born as deviant or nondeviant person, but he/she may learn to behave different ways through social interaction as well as learning from other people. However, social interaction with other people can also influence social conformity.

The second theory is **structural strain theory** (Merton, 1968), which states that people exhibit deviant behavior because of social pressure. I sometimes ask my students a question when discussing this theory: "If you don't have money to buy an iPhone, but would really like to have one, what would you do to obtain one?" I tried to give them an example about the relationship between a goal and the means of obtaining an iPhone. The goal is to obtain an iPhone, and the means are whatever the person chooses to use to reach the goal. To answer this question, some students said that they would work hard and save money to buy one, others said that they would ask their parents to buy one for them as a birthday or Christmas gift. Some also said that they would sell something if they have to purchase the iPhone. Other students, with a smile, joked that they may steal it from a store or rob a bank to get enough money.

Their answers enabled me to teach them how to label people into different groups according to how they deal with the relationship between goals and means. Merton (1968) divides people into five categories under the structural-strain theory. The first category is **conformity**, which means people follow the rules of the society. For instance, if people would like to be rich, they try to conform to the social values and expectations; that is, to get a good education and to work hard. As discussed earlier, my students would make the effort to save money or ask their parents for financial help, in order to buy an iPhone. This behavior, of course, can be accepted by our social values and norms. They can all belong to the category of conformity.

The second category is **innovation**. It indicates that the goal is socially acceptable, but the means to reach the goal is undesirable. People in this category have an objective or a goal, which is approved by society, such as becoming rich or getting an iPhone. The obstacle is that some people use unusual means to achieve the target. A few students previously joked that they would steal the iPhone or rob a bank to have the money for the purchase. In this category, there is nothing wrong with their goal to purchase an iPhone, but the way of acquiring the money is not conventional, which could be deviant or criminal behavior. This means the way people want to attain their goals is not accepted by the social values and norms, so they belong to the category of innovation.

The third category of people is called **ritualism**, which includes people who have no ability to achieve their goal. So after questioning themselves, they simply abandon it. Many people are in this category, because they feel that they have a goal, which they may not be able to achieve in a short period or even their whole life. The people in this category follow the social values and norms and do not want to use any ways of innovation to reach their goal. After realizing they will not be able to achieve their goal, they stop chasing after it. In 1999, my husband and I bought our first house. I really loved it and the neighborhood as well. My husband used to drive through an area to go to work that was well-known because of its large homes and its reputation as the "richest neighborhood" in the metropolitan area. A few months after we purchased our house, we drove to the "rich area" to see spring flowers. I saw many beautiful homes. Among the homes we saw, there was one located at the edge of a river, with trees and flowers everywhere. The house had white siding, big windows, and a balcony around the entire house. I looked at that house from a distance for a while and dreamed of buying a house like that in the future.

"I really love this beautiful house. Can we save money to buy a house like this when we are retired?" I asked my husband.

"Do you want to buy a house like this? How much do you think it is worth?" he sounded like he did not understand me.

"Yes, I want a house like this, but I do not know how much it is worth." I looked at his face and was waiting for him to tell me his estimation.

"It could be a few million dollars." I had no idea if he exaggerated, if he just gave me the average price of housing in that area, or if he just wanted to scare me.

"Do you think if we worked very hard and invested most of our income in stock market or banks we would eventually be able to buy a house like this? I think this is my biggest American dream." In my mind, I almost wanted to beg him to agree with me, even though I understood that to save a few million dollars could be a very hard job for the majority of Americans.

"It is nice that you have a dream, but now we need to go home. If you really love this house, we can stand here for another five minutes while you continue fantasizing about it," he said.

When we drove back home, we both looked at our house from inside the car as we were passing. I felt it was small compared to the dream house we saw. Knowing that I would not be able to buy a multimillion-dollar home, I simply gave up my dream because the goal was too high for me to attain.

The fourth category is **retreatism**. People who belong to this category tend to have various personal problems, such as drugs or alcohol. Many of them are considered society's dropouts, which include people who are abandoned by society and vice versa. This category of people neither has any goals nor believes the social values and norms to achieve the goals. I used to teach a social stratification class and one time during class, one of my students, Eric, told me a story about what had happened to him.

"A few days ago, I went downtown to work. I met a homeless person who asked me for money. I said I was a poor student and had no money, but if he was hungry, I would buy him a hamburger," Eric started his story.

"Did you buy him a hamburger?" a female student asked.

"No, because he refused," Eric replied.

"Why?" I was surprised.

"Because he only wanted cash," Eric answered.

"Isn't it easier to give him money and then whenever he is hungry he will buy himself a burger?" another student said.

"No, I would like to help a person who is suffering from hunger and who needs food to eat immediately, but I am not simply going to give away my money. I do not have a lot of money. Furthermore, those people begging you for money may not need a hamburger, but need alcohol instead. I do not want to help those people with their drinking habits," Eric concluded.

"How did you know he would buy alcohol instead of food later on?" I asked.

"I smelled alcohol on him, and I was really suspicious about why he asked for cash only," Eric said.

On one hand, people who have a serious addiction to alcohol or drugs often have no goals due to their personal troubles. On the other hand, sometimes society does not offer these individuals any opportunities to change their social status. As a result, these people are viewed negatively due to their personal problems. I once asked my students in class, if a homeless person asked them for a job opportunity, whether they would like to consider it as a manager of a fast food restaurant. The majority of them said no. The reasons they argued were that many people, who had a home address and do not have any alcohol or drug problems, also needed a job. One student was a manager and he said,

"I would like to give a job to the people who are the most qualified for the job first."

I really do not think my students just wanted to give me an easy answer. Instead, their answers have represented the general responses of society. However, I feel if there are people who want to make changes in their life or have been corrected from their past life, our society should help them realize their dream too.

The last category is **rebellion**. People in this group are called rebels, who are not be considered that they do not have the ability to reach a goal, such as to become rich. People in the category oppose the social system in their society, the existing social norms, as well as the goals and the means of becoming wealthy. This category of people would like to change the system by using alternative social values and norms. The founding fathers of socialism and communism can be used as an example, such as Karl Marx. He criticized the capitalist system and his ideology was to establish a socialist and a communist society. The founding fathers of socialism and communism were rebels and disagreed with the normative goals and means to become rich in capitalist societies. They denied using any means to reach such a goal. What they advocated was to have a revolution to destroy the capitalist society and build an ideal society with equality.

The third theory regarding deviant behavior is **control theory** (Hirschi, 1969). It states that deviance occurs because society does not have strong social control over people's abnormal behavior (see Fig. 6.2).

Figure 6.2. This is Tiananmen Square. As you can see, smog makes the photo unclear. Beijing has become one of the most air-polluted cities in China. The Chinese government has established many regulations to protect the environment. The building in the photo is Chairman Mao's Memorial Hall, which was built between the late 1970s and early 1980s. In the front of the Hall is the People's Hero Monument. On the left is a police car. The fence is to prevent people from going through the square because of busy vehicle traffic. Pedestrians must use the underground tunnel to go to the other side of the square.

In 1995, My husband called me from our home in Alabama to my Kentucky apartment and said he could not find his car, which was a new Honda Accord that we had bought a year earlier.

"I think you'd better call the police to figure out what happened," I suggested.

After talking to my husband, later, a police officer confirmed that the car was stolen and he was told to contact a detective. Both my husband and I could not believe this happened to us. He kept saying, "I cannot believe that. This kind of thing only happens in movies. How could this happen in a real life?"

Ten days later, the detective called him and said our car was found abandoned on a street in a small city in Georgia. The location suddenly reminded my husband of the burgundy Honda that had a Georgia plate, which was in the parking lot outside our condo after my husband found his car was stolen. The most suspicious thing is that no one had ever closed the window, even though there was a heavy rain two days earlier. Then, police officers verified that a group of thieves drove from Georgia with a stolen burgundy Honda, then parked it beside our Honda and stole it. When we finally got our car back, it was full of trash. When my husband cleaned the car, he found a photo left by the car thieves, and he was excited because he thought the thieves would be arrested and punished, so he turned the photo over to the detective.

A week later, my husband called to check on the status of his case. The detective asked my husband, "Do you know how many cars were stolen last year?"

"I do not know," my husband answered.

"Do you know how many vehicles were stolen last month, or last week, or yesterday?" the detective continued asking.

"I do not know, but I do know that my car was stolen and I also found a photo of a group of young people. The thieves should be punished." In my husband's mind, police officers should have had no problem finding the thieves.

"Look, we are too busy with other cases. Since you have a very good insurance company, you should work with them and get your car fixed." My husband felt disappointed after speaking with the detective.

I have often thought that when the detective asked my husband how many cars were stolen last year, last month, or last week, did he ever wonder why so many cars were stolen? Does our society have a strong social control on stealing other people's property? This is an example of how a lack or failure of strong social control can result in deviant behavior within a society.

Some sociologists believe that deviant behavior is not learned but labeled by people in societies. **Labeling theory** (Becker, 1966) is the fourth theory that discusses why people perform deviant behaviors. This theory indicates that deviant behavior, like conformity, is labeled by other people and society. For instance, once while driving back home after work, the speed limit was 55 miles per hour, but I was going about 65 because traffic was moving at that speed. Suddenly, I heard the sound of a car horn. I looked back in my rearview mirror and determined that the sound was coming from an old Chevrolet, which was directly behind my car. The driver continued honking, which made me angry. I changed lanes to the right and prepared to turn to another road. I also wanted to see who this rude driver was, but the car passed me so fast that I did not get a good look. However, I did happen to see that the driver was a man.

"My God, this is a crazy driver." I said to myself knowing that I could do nothing to correct him.

The next day, I told this story to the class when discussing deviant behavior. A male student, felt reluctant, raised his hand and said, "Do you drive a burgundy Toyota Camry? Did you turn to the road heading toward the city of Ft. Thomas?" It seemed that he was trying to remember something.

"Yes, how do you know? Were you the driver behind me yesterday who kept honking the horn at me?" I suddenly realized why he knew the color of my car.

"Do you drive a big gray car?" I continued.

"Yes, please let me explain. I did use my horn and I drove fast because I was late for work. If I knew it was you I would have definitely driven better. I am sorry about what I did. I will drive more cautious in the future." He tried hard to justify and explain the situation.

"How fast were you driving? I was already going ten miles over the speed limit," I asked.

"I cannot say," he smiled.

"You know the speed limit is only 55 miles per hour," I said. "You should drive more carefully."

"You should do the same because you were also driving faster than the speed limit. It is also a deviant behavior," another student pointed out.

When labeling or defining someone who has deviant behavior, there are two different levels of deviance: **primary deviance** and **secondary deviance** (Lemert, 1972). The former is temporary or minor deviant behavior and can be withdrawn. The latter is continual or persistent deviant behavior as a career or a lifestyle. Therefore, a primary deviant is a person who does it once and then changes. A secondary deviant is a person who keeps practicing deviant behavior and continues through life doing so. For instance, years ago, a friend asked me to go to a department store with her to buy a handbag. She did not find a bag that she really wanted, but I happened to find a small candle for myself. The candle was square-shaped with printed flowers on it, and I thought it was very cute and affordable with the price being less than a dollar. I decided to buy it and I would put it on my desk in my office. Before we checked out, we walked around the store to see if there was anything else we wanted to buy. Unfortunately, we did not find anything we were interested in, so we walked out of the store. When we were in the parking lot, I found that I had the candle in my hand and had completely forgotten to pay for it. I immediately walked back into the store and explained to the shop assistant that I forgot to pay for the candle.

I said to the shop assistant, "I am sorry that I accidentally carried the candle out of the store without paying for it."

"It is okay. Anyone could forget something. I am glad that you realized that you had not paid and came back to pay for it." The shop assistant's friendly attitude really reduced my embarrassment.

I felt uncomforted, but I insisted on going back to pay for it. I felt that if I did not pay for the candle, I would be labeled as a shoplifter. This is an example of primary deviance, which means that if, by mistake, someone has done something wrong, they immediately correct their inappropriate behavior. If they accepted the title of a deviant and continued to behave in a deviant manner, as if they keep stealing, the behavior of these people would be secondary deviance.

In our daily lives, we need to be extra careful while defining or labeling people according to their behavior. This act is described by a concept called **stigma**: an influential mark, which may negatively change a person's ego. When I was in school as a student in China, after each test the teacher would post our names and grades on the blackboard. The students who received good grades, of course, felt happy. Those who did not receive good grades would be disappointed because everyone would know who did not do well.

I still remember when my elementary school teacher exhibited a boy's test grade to the whole class and said, "I will let everyone know that you did not pass this exam. You should feel ashamed of yourself. I hope you will remember your bad grade and you will make a better effort for the next test."

If I recall correctly, this student had a record of poor grades in all his courses. He was always the target in class, and was criticized by many teachers for not passing exams. After learning the sociological term of stigma, I recalled this boy immediately. I do not know where he is now or what kind of job he has, but I hope that such a negative powerful label did not create some pessimistic ego, which impacted him throughout his life. Most Chinese students while in school have experienced the exposure of their grades by teachers. This kind of embarrassment at some points can greatly impact or limit the development process of a child.

When I came to America, I noticed that my department teaching assistants would post students' grades along with students' social security numbers, but I could not understand why they did not post the grades with students' names, which was normal procedure by teachers in China when I was in school.

"This is a student's privacy, which cannot be violated," a graduate student who was a teaching assistant told me.

"Are you saying that whatever grade I receive will not be known by others?" I asked.

"Correct. It is not anyone's business to know your grade," she definitively answered.

I suddenly felt a great relief. As an international student with English as a foreign language, I did not have enough confidence to deal with my graduate school work. Instead, I felt that I had high levels of pressure because I was worrying about my school performance and my grades at the beginning. As soon as I heard that no one would know my grades, I felt relieved! This did not mean that I did not want to work hard, but I felt that if anything happened to my grades, I would not be exposed in front of everyone, giving me a chance to try harder and do my best from then on.

If a person has done something wrong, this individual will be punished due to the results of their deviant behavior and the seriousness of their action will affect others and our society. There are four different types of punishments for people who exhibit deviant behavior in society. The first is **retribution**, where punishment is given in repayment. My students often used an American saying "an eye for an eye" to describe retribution. I had a male student who told me that he was in jail for one night after being drunk and relieving himself in public. Someone reported the incident and the police arrested him. He woke up the next morning in jail, and was terrified. This male student was penalized due to his public misconduct. In a society where people receive punishment, due to their deviant behavior, it is considered a form of crime or retribution.

The second punishment is **deterrence**, which is the effort to detect or reduce criminal activities through punishment. Jails, prisons, and house arrests are examples of this term. After I joined the American society, I heard students often visited prisons with their professors, especially those majoring in criminology or criminal justice. I was invited by my colleagues a few times to go with them to the jail, but never got the chance to make the trip. My students told me that in high school they had visited prisons as well. I would often ask them why.

"I guess our school wanted us to behave and wanted to show us that if people do anything wrong, there would be a place to punish them," one girl said.

"Did you feel scared when you were there to visit?" I asked.

"Yes, because you do not want to stay there for years. The fear of being locked up made us realize that we really needed to behave," she explained.

Each year, there are many students, organized by their schools, visit jails and prisons. The purpose of this is to deter them from engaging in criminal activities and to instead, further enhance the stability of the society.

The third punishment, **incapacitation**, is defined as restrictions on the freedom of the lawbreakers in order to prevent them from participating in any further criminal activity. American television channels have programs that show how police officers protect people and fight criminals. The most popular one is *Cops.* Another one is *America's Most Wanted.* One of the shows not only collect information about criminals by looking for help within society, but they also educate the public by using these negative images of criminal activities in society. I have learned a lot from *Cops,* such as the concept of house arrest. This is an example of incapacitation, because house arrest will keep the lawbreakers in their homes and try to prevent any further crimes, which may happen if they were free to roam around the streets. I had never watched these kinds of shows when I lived in China, because Chinese television shows use positive images. In recent years, it has changed to a certain extent, and I have seen Chinese television report in the news about some criminal activities. I believe it is a positive change because it has given Chinese people multiperspective news in the society.

I once had a male student who came to me at the beginning of one fall semester and asked to change to my other class because of the fact that the class was full and he had to have my permission to attain a seat.

"Why do you have to switch classes?" I did not understand.

"Because I received a restraining order," he felt hesitant to tell me.

"Why?" I had to make sure it was not a made-up story.

"Okay, I will tell you. My former girlfriend is in the same class and her father dislikes that, so he put a restraining order on me. I have to change classes," he tried to explain to me.

"Tell me which girl, and I will separate you because we are in a big classroom." I still did not want to switch him to my other class, which was in a small classroom and full.

"I have already measured the classroom. It's not enough distance," he said disappointed.

"What did you do to make her father so angry at you?" I asked.

"I am not going to tell you. Anyway, it was stupid." I was glad that he learned a lesson. I also helped him switch classes.

A restraining order is another way to understand incapacitation. It requires that a certain distance be maintained between a problem maker and victim. Jails, prisons, and house arrests, all function in an effort to keep people with deviant behavior or criminal behavior from the public.

The purpose of having punishment is to reeducate lawbreakers and avoid criminal activities, which is referred to as **rehabilitation**. This is a difficult process. On one hand, they lose their ego and personal identity, even though they would like to make changes in themselves. On the other hand, society may not trust them anymore. A friend of my mother has a son, who, because of have a record for stealing, was incarcerated for a few years. When released from prison he could not find a job because of his criminal record, his neighbors looked down on him and avoided him. The opportunities become narrow for those who are criminal offenders in society.

One of my students summarized in class, "The opportunities are limited for people who have broken the law before because we have scarce resources and less job opportunities. Even people who have done nothing wrong need to compete with others for opportunities. If someone broke the law, they have lost the chance and ability to compete with others." Although, I agree with the idea of giving second chances, the reality is that our society may not or not be able to offer such a second chance to those people to restart their lives.

Structural-functional theory, social conflict analysis, and symbolic interaction perspective all explain deviant behavior in a society, but the basic analysis of these theories on deviance varies. Summarizing these three assumptions, **structural-functional perspective** uses three different points. First, deviance exists in all societies, even though it is defined differently from culture to culture based on each society's values and norms. In China, there are no laws for the drinking or smoking age, but in America, these rules are enforced strictly. One time I went to a gas station to pay for my gas. I found a calendar with a notice that said, "You have to be born on today's date eighteen years ago." I could not understand this sign, so I asked, "What is this?"

"Are you older than eighteen?" the lady asked.

"Yes, of course," I answered.

"Then you do not need to know," she replied.

"Why?" I could not understand.

"This rule does not apply to you," she was a little bit impatient.

"What is the rule?" I continued, even though I knew she would be mad at me.

"Listen, you must be eighteen to buy cigarettes." She said slowly and spelled out every word with anger.

This was the first time I had received information that there was an age restriction for smoking in America. Later, I learned many rules and I believed these rules would help our society remain stable. The second point of structural-functional analysis is that deviant behavior reminds people about social values and norms, which helps clarify moral boundaries in a society. This can be understood by an example of a student of mine who got arrested due to drunk driving. She had a few peers in the same class I taught. When her friend explained the reason why she did not attend school one day, the class learned that drunk driving was bad and could result in jail time. The moral boundary is this: if you are drunk at home or at a friend's house when you are at legal age, you may not be arrested, however, if you are drunk and decide to drive, you will be arrested if caught.

The third point is that deviant behavior should not be considered all bad and it can be good and result in social changes. This is best illustrated by the work of Martin Luther King, Jr., which I discussed earlier in this chapter.

Symbolic interaction perspective emphasizes that nobody is born as a deviant person, because deviance is learned through interaction with other people. Different people label a person as deviant or non-deviant differently, and one person does not always feel the same as the next. person The popular use of cell phones and text messaging has led to some of my students to check their messages in class. I feel this is not appropriate in the classroom, and I often solve this problem by joking around because I believe those students are not purposefully checking their phones just to annoy me or to break a class rule. Typically, my students will smile and put their phones back; however, there was one student who walked out of the classroom after she said to me that her cell phone use was not my business. The reaction of each person when being labeled as deviant is different. Unfortunately, labeling a person as deviant can sometimes result in secondary deviance, which means the person will adhere to their label and continue to practice deviant behavior.

The last theory is **social conflict perspective**, which connects social inequality to power. This theory indicates that powerful people make social rules based on their social interests. Powerless individuals within the society are more easily considered criminals, compared with those who have more power socially. Powerless people who challenge the social rules would receive punishment, but not the same penalty as those with superior power.

It is important to learn how to define deviant behavior, and to understand its influence on the operation of society as a whole. It is also important to understand the functions of deviance, because these functions clarify the moral boundaries and confirm the social values and norms of the society. The essential point is that deviant behavior may not be bad all the time, and it may create some much-needed changes.

Chapter 7

SOCIAL STRATIFICATION

Key words: social stratification; open stratification system; class system; closed stratification system; caste system; social mobility; structural social mobility; intragenerational mobility; intergenerational mobility; socioeconomic status; social inequality; structural-functional perspective; social conflict perspective

Coming from a socialist country, I had always believed that peoples' jobs were assured no matter which country they lived in. This was true of China at the time I came to the United States in the late 1980s. When I heard that my job as a teaching assistant was not guaranteed, but was based solely on my school performance, I became nervous. This was the first time I experienced uncertainty after coming to America. I approached one of my American friends who was also in the program with my concern, "How am I supposed to finish graduate school if my teaching assistantship is not guaranteed?"

She plainly stated, "Everyone in graduate school has to depend on their performance to keep their scholarships. No one is guaranteed, and everyone has to work hard." That left a heavy weight on my shoulders and an unanswered question, "What would happen if I lost my scholarship?" Now I understand that if I did not perform well, the alternative would have been to discontinue my graduate schooling in America and return to China. However, at that time, I was very naïve, and I still believed my university or the government would eventually help me.

"I will definitely try hard, but what will happen if I do not do well?" I could not understand how my friend could accept this reality and speak so calmly. So when she said "Nothing is guaranteed," it shocked me. "If I knew before I came to America that I could lose my scholarship or that it was not guaranteed, I would not have come. In China, everything is guaranteed, even jobs," I repeated.

"What do you mean that everything is 'guaranteed' in China?" she asked, sounding confused.

"In China, as long as you enter college, it is assumed you will graduate. You are guaranteed a job and guaranteed a salary even though the annual income may not be much," I responded.

"I cannot believe that. What happens if you don't pass your tests?" she replied.

"We are allowed to take a make-up test. A makeup test means that you took the test but did not pass it and you are given a second chance," I answered.

"I see. So almost every one can pass because you have a second chance. Am I right?" she asked.

"Yes, I'm wondering if they do this in America as well. If I fail the test the first time, can I have a second chance?" I asked.

"No, there is no second chance here in America. If you fail, or if you get lower than a 'B', you will lose your scholarship, and there are no exceptions," she answered.

I had no more questions for her as it seemed this was clearly the norm for America's education system. It appeared that everyone here in America felt that this was a fair way to ensure equality in the selection process. They were conditioned to the idea of not having second chances. I, on the opposite, had been conditioned to having more than one chance.

"After graduating from college in China, our government assigns everyone a job with a standard income, pension, and free health care," I explained further.

"But you have an equal pay system with low income," my friend replied. She obviously knew something about socialist China.

"It is *guaranteed.* Even though we do not earn a great deal of money each month, we know we will never get laid off or fired."

Today, due to rapid social changes and development, nothing is guaranteed in China. Unlike in America, college students in China are still allowed a make-up test. However, these days if they fail numerous times they are not guaranteed to graduate with a degree. They may receive a certificate showing that they studied in college but did not earn a bachelor degree. When I attended school in China, college students never had to pay tuition for college. Although, Chinese college students today have to pay tuition, it is much less expensive than the average tuition at American public universities. The average income for a Chinese family is lower than the average American family's income, but the equal pay system in China ended in the 1990s. The most significant change is that the Chinese government no longer assigns or guarantees jobs to college graduates after graduation. Today students must look for work and maintain employment based on their performance, and no one is guaranteed employment.

More than two decades ago, businesses owned by the Chinese government, especially manufacturers, laid off millions of workers with only a limited buyout package. In addition, people in China are now responsible for partially paying for healthcare costs, which was free before the healthcare reformation in the early 1990s. Chinese people must also pay for their future social security and healthcare for retirement as well. The situation of "no guarantee" that I encountered in American society when I first came is now exactly mirrored in China (see Fig. 7.1).

Figure 7.1. In the last three decades or so, China has experienced rapid economic and social changes. In 2008, the Olympic Games were held in Beijing. The above photo shows the main building used for the opening ceremony of the Games. This economic development has gradually led to a widening gap in the Chinese society between the rich and the poor because of their different income, wealth, education, and opportunities. Social stratification has become a social phenomenon in today's China.

As mentioned earlier, China used to have an equal pay system, meaning everyone received almost the same annual income. This system is known as a classless society. However, like the American society, socialist China now has social classes with rich and poor people. For instance, in 2014, China had added one million millionaires, which made China 3.6 million millionaires (Welitzkin, 2015). In comparison, American society had 6.9 million millionaires in 2014 (Welitzkin, 2015) (see Fig. 7.2). Social classes in a society are encompass which is known as **social stratification**: a social system in which people are divided into different social strata (layers) or classes. This is a social label given by a society, which divides people into roughly three categories, such as upper, middle or lower classes. It means that if an individual specifies that he or she is middle class, it only indicates that he or she belongs to the category of middle class. A middle class involves a large group of people in the American society. Within this category people's income ranges are from high to low.

Figure 7.2. This is an Audi car dealership. According to *China Daily* newspaper (2013), "Chinese buyers pay more for Audi, BMW, Mercedes as imported cars because of taxes and other charges." China also produces different kinds of automobiles, however, many families are still interested in imported cars, which not only are a form of transportation, but also represent the owners' economic status.

Different societies have varying ways of grouping people into diverse social classes. A middle class person from a more developed societal background maybe categorized as an upper class person in a less developed country. I had a friend once who graduated from an American law school many years ago, and then went back to China to join a law firm. In the late 1990s, a relative and I happened to run into him in a restaurant in Beijing. When we learned he was divorced, my relative wished to introduce him to her friend, who was around the same age as him.

"Do you have any criteria for a girlfriend?" my relative asked.

"Not really. I expect my future girlfriend to be young and pretty," he said.

My relative did not hide her surprise. "How young should she be?"

"The younger the better," he answered.

"Are you talking about a girl who just graduated from college?" My relative could not believe her ears after learning his age.

"Yes, that would be the best age. Remember, she must be pretty too."

"Then you will be ten years older than your girlfriend. Are you okay with that?" Obviously, my relative could accept that he wanted a pretty girl, but could not understand why he would be looking for such a young girlfriend. Although my relative and my friend had never met before, my relative tried to point out that he was not that young, and that the age difference might not be beneficial for his second marriage.

"That is the perfect age for me. I do not want to marry a person who will soon go through menopause. You know, I work for a law firm," he continued. "I can provide my future wife with a good quality of life. She will not have to work, but will enjoy a huge house, an expensive car, and many other luxurious things."

After talking with my friend, my relative clearly showed her contempt and explained that she had decided she did not want to introduce anyone to him.

"All pretty young girls will become old and may not stay pretty as they age. Do you think he may divorce her when she reaches *menopause* and marry another pretty young girl? Is this simply because he has a lot of money?" she was quite angry.

According to my lawyer friend, his yearly income was as much as I earned as an assistant professor in America in the mid-1990s. This was a big increase compared with what I had earned before I came to the United States in the late 1980s. I was, and still am a middle class person in America. However, my lawyer friend has been, and still is relatively well off by the Chinese standard of living. Different societies have various standards of arranging their members into different strata, based on their living standards, income levels, social statuses, and other factors. Generally speaking, once people are grouped into a social class, it is likely that their children will stay in that social class, but there are exceptions. In America, some individuals may be born into a poor family, but work exceptionally hard and become wealthy later in life. One famous example of this is Sam Walton, the founder of Wal-Mart.

Before I came to the United States I had never experienced social classes. Although I had heard about rich and poor people in America, I was unable to envision the differences. My husband and I used to ride our bikes on the weekends to visit a nearby residential area when we were in graduate school. We called this subdivision the "wealthy people's district." I took photos and dreamed that one day I would be able to buy a house like the ones I had seen. Years later, when my husband and I settled down and bought our own home, I realized that the so-called "wealthy people's district" was just an ordinary subdivision for middle class residents.

From my observations while living in the United States, I realized that as long as we are willing to make an effort, we have an opportunity to change our social status. When I first came to America, I lived in a university-owned family house, which had two bedrooms. I paid $129 a month, keep in mind that this was the early 1990s. Inside of the house there was only one heater, located between the family room and the kitchen. There were no heaters or air conditioners in the bedrooms or bathroom.

The university I attended was located in a cold area with nearly five to six months of snow from late fall to spring. Even with such cold weather, many Chinese students and their families still chose to live in that particular student family dormitory due to the rental price, being much lower than any other family housing. After my husband and I married, we moved to that dormitory. My university furniture exchange center offered us some used furniture for only $30. We got a big couch, coffee table, queen-size bed, breakfast table, four chairs, and two study desks. At the time, my housing situation was not the best and later I heard that my dormitory used to be a soldier's barracks. The outside of the house had an aluminum siding and the walls inside were thin, so in the winter my husband had to put plastic sheeting over the windows to keep the heat inside. We also moved the bed closer to the only heater in the house in order to keep warm. Years later, after I graduated, I learned the university demolished my former home due to unsuitable living conditions.

During this time, the beginning of our marriage, my mother repeatedly asked me to send photos of our residence so that she could see a bride's house. I never sent any photos to her because I did not want her to feel sad. Nevertheless, we had faith that if we received our education and graduated with our degrees, our status and lives could change. After my husband found a job as an engineer, our lives immediately improved due to his increased annual income. This example illustrates the social stratification system in American society and the important function that education plays. It displays that if a person has a goal and works hard toward that goal, then he or she can eventually change their social status.

The social stratification system in American society is called an **open stratification system**. This is a social stratification system that allows people to move between social strata. An example of an open stratification system is a **class system**, or a system in which a person's hard work and success are emphasized. The significance of a class system is that everyone is encouraged to make an effort to work toward their goals and dreams.

When I first came to the United States I had virtually no money with me due to China's equal pay system. My family, like most other Chinese families, did not have the financial ability to support their children's education abroad. Upon my arrival to America, I only had $30 in my pocket, which I exchanged from the Bank of China. In the late 1980s, $30 was the maximum amount of money a citizen could exchange. In addition to the $30 I had, I also borrowed $200 from a friend who was already in the United States attending graduate school to pay the deposit for my apartment after my arrival.

Before starting graduate school, I had to apply for a short-term loan to cover tuition for my summer classes. My life was difficult in the beginning due to pressure from limited financial resources, schoolwork, and a brand new environment. I understood more about the American society within a year or so and I found that I could accept the idea that nothing was guaranteed. I also understood that individually I must work hard and get ready financially and psychological for different possible situations to come. Having lived in both socialist and capitalist countries, I became acclimated to the differences between these two types of societies.

One of the advantages of the capitalist system is that it encourages people to work diligently for what they want. However, even though I take this "nothing is guaranteed" system for granted, I still believe that there should not be such a disparity between rich and poor in our society. For example, some CEO jobs pay more than a few million dollars annually, with another million-dollar bonus at the end of the year. If a company has to terminate their CEO's job, then the CEO will receive millions of dollars as reparation. On the opposite, the current minimum hourly wage in Kentucky is $8.20. Those people who are paid that rate of wage will have to work for more than 62 years without any holidays or sick leave to earn one million dollars before taxes.

People have differing opinions about those who have a poor quality of life. Many people believe that being homeless is that person's fault. Others may believe that it is society's fault, or a combination of the two. On one hand, some people may feel that those in poverty have the responsibility to work hard and improve their situation. On the other hand, some other people may believe that American society is at fault for not offering enough opportunities, such as jobs, medical assistance, and better living conditions to these disadvantaged groups of people.

The problem with socialist China was that the equal pay system actually worked as a hindrance for people to work hard, because everything was "guaranteed" and the system did not allow people to have a better life than others, no matter how hard they worked. Now that China has modified the equal pay system, many people have prospered while many others have remained stagnant. China has created a social stratification system, which is similar to the American class system now, even though wage rates for the Chinese are relatively lower (see Fig. 7.3). Due to recent globalization and the availability of the Internet, Chinese people have become familiar with some of the wealthiest people in America and their success stories, such as Bill Gates, Warren Buffet, and Mark Zuckerberg. They have become role models for the younger Chinese generations to follow.

During one of my visits to China back in the 1990s, a friend's seven-year-old son told me that when he grew up, he would earn a lot of money so that he could buy his parents a big house. I will never forget how he stretched his arms out as far as he could to show me how big the house would be. Knowing what I knew about China and my experiences in America, I wanted to cry because of what the boy had said and the significant social changes that had occurred in such a short period since I had left the country. As a sociologist and a Chinese, I regretted that I missed my chance to observe such rapid social changes taking place in China. When I was at the same age of my friend's son, I was taught to serve people and our country. Chinese people, especially children in schools were all educated by the Communist Party that we needed to sacrifice our lives for the interest of others.

Today in China, even though the ideas of serving people in the country are still taught in schools, children are also influenced by society and their family to become responsible for their own prosperity. When I was growing up, my generation was criticized for dreaming of being wealthy since it was seen as a capitalist belief, but in today's Chinese society, this conviction is now being coveted. To become rich is considered successful and admired by other people. This phenomenon not only indicates that there is a new social stratification system in place, but also new possibilities for people to change their social class through social mobility in China; China now has an open stratification system.

The opposite of an open stratification system is a **closed stratification system**. This term is defined as a social stratification system that does not

Figure 7.3. With the social development and economic growth experienced in China, some people have become rich and the number of people in the middle class is increasing. However, there remains a group of people who have become even poorer because of their low education levels, various health issues, and lack of job opportunities. The above photo shows a man in need of help not only because of his health issues, but because he did not have children, and therefore has no financial support from his family. In China, if the elderly parents do not have enough economic resources, the adult children have to financially support them.

permit a person to move between social strata. The open stratification system allows an individual to have social mobility between classes, whereas a closed stratification system does not. One example of a closed stratification system is a caste system.

India used to have a **caste system**, which is a system of social stratification where people must remain in the social strata into which they are born. The caste system is no longer legal in India. When mentioning that a person is "born into" a social layer or strata, it is also called "ascription." This means that a person is born into a specific social class. It does not matter how hard he or she tries, since the system is set in place by society and will not allow this person to move to any other social classes due to the social layer they were born into.

I had a female student whose family originally came from India. One day, she came to me after I discussed the caste system in class. She told me a story about her boyfriend whose family was also from India. She showed me a photo of a handsome young man.

"Congratulations! He is very handsome," I said.

"I know. He is now in graduate school. I believe that he will have a bright future," she continued.

"It is likely that you will have a wonderful future. Are you going to get married soon?" I asked.

"No. There are some problems. My parents do not agree with our relationship," she was almost crying.

At first, I could not understand, "Why?"

"Although we are in the same social strata, we are at different layers. My family name is much higher than his family name. That is why my parents disagree with our relationship. I really do not know how to solve this problem," she said sadly.

I was surprised by her situation, "Wait a minute. Have your parents been in the United States for a very long time?"

"Oh yes, but we still keep strong Indian traditional values," she replied.

"According to what I know, the caste system is no longer legal in India." I told her what I learned from a book.

"I know, but many people like my parents' and grandparents' age, are still keeping such traditions."

Later, I heard that she married this young man after successfully persuading her parents that the social strata were not an influential factor, and they now enjoy a happy life together. Most societies in the world today allow individuals to move or change their social strata through personal efforts. As mentioned earlier, this can only happen in an open stratification system, also called a class system, which allows social mobility and focuses highly on individual achievement. **Social mobility** is defined as the movement of an individual's social position within a stratification system. Social mobility is an important concept when distinguishing between caste and class systems. In a caste system society, as previously discussed, people are forbidden to move between social classes, so social mobility is not available. If a person is born into a slave's family, not only will he/she be a slave, but his/her children and future generations will also be slaves. They will not be allowed to have an education or even marry someone outside their social strata to make changes in their social position. In a class system, social mobility is available if a person makes an effort and has opportunities to change his or her social status.

There are three kinds of social mobility: upward, downward, and horizontal. The first two can also be called vertical social mobility. As I previously discussed, when I first came to America, I did not have much money. However, with my hard work, I have become a professor and I am considered a middle class citizen. This is the typical upward social mobility that happens to many American people. There are also people who have moved down from a higher social status. Years ago, I met a CEO of a high-tech company and later, because of the competition in the market, the company filed for bankruptcy and closed down and the CEO lost his job as well as the standard of living he had become accustomed to. This is an example of downward social mobility.

There was a period of my life, where I experienced horizontal mobility, meaning that social mobility moves in a parallel-manner. I taught in college as an instructor before I came to America, and I was sure that my career development path would go from a lecturer to being a full professorship in China. After years of graduate school in America, I received my Ph.D. and am now teaching in college and have received a full professor position. This change in my status is called horizontal mobility.

In China today, a person must have at least a master's degree and most likely a Ph.D. in order to teach at a college, even though colleges still keep some older professors who have only received bachelor degrees. This is because a great social change has taken place and the requirements for educational qualifications in China to be different now. This adjustment has significantly influenced the opportunities for many people who are trying to find teaching positions with a higher education. These limited opportunities are not the result of an individual's lack of trying, but instead are due to rapid social changes. This social movement is called **structural social mobility**, that is, social mobility that is not based on individual effort or achievement; but instead, a result of social changes in society as a whole.

In the early 1980s, television became popular in China. I remember the first TV I saw was bought by my neighbor, which was a nine-inch black and white one. Later, my family bought a 14-inch black and white TV, it was considered to be the biggest one among my neighbors. In 1992, when I first went back to visit my family in China, my mother had a 27-inch color imported TV. She continually complained that she disliked the remote control because of English words on the device, which she did not understand. She told me that she missed the buttons on the television where she could push to get different channels.

"I tried to buy a television with all the buttons on it so I could change channels, but I could not find one. Now, every TV must use a remote control," she complained.

"Mom, you have to realize that there are many channels now. You do not want to stand up and change the channel and sit down, and stand up again, and change it again, and sit down again. A remote control is a useful device for you to save your energy." I attempted to persuade her to accept the new device, which I really loved to use.

"There are so many new devices now. If you try to learn how to use them, your life will be much easier and you will feel more comfortable," I concluded.

From the "biggest" fourteen-inch black and white TV in the mid-1980s to a twenty-seven-inch color TV in 1992, rapid social change and technological advancement in China obviously altered my mother's life dramatically. Today, most Chinese families watch flat screen TVs at home, which further represents how social development has improved their quality of life.

Another example occurred in 1995, before I went to China to complete a research project, I wanted to take some black and white photos to make some slides. I went to department stores, and specialty shops selling cameras and accessories. However, I could not find any black and white film and they had to special order it for me. Later, I was also told that the development of the film would be expensive.

Today I could not explain why I had insisted on taking black and white photos. I think it was because I believed the effect of the slides would be more impressive. I recall from my childhood that photos were always black and white until the day I saw a colored photo of a newly married couple. I kept asking my mother how people could take color photos. My brother helped with the answer, stating that when the photo was taken it was black and white, and later, the person who developed the photo had to add different colors. This reminded me of when I took drawing classes and had to use watercolors. One day, when my mother was not at home, I put some watercolors on a photo only to find myself in trouble because it was not waterproof. My experience with the film going from black and white to color illustrates social structural mobility. The changes were not due to any one individual wanting to use colored film. This change was due to the needs and wants of technological improvement in society. Nowadays, advancements in photo technology are such that one does not need to develop film at all. Rather, most people are likely taking digital photographs now, and more likely to take so with their smart phones.

Social mobility includes two concepts: **intragenerational mobility** and **intergenerational mobility**. The former is defined as a change in social position within an individual's own lifetime. The latter is defined as a change in social positions that took place over generations within a family. For me, my intragenerational mobility is represented by the changes from an elementary school teacher, to a college student, to a college instructor, to a graduate student in America, and then a college professor. I always imagined that if I had never gone to college I might be a happy elementary school teacher in China, but I would regret that my life had not been different. Without these position changes in my life, I would have not been able to receive more education, establish my career, accomplish my goal, or even travel to see Banff National Park in Canada, Niagara Falls, the glaciers in Alaska, the beautiful ocean on the Atlantic coast of Maine, the Caribbean Sea, as well as the Maya Pyramids in Mexico.

Compared to my parents' generation, I have received a higher education, earn higher wages, and have a better quality of life. Now, when comparing my parents to my grandparents, I think my parents feel they are better off than my grandparents were. This generational comparison is called intergenerational mobility. When I was in graduate school, a few graduate students performed a survey that contained a question, asking close to 600 undergraduate students what social class they believed their families belonged to. The statistics showed that about 96 percent of the respondents said that they came from middle class families.

American society has a big middle class with a large range of family incomes. Based on the analysis by Kiersz and Kane (2015), the middle class has shrunk in the United States between the years 2000 and 2013. Kiersz and Kane (2015) point out that in order to be considered the middle class in the 50 biggest American cities, a household must earn at least $30,587 (Temper, FL) to $183,066 (San Jose, CA) in 2013. The wide range is not only based on different living standards in different regions/cities in America, but it also demonstrates that the middle class includes the majority of the American people. Therefore, I assume that most people's intergenerational mobility today will not change, due to the fact that their parents are in the middle class, and their children are in the same middle class, even though education and income levels have changed. Again, this is because the middle class is a large social group within the majority of Americans.

In sociology, an important concept is called **socioeconomic status**, which refers to a combination of variables used to measure different dimensions of social inequality, such as education, occupation, income, and other social factors. I once had a professor who worked for many years in college with a relative higher income. His son, after graduating from high school, went to work instead of going to college. His job was dangerous, because he worked in mountains and established electrical power systems from one part of a mountain to another. His father said that his son's initial yearly income was close to his. Therefore, a single social factor, such as income, may not be used as the only indicator with which to study people's social status. Other aspects, such as education levels, occupations, and other factors like residential area can also be used as social indices.

We measure people's social statuses because social inequality exists. Many students have told me that people are equal, but I disagree. A student once asked me about the idea that people are born equal. I have to say this is a common idea amongst many different people, because we often hear, when referring to someone born into wealth, that person "is born with a silver spoon in their mouth." Why isn't everyone born with a silver spoon in his or her mouth then? Simply because the odds could be against them when they are born into poor families. I do agree with the idea that people can always make an effort to compete with their previously designed statuses and make a better life for themselves than what was initially established by their parents. However, people are not born equal and they have unequal statuses during their entire life span. This is known as **social inequality**, defined as the uneven distribution of wealth, status, and power in a society.

Wealth determines a person's social class, status is an individual's degree of social prestige, and power represents an individual's political status. For instance, when I was in graduate school in a small town in the Midwest town, I had heard about homeless people, but had never met one until we moved to the South. A man and a woman stopped me when I went into a small store and I was scared because I did not realize they were homeless. I could not believe these two strangers were asking me for money, and I asked why they approached me, thinking they wanted to rob me. I could not stop shaking and quickly ran back to my car. Ironically, later my husband and I drove to a small hill where we saw many expensive houses with fenced yards and gates. I could see clearly the differences between the rich and the poor.

In my class I always use an example of social inequality by discussing my students' minimum pay per hour wages. In Kentucky, it was $5.25 in 2008 and it increased, for example, to $8.20 in Lexington and $8.25 in Louisville Metro an hour in 2016. Compared the minimum hourly pay for a person with $8.20 as an example and a person who earned about $60 per hour at the same time, if it is not taking tax into consideration, how far could $8.20 go? At the same time, in the fall of 2016 gas was about $2.40 per gallon. This means that a person with the minimum hourly pay could purchase about three gallons of gas for an hour of work. This is barely enough for a couple of round trips between home, work, or school. Earning $60 per hour would not only fill the gas tank of a four-door sedan, but there would also be at least $30 left over for other needs.

To buy a $600 laptop computer, if earning the minimum hourly pay for $8.20 per hour, a person has to work for nearly 73 hours, again it is not taking tax into consideration. That would be more than nine days of work, eight hours per day in order to purchase the laptop. The person who earns $60 per hour will only need to work ten hours to purchase that same laptop. If they were to see a doctor, and the co-pay is $30, the person with the lower wage has to work for 3.65 hours to cover the co-pay. The person earning $60 per hour just needs to work for about 30 minutes. Of course, if the person who earns the minimum pay worked hard and eventually got promoted, he/she could possibly earn even more than $60 per hour. The above comparison shows that there is a big gap between hourly wages in many societies, resulting in people's unequal social statuses.

Structural-functional theory and social conflict perspective explain the same social phenomenon of social stratification systems differently. Based on **structural-functional perspective**, a social stratification system is useful for people who want to make changes to their social status. No one in the system can avoid being placed in a social class. That is, if a person is not rich, this person might be considered average or poor. If this person is labeled poor, their opportunity to move up in the system may be greatly limited. However, to make an effort to climb this big social stratification ladder and to be better off in the future has become a common American belief. My experiences while progressing in life are examples of this perspective.

During my first winter in America, like most of my Chinese schoolmates, I did not know how to drive and did not have enough money to purchase a car. I was lucky enough to live near campus. In order to carry more groceries, I bought a brand new bicycle and a big chain to lock it up. One month later, I found that the chain lock had been cut into pieces and my bicycle was stolen. So, I had to carry my groceries from a nearby grocery store, which was about 30 minutes away. By this time, I really wanted to purchase a car, and it did not matter it was an old used car. A few years later, my husband and I bought our first car. It was an 8-cylinder Ford LTD used car. Fortunately, gas prices were not a factor since it was only $.79 a gallon at that time. Eventually, we bought our first new car and our house. This story demonstrates that sometimes with hard work and effort, situations such as living conditions can be improved. However, because we live in a society with different social classes, some people begin life with greater access to social resource than others, hence the "silver spoon" saying.

I believe that if someone works hard to achieve a goal, eventually they can reach that goal. Nevertheless, this has become partially true in my life because I have a bigger goal that has not been realized yet. My personal experiences may not be true for everyone due to different individual situations and goals. I know a little boy in China, who started to learn violin at the age of four. His dream was to be a famous violinist.

"How famous do you want to be?" I asked with curiosity.

"As famous as Yo-Yo Ma," the boy told me. "He is a French-born Chinese American cellist. He is a worldwide famous musician."

His mother told me she really wanted her son to emulate Mr. Yo-Yo Ma, who began studying violin at a very young age and later changed to viola. At the age of seven, he became famous and played for President John F. Kennedy. At the age of fifteen he performed as a soloist with the Harvard-Radcliff Orchestra. My friend's son has now graduated from college, and he seldom practices violin at home due to his commitment to his career. He still works with his hands, no longer as a musician but as a quality control engineer. I once asked his mother why he did not try to continue to perform violin. She explained that it would be extremely hard for her son to have a career as a violinist if he cannot be selected by a famous orchestra in China. The truth is that each year there are only a few people who find a position in the limited number of orchestras in China. The people they select have to be excellent. Obviously, the boy's mother felt the goal was too high and too far out of reach for her son. This shows that, even though everyone may have a goal and work hard, some goals may be unobtainable.

Structural-functional theory also explains that the social stratification system has a positive function for the operation of a society. Because everyone is encouraged to do a good job, this allows society to progress. In this process, those who make a greater effort and contribute more to society receive more rewards, such as, a CEO who has a prestigious status and is also highly paid. Whatever goals one has and achieves not only benefits society, but is also beneficial in their own lives. Based on this structural-functional theory, social values, people's beliefs, and achievements benefit both society and individuals, so this stratification system will remain stabilized.

Social conflict perspective, the opposite aspect, disagrees with the explanation offered by the structural-functional analysis. Social conflict theorists believe that people are divided into different social strata due to conflict. Because of this, different people have different social resources. People with more wealth, higher prestige, or more power have access to more resources, which allows them to be more successful than those with lower incomes or statuses and less power. I used to believe that if someone wished to attend school for higher education, that person would have the ability to move to a better status. However, I now have a different understanding because of my life experiences.

Years ago I had a student who was deaf. He began college with the dream of graduating and finding a good job. As there were no computer-connected projectors available at that time, he attempted to read his professors' lips to write down class notes. To help him, I asked a student to sit beside him to make sure he had written down everything. After the first test, he missed two weeks of class. When I called him, forgetting the fact that he could not hear, a female answered, and I told her I would like to speak to him.

"Could you talk to me so I could relay the message to him via sign language," she asked.

"To whom am I speaking?" I asked.

"This is his girlfriend. Could you please tell me why you want to talk to him?" she asked again.

"He has missed two weeks of class. I am worried that he will fall behind," I explained.

"Well, our family has run into a serious financial problem, and we all have to work longer hours. He has dropped out of school," she told me with a sad tone.

"I am sorry to hear that. If he comes back, please tell him to take my class again." I really tried to convey my sympathy to them.

Like many others, I used to believe that if you could not afford to go to college, you could just take out loans, and that would allow you to go. Looking at the bigger picture, I now understand that the lack of money may not always be the reason for the inability for someone to attend college. I have a friend who is now a nurse in a hospital. She always wanted to attend dental school in America and receive a dentist degree. This is because her previous occupation was a dentist when she was in China. She could not reach her dream to be a dentist in America, simply because she did not have enough money to go. I told her that she could get a loan from a bank.

"Well," she explained to me, "I know that I can borrow money from banks, but I have two kids and they need money, too, plus we have a monthly mortgage. I will have to shelve my medical school dream due to a lack of finances."

Social conflict theorists believe that only some people in society can use the system of social stratification as a tool to mobilize and benefit their social status. This means that those people who have more social resources have more opportunities to make such a change. According to social conflict theory, social stratification can be avoided. How? My understanding is that socialism, with an equal pay system, diminishes different social classes. The ideology put forth by Karl Marx has proven that even in a socialist society it does not end social stratification. China is a good example of this situation.

Before the rapid social change and development in China, an individual's status was based on power. I had a neighbor in China who held a high status as a government minister. He had two children, who went to prestigious schools. Although these schools were public, they admitted many high officials' children. The minister was provided a driver and a car with free gas, all paid for by the government. The government even paid for their housekeeper. With this information, it is hard to say that a socialist society is approaching equality. However, with rapid social change in China, social status is now linked not only to power, but also to wealth.

According to social conflict theory, social stratification represents only a part of people's interests in a society. These groups of people include those who have access, ability, or opportunities to change their social status and classes. Their interests of social stratification and social mobility do not reflect the entire population in the society. Based on this theory, only certain parts of society and only certain individuals are receiving benefits from this social stratification system. Therefore, both the society and the system may not be able to remain stable.

It is an important topic in many societies to study social stratification system and its impacts on people's behaviors, attitudes, as well as their daily life. Some people feel that it is fair to perpetuate the system of rich and poor because they think that each person has different contributions to society. It also reflects varieties of individuals' abilities as well as social rewards to their contributions to their society. This stratification system keeps society operating due to most people's beliefs that hard work will lead them to become wealthy. Others feel it is not right to divide people into different social statuses according to their personal abilities, wealth, political positions, and social classes, even though many people feel it is natural. Individuals with these ideas argue that people are not born equal based on their family socioeconomic statuses and therefore, should not be forced to stay in these unequal positions throughout their lives. I feel that society should embrace the idea of equality.

Those opposed to social stratification believe that it is the duty of a society to eliminate inequality among people. However, social stratification system exists in both capitalist and socialist societies. In order to move the world toward more equality, it is essential to understand the issues first. Why does inequality happen? How can inequality exist in human societies for thousands of years? How can different sociological methods that are practiced help narrow down unequal social sharing, in terms of privilege, wealth, and power?

Chapter 8

RACE AND ETHNICITY

Key words: race; ethnicity; stereotype; segregation; minority group; prejudice; racism; discrimination; amalgamation; pluralism; assimiliation; annihilation

I learned that the American society was known as a melting pot a long time ago while I was in China. I remember hearing about the term, "melting pot" during my American History courses in college. At that time, I did not understand the real meaning of the term because even though China is a country with fifty-six nationalities, we are all the same race. My nationality is "Han." Han people are located almost everywhere in China and are the major nationality, which includes about 91.6 percent of all the Chinese people (Central Intelligence Agency, 2015). I have met many other nationalities as well, the Tibetan people being one of them. They wear traditional clothing that has been originated from their ancestors, without their unique clothing I would have not been able to recognize their nationality by sight. Although some people may have different accents or dialects, that does not mean they all belong to any particular nationality. Instead, I would think that they are from different regions in China.

There are actually more than 80 different languages and dialects in China, even though many Americans only recognize the two main languages: Mandarin and Cantonese. Mandarin is a standard official language used by broadcasting, such as television and radio. Mandarin is the most popular language in the world since China has more than 1.37 billion people as of 2015 (Central Intelligence Agency, 2016) and 91.59 percent can speak Mandarin. Dialect is a regional language. It is said that people may live less than ten miles from each other but speak a different dialect. I do not know if this is exaggerated, but it does describe the many different dialects in China. I have traveled to many cities in China before, such as Guangzhou, and unless they spoke Mandarin, I could not understand them. Due to rapid social change like the availability of modern transportation and migration of people, more people who spoke Cantonese can now also speak Mandarin (see Fig. 8.1).

When looking into China's history, we discover that there are many different reasons for its regional dialects. In ancient time, mountains and rivers made transportation difficult. Also, the geographical size of the country deterred people from being able to communicate and interact with each other, which facilitated the formation of different dialects. China is a huge country with many mountains and two main rivers, the Yangtze River and the Yellow River. The Yangtze River is the longest river in Asia flowing from Tibet into the East China Sea. China is slightly bigger than the size of the United States (China is about 3,696,100 sq. mi. while the United States is 3,676,487 sq. mi.) (see Fig. 8.2). However, China has four times of the population compared to the population in the United States. At the same time, the

Figure 8.1. In Beijing, McDonald's and Starbucks, as well as imported cars and other products, are often seen. Mandarin is the official language in China, however, English has become more popular in recent decades. Many young Chinese people have an English name they use at work.

Figure 8.2. This is the Great Wall, on which construction began about 2,300 years ago. Over time, different dynasties in ancient China continued to build the wall in order to protect different territorial borders. A recent survey found that the total length of China's ancient Great Wall with all of its branches is 13,171 miles. The Great Wall, like a dragon, meanders over mountains, deserts, as well as grasslands. It runs across 15 cities, provinces, and autonomous regions in the Northern part of China.

total population in the United States was close to 324 million. As of July 1, 2014, the top city in the United States by population was New York, NY, with a total of 8.49 million people (Infoplease, 2014). While China has five cities, their total population ranges from 10 million to 22 million (Chinahighlights, 2014).

Once while I was walking on the campus of my university, I saw an Asian student in the distance. At first, I thought she might be Japanese because nearby the university I am working in there was a big headquarters and manufacturer of Japanese automobiles. I nodded my head to her with a smile. She stopped and asked in English, "Are you Chinese?"

"Yes. Where are you from?" I asked, also in English.

"I am Chinese too," she replied.

Normally, if I know that we both come from the same country, I would immediately use our native language for communication. Since Mandarin is the official language in China, which is what I meant to talk to her in, but I continued in English instead, "Which part of China are you from? By the way, I am from Beijing." The reason that I continued to use English because I had a feeling that she didn't speak the same language as I did.

"I am not able to speak Mandarin. I am from Hong Kong. I can only say 'ni hao' in Mandarin," she smiled.

"Ni hao" translates to "How are you" in English. We continued to use English so there was not a language barrier between us. It was amazing that we were both Chinese, but spoke different Chinese dialects, and we had to use English to communicate with each other. After our conversation, she enrolled in my class and also recommended my class to her younger brother. Again, English was still the only form of communication for us.

Although there are many dialects, China has at least 30 different written languages. However, we have only one standard official written language: Chinese. There are two different ways to write in Chinese, the traditional and the simplified versions. Mainland Chinese use the simplified version of written Chinese, whereas Taiwan uses the traditional version. Living on the mainland, I learned the simplified version and am only able to recognize and read the traditional version, but not write in it. In the United States, the most popular written and spoken language is English. There might be subtle differences in pronunciation between the people in the North and the South, but they are all understandable. Some people may speak other languages, such as Spanish or Chinese, but those are not the majority's language, although Spanish is quickly becoming a prominent language in America. According to the American Community Survey (U.S. Census Bureau, 2014), there were 38.3 million people aged five or older, who spoke Spanish as their primary language at home. Another popular spoken language is Chinese with 2.9 million people using this language at home (The U.S. Department of Commerce, 2013). However, people still have to learn English in this country in order to communicate.

America is a melting pot due to its diverse racial groups and ethnicities. **Race** is defined as a group of people who have the same biological characteristics from one generation to another. The definition of **ethnicity** is a cultural inheritance, which is distributed by a group of people. These two sociological terms are often used together, but they are completely different from one another. Race is based on biological background, such as a person's skin color, while ethnicity is primarily based on an individual's cultural inheritance. For instance, I can only eat pizza for two meals in a row until I get tired of it, whereas I can eat rice for years and never get sick of it. This is because rice is a traditional Chinese food, and pizza is a food commonly consumed in America. Due to my Chinese cultural background, I always eat rice with other Chinese dishes.

An American colleague asked me if I liked to eat rice, and I said yes. Then she asked me, "Do you have a rice cooker at home?"

"Yes, I do not know how to cook rice without my rice cooker," I answered.

"Could you please bring your rice cooker someday and cook some rice for me for lunch?" she asked. "I really like rice, but I do not have a rice cooker."

"That is not a problem. I can bring in my rice cooker tomorrow. Do you need me to bring a Chinese dish, such as pork and vegetables?" I also asked.

"No, thanks, I just want to eat the rice," she laughed.

"I have never heard of that. Are you going to eat the rice only?" that was unbelievable to me.

"Yes, I only want to eat the rice with my recipe."

"What is that?"

"You will know tomorrow," she said.

The next day I brought my rice cooker and rice. After the steamed rice was ready for her to eat, I found that she had some sugar and butter on her desk.

"Are you going to eat rice with these?" I was surprised.

"Yes, have you ever tasted rice with this?"

"No, I have never had rice mixed with sugar and butter in my life."

The taste was really good, but that was the only time I ate it. When I talked about this story to my class, a student commented that this was a common way of eating rice back when her parents were children. I do not think I will ever try it again because it is not the traditional method in which Chinese people eat rice. Not having been socialized on that track exemplifies my cultural heritage, the way I was raised and what I learned while growing up. In certain circumstances, a person belongs to a racial group; however, he or she may not automatically learn the cultural heritage from that racial group. An example of this is that many Chinese children, who are born in the United States and can speak and write well in English, may learn American cultural traditions more than the practice of Chinese culture. They might not be able to speak or write well in Chinese, even though both their parents' native tongue is Chinese. Therefore, a person belonging to one racial group may not necessarily belong to that same ethnic group.

I met a professor a long time ago, and she asked me if I was Korean.

"I am Chinese. Why do you ask this question?" I asked surprised.

"My daughter, I mean my adopted daughter, Tammy, came from South Korea. She is eighteen now. I want to find someone who is familiar with the

Koreans here and can introduce her to a Korean boyfriend. Since you are not Korean . . .," she stopped and felt hesitant to continue the conversation, and looked a little disappointed.

I immediately said, "No, I am not Korean, and I do not know any Koreans personally. But the good news is that I know an oriental church and there are many Koreans who attend that church."

"Really? Could you please tell me the address?" she asked.

A few weeks later I met her again on campus, and asked her if she had found a boyfriend for her daughter. She said, "I did not go to the church."

"Why?" I asked surprised.

"I went home and told my daughter that I would like to go to an oriental church with her the following weekend. She asked me why so I told her I wanted to find a Korean boyfriend for her. She again asked me the reason and she said she is not Korean but American and doesn't speak Korean or eat dog meat," the professor tried to explain.

Before continuing the story, I have to talk about a term, **stereotype**, which is defined as a generalization on a category of people that persists even in the face of opposing facts. Eating dog meat actually is a stereotype placed on Korean people. So I tried to correct the professor by stating that, "I think it is a biased idea that *all* Korean people eat dog meat. The people I have met before have never eaten dog meat in their lives."

"Yes, I know. My daughter and I seldom talk about Korea because she was abandoned on the street the first day she was born. She had lived in Korea for only three months when we adopted her, and she has never been to Korea since. Therefore, I gave up trying to find a Korean boyfriend for her, because she has very limited knowledge about Korea. She persuaded me that she is a girl who was born in Korea, but her ethnicity is American."

Another example about stereotype is when my husband and I used to live in Alabama. We often went to Chinatown in Atlanta, Georgia in order to buy Chinese groceries. One afternoon, while driving to Chinatown, we noticed that we were going seventy miles per hour, and suddenly my husband had to use the brakes and slow down to about forty-five miles per hour. There was a car in the front driving slowly. My husband, while changing to the left lane, said, "My god, I cannot believe these senior citizens. They drive so slowly."

"How do you know they are senior citizens?" I asked. Most of my research projects focus on elderly studies, so I wanted to know the reason why he had such a stereotype about the elderly people.

"Please keep the same speed with the car when passing, I want to see if they are seniors or not," I continued.

When the two cars were side-by-side, my husband and I both looked through our right window and tried to figure out who they were. To our surprise, there were two people in the car, and their ages added together were not even older than forty. The reason they were driving slowly was they were kissing while driving. I knocked at my right window and said loudly, "Hi, take it easy. You are driving now." I was not sure if they heard me or not, and we soon passed their car.

"They are not senior citizens," I said and gave my husband the evil eye.

"Senior citizens always drive slowly," he answered.

"That is not true all the time. I do not think all senior citizens drive slowly. Let me tell you a story," I continued.

I had a female student who had never missed class. One day, she told me that she had to miss one class because she needed to go to court. I asked her if she had any legal problems, and she said both yes and no. She explained that she had to be there, but she was a witness for a car accident. She said that a few months before, she stopped at a stop sign and another car rearended her. She looked back and saw that a big, old green car immediately backed off, turned around, and left. She was so shocked that she did not even pay attention to the license plate number. She reported the incident to a police officer, and paid a few hundred dollars to have the car fixed. The student felt that the police officers would never find out who drove the big green car.

After a few months, she was called and informed that they caught the person who had hit her car. This person had four or five reported car accidents in the prior months, but each time she turned around and drove away, until the last accident. It had occurred in a parking lot from which she could not escape, so she was easy to catch. The person was an elderly woman about eighty-seven years old. According to my student, this elderly lady was just cognitively slow and was hitting people because she could not drive well anymore and it had nothing to do with speed.

"Do you still say that elderly people drive slowly?" I asked my husband again after I told him the story.

"Yes, I still feel that seniors drive slowly," he insisted.

"Well, you need to understand that this is a stereotype of elderly people?" I started to feel he was arguing with me on purpose.

Stereotype often defines a group of people's behavior due to their age, skin color, or even where they were born. Back to discussing ethnicity, I often hear from my Chinese friends in the United States that their children are "bananas," which means that although their skin color is "yellow," their way of thinking, social values, and beliefs have become "white." My understanding of the term "white" does not mean the color of skin but the American culture in general. They are born in America, Chinese children and their ethics and attitudes are strongly influenced by American culture rather than the Chinese traditions they learned from their parents at home. When I first heard this term, I was surprised. However, when visiting my relatives on the East Coast, I was convinced that this "banana" description was an appropriate term. We started serving different Chinese foods for dinner one night when Jennifer, a six-year-old Chinese girl, said, "I want to have chicken nuggets."

"There are no chicken nuggets. We have only Chinese food today," her mother said.

Jennifer reluctantly picked up some of the food. She was the first one to finish the dinner and leave the table. I stopped her and said, "A kid needs to eat more food in order to grow big and strong." This is absolutely a Chinese value and most Chinese parents often ask their children to eat more than they want.

Jennifer stared at me and said, "It is my choice whether or not I want to eat more. If I do not like the food, then I will eat less. Why do you force me to eat something I do not like?"

I could see there was a big question on her face, but I had no explanation. My relative started to laugh and said, "She is an American kid. We are used to her challenging questions about our Chinese values."

At this moment, the term "banana" suddenly came to my mind. Although the girl's race is Chinese, her cultural heritage is from America. For my generation, it is hard for us to become a "banana" type of person even though we have settled in America for years, because the Chinese traditions and culture have been strongly rooted in us. I remember the first time I went to a Chinese restaurant with an American professor and his wife. A waiter talked to my professor first in English, and then turned to me in Chinese by asking what I would like to order. I was surprised and asked, "How do you know that I speak Chinese?"

"Look at our appearance. We are about the same because we both have black eyes, black hair, and yellow skin. We are all the children of the dragon, am I right?" His answer was so cordial, which made me burst into tears as well as made me homesick. The reason the waiter said that we are all the children of the dragon is because dragon is the traditional Chinese totem. It is not necessarily that we are the children of the dragon, but instead, we are the inheritors of the Chinese skills, habits, customs, and cultural connotations. The waiter recognized me as Chinese, not only because of my facial features, but also because of the way I spoke to the professor I was with, and the clothes that I was wearing, which represented the culture I am from. People who are familiar with the culture are able to recognize all of these.

I gained my basic understanding about American racial issues while in China. My knowledge was expanded from three different ways: An American Civil Rights activist, an English book, and an American play. Dr. Martin

Luther King Jr. was the name of the person that came to my mind. I had first heard his name when he was assassinated. Many Chinese newspapers put it as headline news, but at that time I was too young to understand what was going on. When a teacher in my history class talked about Martin Luther King, Jr. years later, I learned a word in Chinese, **segregation**. It is defined as the separation, either physically or socially, of different categories of people. At that time, I could not imagine how a society could have separate waiting rooms in a hospital, or separate schools, simply based on skin color.

The second way I learned about American racial issues and history was from, the English book, *Uncle Tom's Cabin,* written by Harriet Beecher Stowe in 1852 that was translated into many different languages including Chinese. When I started reading the book, I was already in junior high and I had a better understanding of racial issues. The third was a play called *Guess Who's Coming to Dinner,* which was about a young Caucasian girl who brought her boyfriend, an African American, back to her home for dinner. If you listen today, this story should not be any surprise. This movie was made in 1967 and involves a positive discussion on the topic of interracial marriage. Historically, this was illegal in most states in America. I thought I understood the meaning of the movie well because I was a college student when the movie was introduced to China in the mid 1980s. It was not until I came to the United States where I realize that I obtained personal feelings about racial issues in this society. I am not saying that I personally have experienced racial discrimination, but I did have an experience where I was unsure whether it was discrimination or not.

It was the third day after I arrived in the United States, and I wanted to take some photos to send back to my family. I went to a large department store in my town, and there was a lady in the electronic department, who was helping everyone standing in the line before me. After that, she started to check on something else in the store without helping me. I waited for a few minutes and finally, I said, "Can you help me?"

"WHAT do you want?" she answered me with an impatient voice. "I would like to buy some film. How much is it?" I responded back. At that moment I just wanted to get the film and leave.

She told me the price, let's say it was $3.00 even, and then she gave me a receipt and said $3.15.

"You said $3.00 just a moment ago. Why is it $3.15 now?" I said confused.

"Have you ever heard of sales tax?" she asked.

"No, I do not know what sales tax is. I just came to this country two days ago. Can you tell me about sales tax?" I really wanted to know.

"Go and ask your professor. That is not my responsibility," she said.

When I chatted with my other friends at school, to my surprise, quite a few foreign students knew her. They all said, "Next time try to avoid her. There are so many nice people around."

After coming to the United States, I did not feel very comfortable because I had become a minority. Even though I sometimes feel uncomfortable, I have to deal with it. The definition of **minority group** occurs when people are categorized by their physical being and sometimes, cultural characteristics, which put these individuals at a social disadvantage. However, sometimes, the feeling of being in a minority group often occurs which is not necessarily discrimination.

One day, I called my county courthouse for its address in order to mail a file to their office. The receptionist was friendly, nice and she explained the procedure of how to submit my document. At the end she told me the office address, spelling out every single word. I am sure that she recognized my foreign accent, and after a few words I started to follow her spelling out the words while writing,

"Division, D, I, V, I, S, I, O, N."

"Very GOOD!" she said.

I really appreciated her patience in helping me. But I also felt that she went too far, which made me feel like I was unintelligent because of the way she reacted to me. She behaved as if she were talking to a child or a mother who was happy because for the first time her daughter could correctly spell a word. Being an immigrant from a foreign country, I felt that people often question me about my ability to read, write, and speak English. I have heard many times when people speak to me that my English is good, but I understood that their meaning of good was a double standard of judgment.

People understood that I was not born in America; therefore, compared to some foreign-born people with a native language other than English, my English sounds good. I was never expected to have the same level of English ability as native-born Americans because of the fact that I am a foreign-born person. The term of this phenomenon is **prejudice**, which is a speculative overview of people who are categorized, based on their physical and cultural characteristics. Many citizens often have prejudiced thoughts against foreign-born people because they lack the ability to speak English well at times. Prejudice is normally a negative viewpoint of a social phenomenon. However, it also sometimes represents certain ideas formulated by people or social values, such as the above example of foreign-born people and their ability to speak English.

When discussing the topics of race and ethnic groups, there are two important sociological terms: racism and discrimination. **Racism** can be defined as beliefs that attempt to justify different racial groups in a socially disadvantaged status. I personally have experienced racist comments from two students I have taught. First, from a female student, who often used her cell phone during class, I had asked her to put her cell phone away quite a few times. One day, she was so mad when I told her to put her phone away again that she responded by telling me that it was none of my business. I said that in my class it *was* my business, so she should follow school policies and my classroom rules. She was so angry that she stood up and left the classroom. My department chair talked with her and told her that she needed to apologize to her classmates and the professor, but she came back to the class without saying anything. I did not want to take the incident any further because I assumed that she had learned a lesson and knew that it was not appropriate behavior for the class.

A few weeks later we had a test. The female student I previously mentioned left the class with another male student after submitting their exams. The male student said to her, "This Chinese bitch gave us tricky questions. She should go back to where she came from."

"Yes, she is a bitch," they laughed and left.

I was not there when this happened, but another student overheard their comments and felt uncomfortable. She not only wrote me an email, but also came to my office and spoke to me about it. This is the first time I had ever heard such nasty words, like "a Chinese bitch." I was very aggravated and hurt for a while because I had never heard these kinds of racist comments in my life. I understand that there are people who have racist feelings, comments and beliefs, and feel minority groups are inferior. However, many American people believe that all racial groups should be equal. I felt relief a few days later, because this incident made me have a better understanding of American racial issues. There is still a long way to go before America reaches a pluralist society, in which people will respect each other's traditions and not be identified by their skin color or their nationality.

If we say the concepts of prejudice and racism are ideas, discrimination is considered the actions that will most likely be based on those particular beliefs. The definition of **discrimination** is treating distinctive racial groups differently. Racism and discrimination were the dominant values and behaviors during a period of American history. *Uncle Tom's Cabin* describes a time when racism and discrimination were common and acceptable in America.

I read an introductory sociology textbook before. The book showed a black and white photo on one page with three restroom doors. One door had the sign, "Gentlemen," the second door said "Ladies," and the third door was marked "Colored." The meaning of these three signs was that if you were white, you needed to use the restrooms according to your sex, but if you were a person of color, you should ignore your sex, and use the third restroom based only on your skin color.

When I visited the museum center of the city I live, one of the exhibitions was on "Race." There was an older sign with two lines of words. The top one was: Public Swimming Pool; the bottom words were: Whites Only. The question I had to ask was: Was it really a "public swimming pool"? This is an example of racism and discrimination from the past. Today, with rapid social change and the Civil Rights Movement, the separate restroom for "colored people" has since disappeared. The public swimming pool is now truly for the public. Many job application forms even suggest that if the applicant is from a minority group, he or she should mention that, because they may have a better chance of being considered. Even with all of the changes, today we still hear of discrimination cases.

Years ago, the area where I lived had a conflict that revolved around a racial issue. Later, the National Association for the Advancement of Colored People (NAACP) started a campaign to boycott any social activities in this area. One day, I called my mother-in-law in Beijing. She said, "I heard some news about the city you are living in."

"What is the news?" I started to pray that she would not mention anything about the racial conflict.

"I heard from CCTV (the Chinese Central Television) that your city had a racial conflict and now you have a boycott," she said.

"Oh my God!" I felt disappointed.

CCTV is a television station run by the Chinese central government, and owns quite a few channels. All Chinese families will watch CCTV programs, and there are not likely to miss the news. This worried me because most people I knew in China were familiar with where I resided, and I did not want anyone to have a negative opinion about the city I lived in.

After living in the United States for many years, I now understand that the American society has made significant progress with civil rights of different racial groups. At least, most American people I know have a very positive feeling as well as actions toward different racial groups. It is likely in my classroom, I can feel kindness toward me and other minority students. Another example is that every Thanksgiving since I started to work in my university in 1994, my family would be invited by my colleague and friend, Joan and her family for Thanksgiving dinner. We know everyone in the family and we call Joan's mom mother. Mother knows the cookies I like the best and always gives me extra to bring home. From this story, you can see a vivid picture of the ideal melting pot in American society.

With this, I understand that we all trying hard to work together but still have a long way to go. In the spring of 2015, a white former police officer in North Charleston, S.C. shot an unarmed black man. The death of this man as well as a few other unarmed minority people has caught many American's attentions because of the mistreatment of minorities. Following these incidents, there were numerous activists who spoke out against these harmful actions. The recent movement that promoted the Black Lives Matter mantra is one of the reactions which formed to fight the racially motivated negative behavior.

After coming to the American society, I have found that many people have mixed racial backgrounds. What I mean is those people's parents are from different racial groups. In a sociological term, this phenomenon is called **amalgamation**, which means the intermarrying or interbreeding of different racial groups. When it comes to the social meaning, amalgamation is defined as a child's parents being from different racial categories. I used this word for many years, and none of my students questioned it until one day a specific student did.

"What do you mean amalgamation? I do not like this word," a student said.

"It means merger or consolidation. Why don't you like the word?" I asked.

"It means blend or mixture. This word can be used for everything, for companies, and for animals. We are humans, so we should not use the same word that can be also used for animals," she answered.

Later, she went to the library and found a few words that could be used instead of the word amalgamation, such as hybrid, merge, or combination. We use amalgamation, or any other word with a similar meaning, to indicate that many people from different racial groups are married or choose to be together to have the next generation. This is an especially important and a popular social phenomenon in American society.

I have known many families in this situation: An American white husband and a Chinese wife, an American white husband and a Japanese wife, and a Chinese wife and a Japanese husband. All of their children are able to speak two languages and recognize two different cultures. I personally think that it does not matter what kind of term we use to describe this social experience. With the increase of globalization and social development in the world, more and more societies and people will accept the occurrence of amalgamation. I also believe that many people will mark the race categories like "other" when filling out a questionnaire or an application before we have more categories to define people's racial groups. Even today, any survey on racial groups cannot cover all the categories of combinations of different race. This has become a special characteristic of American culture. However, there are so many situations surrounding the concept of "other," this category is continuing to evolve and covering a broad range of people. Realistically, nearly everyone could define himself or herself as "other."

In my class, I asked a student after he told me that his mother was white and father was African American, "Do you think you are white or African American or other?"

"I think I am African American, because my father is African American. I have 50 percent from him," he said.

"Why don't you think you are white since you are 50 percent white?" I continued.

"I am not white. I am sure about that," he answered immediately.

"Your mom is white," I said.

"Yes. She is, but I am not," he responded.

"What would happen if your father were white and your mother were African American?" I asked.

"I would still be African American," he said.

"When you fill out a form about your race, are you going to mark the category 'other'?" I asked.

"Sometimes, if there is a category of 'other', but most of the time I mark 'African American,'" he said.

"How many students in your high school are in this situation like you?" I have heard of his school because I used to live in his community, which was rated as one of the best places to live in. In this neighborhood the majority of residents are white.

"Not many. I guess I was the only one in my high school. But here at college, I have found more people like me," he answered.

Most biracial people with African and European ancestry consider themselves African Americans rather than Caucasian due to their skin color. The relationship between people from different racial groups is a type of interaction between minority and majority groups. As discussed earlier, my nationality is "Han." However, I personally have one-quarter of a different nationality as a Chinese, because my grandma was from the "Man" nationality. She married my grandpa, who belonged to the "Han" nationality, the majority in China. My mother has 50 percent of each, but my mother declares that she is from the 'Han' nationality, even though she is mixed. I have one-quarter of the "Man" nationality, but I have always the thought that I am 100 percent from the Han nationality. After growing up, I started to be very interested in the Man's culture and history because I started to realize that I have some connection in my bloodline. Man nationality, as a minority, ruled China for 268 years with 12 emperors (1644–1911), which are called "Qing Dynasty." Through learning many facts about this last dynasty in China I now strongly recognized the connection between myself, my mother's family, and this part of Chinese history.

The ideal type of interaction between minority and majority is **plural-ism**, defined as a situation in which different racial and ethnic groups will maintain their own traditions, beliefs, values, and identities. American society is a melting pot, but it is also a "salad bowl." The meaning of melting pot is that people who emigrated from other countries bring different cultures to this country, influence each other, respect each other's cultural background, as well as learn American dominant culture.

This is also the meaning of a salad bowl. Due to the fact that people ideally should keep their own cultures, traditions, and identities, while at the same time they can also maintain equal social positions and contribute what they can to the future of the American society. I come from China, so I will keep my identity as Chinese and my traditions. As a result, I still have the same equal standing as others. I think this is an ideal type of interaction between the majority and minority groups in the society. The fact is the way that most people, especially immigrants, will be more or less absorbed into the dominant culture.

This social process is called **assimilation**, which is the procedure of a minority group increasingly changing their way of life in order to conform to the dominant culture. It has the meaning of merged or mixed. The process of assimilation is that the minority groups in order to fit into the society must alter their life styles, social values, and beliefs, due to the influences of the majority. This is likely a gradual process of change, so people may not recognize the change by their day-to-day life.

In the early 1990s, my husband and I went back to see our families for the first time. Before the trip, I told him that I would eat at all of the restaurants in Beijing because I missed authentic Chinese food. After our arrival, we did go to a few restaurants. One day, my best friends called and said they would like to invite us for dinner; all we needed to do was find a restaurant and they would pay for it. I thought for a while and then suggested Pizza Hut.

"Hello, please wake up. You are in China now. Pizza Hut is not a Chinese restaurant." My friend who called me could not believe her ears.

"Well, I know Pizza Hut is an American restaurant, but the other day I saw one in Beijing. I really want to have pizza," I answered with a little bit of guilt, because I had told her previously that I really missed Chinese food.

"Okay, if you like pizza, we will go to Pizza Hut. I cannot believe that you are that Americanized."

At Pizza Hut, we ordered "meat lovers" and "pepperoni" pan pizzas and we had a wonderful time. After years of settling down in the United States, I felt that even though I still spoke fluent Chinese I had already assimilated to American values, beliefs, and traditions. This kind of assimilation includes the acceptance of American food, lifestyle, major values, and religious beliefs. For instance, I noticed that my family often said to me, when I offered suggestions to them back in China, "What you said may be okay in America, but you do not know the situation in China. This idea is not applicable here."

At the beginning, when my family and friends said that, I just thought it was a communication issue by phone calls. Later on, they often made those statements and I started to realize that I am not only physically and geographically away from China, but also culturally. The latter is not due to the distance between America and China, but because I have assimilated into the American culture. Therefore, when I communicate with my family and friends, my way of thinking is Americanized, which differs from theirs in China.

The third term is amalgamation which was discussed earlier about the relationship between people from two different racial groups who are married or together to have children. The fourth term discussing the relationship pattern between the majority and the minority is **annihilation**. This concept is defined as exterminating another racial group by using violent behavior. An example of this category is when Nazi Germany, ruled by Adolf Hitler, killed countless Jewish people as well as other people during World War II. As a Chinese person, I did not know too much detailed information other than what I learned from my history book. Now I understand more about this part of human history from a trip I took to Washington D.C. in 1996.

We had tickets for several museums and felt that we had to stay in each museum for a short time in order to visit every one. We went to the United States Holocaust Memorial Museum first in the morning. Before we entered the museum we scheduled our stay for about twenty minutes, and then we had to go to the second one. We were really shocked by what we saw when entering. We slowed down and started to read the plaques and signs and walked through in awe. In 1933, there were about nine million Jewish people living in Europe, but by 1945, the Nazis killed almost two out of every three Jewish people. Nazis believed that the German race was superior and that the Jewish race, along with several others, were inferior.

Studying this part of human history shook my whole being. By the time we walked out of the museum it was already early afternoon. We missed our visits to the other museums, but I felt it was worthwhile. I even believe that if we made a trip to Washington D.C. just for this museum, it would have been worth the visit. I not only learned about this part of human history, but I also learned to cherish peace and to respect others as well as their racial groups.

This world is consisted of many racial groups. We are different because of our physical and cultural traits, but we are similar because we are all humans living in one world with similar dreams, which can be the hope for peace, a happy life, or simply be successful. I still remember one of my students said that our race is human, not white, black, or yellow. I also believe this is true. If we have to divide people into different categories to define their physical and cultural traits, I think we need to have more categories than what we have now, such as African American, white, Asian, and Pacific Islander. More and more people today have to use the category of "other," which does not identify any detailed information about their racial groups, neither their physical, nor their cultural traits. In brief, the category of "other" will present limited data for sociologists and society to study racial issues.

The topic of race and ethnicity is always an important topic in American society. I believe there are both positive and negative aspects to this topic. The negative part is due to historical reasons, since racial conflict has been deeply rooted in the American society for a long time. We had the Civil War, Civil Rights Movement, and racial boycotts because of America's racial issues. The positive part is that this society is a melting pot that involves not only people from different countries, but also from different racial groups. They have not only contributed all their efforts for the prosperity of this country, but also assimilated with the dominant culture. American society is also called a salad bowl because of these different racial groups and immigrants from all over the world, which enable the American society to absorb the advantages of other traditions from different cultures and different racial groups. The salad bowl phenomenon also allows different racial groups to maintain their own identities and traditions as well as remain a peaceful and equal social status in American society.

Chapter 9

SEX AND GENDER

Key words: sex; sex characteristics: primary sex characteristics, and secondary sex characteristics; gender; gender roles; gender identity; patriarchy; matriarchy; sexual orientation; sexism; gender stratification; feminism; three types of feminism: liberal feminism, socialist feminism, and radical feminism; structural-functional perspective; social conflict perspective

In the prologue, I told a story about how my mother did not want me to pursue my Ph.D. simply because at the time I was an unwed girl. She did not believe that if I continued to work on my academic development, I would be able to find an ideal husband. She had no expectations for me to further my educational degree after I graduated from college, because she expected that I would get married. I, of course, disagreed but I never argued with her. When I told her that I would like to attend graduate school, either in China or the United States, it took her a long time to finally agree. In the meantime, she continued to attempt to persuade me that as an unwed female, I should not be so aggressive about working on my academics. She also told me that if I were a boy, she would have been more supportive towards me in gaining higher educational degrees. She felt that marrying a good husband would lead to a peaceful and happy family life for me. My mother's thoughts were essentially representative of a social expectation for unwed daughters in Chinese society. If this is true in China, is it also true in America? What kind of expectations would American parents place on their sons and daughters? What kind of expectations would be placed on the social roles of American men and women in our society?

In the year of 2000, I taught a male student in my Introduction to Sociology class. He was very active in the class One day, he came to the

141

class, sat in his seat, and asked me very loudly, "Do you know that Bob Dole's wife announced that she had decided to run for president?" It was about two minutes before the class, so I decided to chat with him.

"Who is Bob Dole?" I replied even though I knew who Bob Dole was. He was a United States Senator from Kansas. The reason I asked is because I believe everyone should be addressed by their given names, and not be called someone's wife, as if they are property. Former Senator Bob Dole's wife, Elizabeth Dole, was well known as Secretary of Transportation with Ronald Reagan's Administration, Secretary of Labor under George H.W. Bush, and then she became the president of the American Red Cross. Later on, she also served as North Carolina's first female Senator from 2003 to 2009.

"You do not know who Bob Dole is? I cannot believe that. He was a Senator and the Republican presidential candidate in 1996," he tried to explain to me.

"Whether you believe it or not, I do not know this person," I said. "Since I do not know who Bob Dole is, of course, I do not know who Bob Dole's wife is either. Since she may have a chance to be the president, could you please spell out her name to the class? By the way, if she became the president of the United States, are you going to call her President Bob Dole's wife? Does she have her own name?" I replied sarcastically.

By this time the class had already started, and it so happened that everyone was listening to our conversation.

"Yes, she does have a name," he replied, and realized that I did not like the title "Bob Dole's wife."

"Please tell us her name," I continued.

"Her name is BOB DOLE's wife," he answered.

The entire class began laughing though I did not laugh. I knew my student was being sarcastic.

Then I said, "I personally respect that Mrs. Elizabeth Dole is running for president. It does not matter whether she will win or not. We should admire what she is doing now."

Years later, when formal Senators Hillary Clinton and Barack Obama campaigned for the 2008 Democratic presidential candidacy, a student told me, "I will support John McCain, although he is much older than the other two. I am not going to support Hillary. This is because, if she became the president, other countries would not talk to us. I think other countries would rather talk to men."

I could not believe my ears, "Are you sure? The prime minister of Germany is now a female."

"I do not think American people would like to have a female president," he told me clearly.

"Are you sure? I do not care if our future president is a male or a female. I think I am going to consider voting for a president based on his or her individual qualifications, ability of leadership, and political thoughts as well as decisions on how to run a country. The sex of the presidential candidate will not be in my consideration at all," I said.

I knew I would not be able to persuade him to agree with me, because his opinion was not only with a personal political affiliation, but also represented the thoughts of other people, who oppose the idea of a woman leading our country.

The reason I continued the conversation with the above student was simply because it had nothing to do with which presidential candidate I was voting for, but my personal belief from sociological perspectives. I do not believe that people's sex should be considered when judging a person's ability; I also do not believe that national and world affairs are only the business of men. This is because sex is not a symbol of people's capability for managing domestic or international politics. Using one's sex as a weapon to stop any female from fulfilling a goal or realizing a dream is a detriment and should not be used as rationale in today's world. My thoughts are not to convince everyone to vote for a female president, but to say no one should judge a person's ability based on sex alone. I also feel that the sex of the candidates should not be a topic when discussing political issues. In the year of 2015, when Hillary Clinton, Carly Fiorina, and Jill Stein announced their presidential candidates; I felt that there was less discussion this time about the sex of the candidates, which showed that our society has been making progress in accepting more females who seek various levels of leadership positions in the nation.

Humans are divided by two different kinds of sex, due to their biological traits. Sex is defined as categorizing people as male and female, based on biology. There is a movie from the early 1990s starring Arnold Schwarzenegger titled *Kindergarten Cop*. One scene in this movie depicts a little boy asking Schwarzenegger, the cop in the movie, if he knew the differences between a girl and a boy. The boy immediately tried to answer his own question by shouting, "Boys have a penis and girls have a vagina!" He was stating the biological difference between a male and a female.

There are two types of sex characteristics: primary and secondary. The **primary sex characteristics** are the differences between reproductive organs, making one male or female. The **secondary sex characteristics** are the biological differences between males and females other than reproductive organs. Generally speaking, according to the secondary sex characteristics, we often say that men tend to have thicker chest hair and facial hair than females or that most males are generally taller and stronger than females.

However, these generalized statements are not as accurate as they used to be. There are a lot of taller women now and some of them are even stronger than some men.

If sex is a biological definition of a person, then, **gender** is a cultural definition of behaviors or attitudes attached to each sex. An example of this is that, some women may shave their body hair, whereas most men do not because societal culture expects the different behaviors. In 1992, when I first went back to China to visit my family, I called one of my best friends and wanted to meet her at a public bus station. She told me that I just needed to wait for her once I got off the bus, and she would come across the road to meet me.

"Hi, I am over here," I saw her wearing a short dress with no sleeves, waving her arms, and running toward me. I was very happy to see her after six years of not seeing each other.

When we were face-to-face, she stretched her two arms and prepared to give me a hug. After that, I surprised her by saying, "Hi, I am very happy to see you, but you need to shave your armpits!"

"What did you say?" she was shocked by what I said.

I repeated, "I said that you need to shave your armpits."

"What do you mean?" she seemed puzzled. I then explained American customs to her. The reason I did this was because she was an English tour guide, mostly for tourists from Canada and America. If she shaved herself, most of the tourists would feel that she was "clean," which would help her better connect with the tourists.

Most Chinese females do not have thick body hair, so in the past they were not accustomed to shaving. More recently, the idea of shaving body hair has been accepted by the Chinese culture, especially the younger generations. Most young women living in urban areas now feel the need to shave their body hair due to the influences from outside of China, which demonstrates the expectations that gender roles are set on them. But at the time I told my friend to shave, it did not seem to be as popular yet for Chinese females. With rapid social change in recent years, many international tourists now visit China, which has influenced the younger Chinese people to shave their body hair.

Typically, most Chinese men choose not to shave their body hair. I once saw a Hong Kong comedy movie, where a man had a date with a woman at a swimming pool. In order to impress her with his strong masculine body, he glued some artificial hair to his chest. Suddenly, a cat came out of nowhere and jumped into the water. As a result, the man lost his balance and fell into the swimming pool with the cat. When he climbed out of the water, all his chest hair had simply disappeared. Although this was a funny movie, it represents the definition of gender well. It also indicates how people think of themselves according to their sex within their culture and how their particular culture influences their thoughts and behavior (see Fig. 9.1).

In most countries, males and females are expected to have certain behaviors and attitudes based on their sex by the influence of their culture. For instance, in May 2007, CNN reported about the death of a soldier in Iraq

Figure 9.1. This photo shows that many migrant workers who come from rural areas to larger cities for jobs, such as construction workers, home caregivers, waiters/waitresses, and other service jobs. Without services offered by those migrant workers, the city of Beijing could not run as it does today. Note that this photo shows a female coming to work in Beijing. This was not the situation in China more than 100 years ago. In Ancient China, females seldom went out of their houses because of the tradition known as foot binding. Performed for beauty enhancement purposes, foot binding resulted in females being unable to walk for long distances. Foot binding originated in the Northern Song Dynasty and ended in the beginning of the 1900s. Once a young girl became 5–8 years of age, their mothers or maids, who were familiar with the foot binding process, would bind their feet. This process involved bending and wrapping all five toes with a long cloth that would then be sewn together with a needle and thread. Once the foot binding process was complete, the feet became very small and the ideal length of a bound foot was approximately 4 inches long.

(*Newsique*, 2007). There was a photo of the memorial service with a coffin and a few people around it. The most notable people at the funeral service were a young woman and a young male soldier conveying sympathy to each other during this incredibly difficult time. The young woman was crying and the male soldier lent his shoulder for her to cry on. The soldier looked extremely sad, but was not showing any tears in public most likely due to the gender roles he learned from society.

I showed this photo to my students because I felt this picture was a perfect example of the two sociological concepts: **gender roles** and **gender identity.** The former, gender roles, is based on the cultural definition when people in each sex are expected to have different attitudes and roles. The latter, gender identity, describes how people think of themselves based on their expected attitudes and behaviors according to the cultural definitions of each sex in a society. For instance, a male student told me that he never remembered his parents helping him to stand up if he fell down when he was a young boy. His parents always said, "You are a big boy now. You need to stand up yourself."

"But to my younger sister, it was very different," he continued. "My parents not only helped her stand up, but also gave her a hug. She is nine years old now! Is this how treatment differs between girls and boys in this society?"

I had no answer for his question because this is true for most human societies. Children are socialized in different ways when growing up based on their sex. People are also treated differently due to their sex at work, in their homes, and the process of social interaction with each other. At work we see different treatment between males and females, such as unequal pay. We also see this treatment in homes, for example, my mother disagreeing with my decision to continue my education for a Ph.D. As well as in the process of social interaction with each other, such as, the idea that gentlemen should hold the door open for females.

I have often heard from my students that they felt males and females were equal in America. They felt that their parents have equal expectations for both sons and daughters. I used to have a retired American couple as my neighbor and one day at a neighborhood party, they told me that their daughter was working on her Ph.D. I could tell from the conversation that they were proud, yet regretted their daughter's continuity of her education. Their daughter was 34 years old and not yet married. This couple told me that they were worried about their daughter, and felt that a girl should not work that hard, but have a happy marriage and peaceful family life.

The couple continued to complain, "Compared to our daughter, our son never worked hard for his education and career. Now he lives with us and does not even want to move out."

I asked, "I know you are selling your house now. What will happen if you move to Florida?"

"We think our son has to be on his own. One day he will have his own family. He will be a husband and a father. He should work as hard as possible to support his own family," the wife said.

From what they expressed, people can see the different expectations for the future of their son and daughter based on their sex. This has reflected gender roles and social values, even though these social values on genders have different levels of expectations in different societies. In addition, I also think that in America, parents have more respect for their children's choices because of the strong values of individualism. In China, parents may have more control of what their children would like to do. For instance, a Chinese student, who is in the music department of my university, told me that she started to learn how to play piano when she was only five years old. She did not want to learn but was forced by her mother to learn how to play piano. This was her mother's dream when she was a young girl. So she felt it was good for her daughter to learn. In China, most parents think children are their property and they need to make decisions for them. In America, most parents think their children belong to the society as well as them. Therefore, their children have more freedom to do what they find interesting. However, each society has its essential social values and expectations which strongly influence gender roles.

Under the influences of gender roles, gender identity is how people behave and think about themselves. As a female, I had never been taught by my parents that I should hold back my tears in public. In the spring of 2007, a student at Virginia Tech shot and killed thirty-two students and professors. It was a big shock to me because I worked in a college, too. I could not believe so many young lives with beautiful futures were gone within a few minutes. The next morning in class, a student began a discussion about this tragedy, quickly joined by many others. I started feeling sad and began to cry in front of the class. The whole class became quiet for a while as I took a moment to regain my composure and a few minutes later, I resumed the class. What really touched me was that quite a few students came to me after class, gave me a hug, and patted me on my shoulder to show they had similar feelings. Even though I felt a bit embarrassed, I have never regretted crying in front of them. I did it because of my understanding of gender roles. I feel that I do not need to hold my feelings in and that it is okay for me to cry in front of people because I am a woman. In most societies, the social values, norms, and expectations on the behaviors of males and females are different, which definitely has an impact on their gender identity. When working on my house, my husband never asked me to climb the ladder to repair the house. He automatically thought that it was his responsibility as the man in the house. This is because of the influence of gender roles on my husband's gender identity.

I remember years ago Disney produced an animated musical-comedy-drama film named *Mulan*. Mulan's last name is Hua (same as flower), who is a legendary woman warrior in Chinese history (the Southern and Northern Dynasties, which is between the years of 420 and 589). The historical setting of Mulan is indeterminate. The story of Mulan comes from a famous Chinese ballad, which says that because of a war, Mulan took her elderly father's place in the military and dressed up as a male soldier fighting against enemies for twelve years. She received high merit as a warrior but was found out to be a female after the war. She refused to receive any reward but asked to go back home to be with her family. I believe one of the reasons that this story is famous for more than 1,000 years is because in Ancient China, soldiers were all males. This story not only represents the Chinese traditions of filial piety, but also, Mulan, as a female solider fighting for her country, has changed her gender identity against the status quo of the gender roles during her time. Her behavior has been highly respected by Chinese people. The term of filial piety means that because our parents gave us life and took care of us, we should pay them back by taking care of them when they are elderly. In China, filial piety is considered a strong social value and tradition, which expects that sons should do more than daughters for their parents.

In most human societies, the power or leadership is controlled by males. One time, a student asked me an interesting question when former Senator and the Secretary of State, Hillary Clinton announced the second time that she would run for president in the election of 2016. Her question was, "If former Senator and Secretary Clinton won the election and became the president of the United States of America, would you say that our society is a male or female-ruled society?"

"What do you think?" I asked back.

She thought for a moment and answered, "I would feel that our society would be a female-ruled society."

I told my class, "No, it would not be called a female-ruled society." The reason being, when deciding if males or females rule a society, it does not depend on who the president is, but rather on the social system in place. In American society, the majority of the Senators, the House Representatives, and the Justices of the Supreme Court are men. There was not a female senator elected to the Senate until 1932. Her name is Ophelia Wyatt Caraway, a Democrat from Arkansas. In 2015, out of one hundred of the United States Senators, only twenty were females and out of 435 members of the House of Representatives, there were eighty-four females. Compared to twenty years ago, in 1993, there were only seven female Senators and forty-seven female

House Representatives. This does show the progress that women have made in politics, though this is far from balanced.

"Therefore, even if former Senator Hillary Clinton won the election and became the president, we would still call American society a patriarchal society," I responded.

In American society, obviously we can tell that it is a male dominant society. A term, **patriarchy**, represents this social phenomenon, which is defined as a form of a social association where males govern females. This is almost a universal power pattern in today's world, usually called the male dominant society. Were there any times or any places in the world where there were female dominant societies? This type of social phenomenon in a sociological term is **matriarchy**, which is defined as a form of a social association where females govern males. It is believed that this kind of power pattern happened in history in certain places.

There is a nationality called Mosuo in China. This small group of people lives in the provinces of Sichuan and Yunnan. In 2007, the estimated number of Mosuo people was 40,000. Today, they still keep the matriarchal form, which is the female dominant society. In this particular group, children do not have fathers and women do not have husbands. Males will go to females' houses at nighttime and go back to their own homes in the morning, which is called a "walking marriage." Females are respected in the family and the children all have a blood connection with their mother's side. The mother or other respected females control the family and uncles will assist in other ways, such as land work. Uncles in the family may be the fathers in another female dominated house; however, they normally stay with their sisters. This is the reason, when answering my student's question about former Senator Clinton, I proclaimed that a female president would not change American society into a matriarchal society, because we have to look at all the institutions of the governing system.

When I first came to America, I learned about the word, "homosexuality." I asked an American student in the same office, "What is the meaning of homosexuality?"

She paused and said, "Do you have gays and lesbians in China?"

"I do not know the meanings of these words, so how do I know if China has them or not?" I started to think she did not want to tell me.

"I think you should check your English/Chinese dictionary first," she told me.

"I checked. It says homosexuality in Chinese." I gave up on finding an answer to my question because she obviously did not want to answer me.

I wondered for a long time why she was not willing to answer my question. After years of living in the United States, of course, I now understand the meaning of those words. A gay officemate I once had told me that his identity was the same as others, he just had a different **sexual orientation**, which is defined as a method that people practice to attain sexual satisfaction. When discussing sexual orientation and homosexuality, my students always provided me with their different attitudes towards these issues. I have seen that people now are more accepting of their LGBTQ communities. Before the same-sex marriage was legalized by the Supreme Court in a 5–4 decision in 2015, gay marriage was only allowed in 37 states. However, as a society we still have a long way to go regarding the rights of people in the LGBTQ community. When discussing sexual orientation, there are also other terms used frequently in recent years, such as the terms of transgender and transsexual. Transgender is considered an umbrella term that includes the multitude of gender variants and identifications. The term of transsexual refers to someone who has medically transitioned, or is willing to transition with hormones and/or surgery. Transgender and transsexual behavior is now becoming more accepted within our society.

Before coming to my current university, I taught sociology classes at another university in the early 1990s. One day, I asked my students a question, "What is deviant behavior you observe in our daily life?"

"You have deviant behavior," a student in his late forties pointed at me.

"What?" I could not believe what he had said. "Could you please explain what you mean?"

"Look, being a female, you should wear a dress or skirt, but you are wearing slacks. This is men's clothing and not for women," he said.

I thought he was kidding, "Are you sure? I think almost all of the females in this class are wearing slacks. Do you think we all have deviant behavior?"

He continued, "I feel sad to see women who have to go out to work. I think they should be at home taking care of their husbands and kids. Let men do the work because we can be depended on."

I wanted to say something to convince him, but I really felt that I would not be able to persuade him to believe that males and females should be equal. I did not want to declare his remarks as sexist because his belief is that males and females should have different responsibilities; however, I disagree with what he said about the deviant clothing. Why should women wear dresses or skirts, and why should women depend on men? I do not think it is appropriate to discuss which sex should be dependable or be depended on. I believe that men and women should respect each other. Any debate discussing whether males or females are dependable or depended on would be meaningless in my opinion. I believe that males and females should be depend on each other and have different division of labor at home and work.

There is a sociological term, **sexism**, which is defined as the belief that one sex is innately superior or inferior to another. I once had a disagreement with a male colleague when I worked at a college in China. I kept sharing my ideas with him because I felt it was important to let him know that I had a different point of view about the situation we were facing. Another female colleague at the meeting, who was much older than myself, said to us, "How about you stop the argument?" Then she turned to me and said, "As a female, I think you should stop first."

"Why? I believe I am right. I should let him know that," I did not understand why she asked me to stop first.

"Being a female, you should stop first even though you are correct," she attempted to explain to me. "You do not want to keep the argument going because you are a female."

I replied, "I think the point is that he got things wrong, which has nothing to do with our sex."

The reason I was asked to stop first is because based on the traditional Chinese values, men should be in control and women should agree with what men say. This is not only true at home between husband and wife, but also men and women at work and in society in general. Even today, I still feel it was not reasonable to ask me to stop the conversation first; however, I understand that this is an old Chinese cultural tradition, that females are treated inferior to males. That is, being a female, you do not want to be too aggressive, even though you may possess such ability. I do not think this tradition is popular currently in China.

My husband has a friend, who was born and raised in a small rural village in China. He was sent to an America university to earn his Ph.D. and financially supported by the Chinese government because of his excellent undergraduate performance as an engineering major. His siblings consisted of two brothers and one younger sister. His oldest brother, because of his responsibility, as the caretaker of their parents, did not receive much education. Their parents also thought that they should not spend any money on the education of his younger sister, because she would eventually get married and his family would receive no benefits from the expenses of her education. His sister married at a very young age and learned only to write her name. Isn't it strange that a brother with a Ph.D. has a younger sister who does not know how to read and write? Even though this story happened many years ago and may not represent the exact situation in China today, it illustrates an example of sexism (see Fig. 9.2).

Due to the formation of social classes in capitalist society, women's statuses are much lower than those of men. This means that males possess more wealth and have more power and prestige compared to females. For instance, a magazine publishes the top one hundred richest people in America each year, and a large majority of them are men. The magazine also lists the fifty richest women. Compared to the possessions owned by the one hundred richest men, the fifty richest women's wealth is, of course, is lower.

In general, women are seen poorer compared to men. This is true not only in America but also worldwide. A sociological concept, **gender stratification**, reflects this social phenomenon. This term defines the unequal social statuses between men and women in the social stratification system. In my Introduction to Sociology class, I always use data to demonstrate the term. Like other societies, males and females are not equal in America neither. Some of the data is categorized by having the same degrees of education, but with different levels of income and the same job positions with different levels of salary.

Figure 9.2. The photo shows a woman using a tricycle as a means of transportation in Beijing. This practice is especially popular for those who work manual labor jobs. In China, there is a famous slogan which says that males and females are equal and women hold up half the sky. This belief makes apparent the fact that women's social status has been recognized by the Chinese society.

"So for every single dollar a man earns, a woman earns about 75.5 cents," I summarized and told the class the data was from 2003 (Infoplease, 2014).

A student obviously disagreed with me, "Professor, I think your data is very old. It is 2016 now, but you still show data from the 2003. I think there has been a big social change that has taken place in America."

"I am sorry that I do not have current data for the change. What is the change? Can you tell us what you know?" I prepared to tell the class the current statistics in 2016. However, because he mentioned the change first, I thought he might know something.

After checking his cell phone from CNN Money (O'Brien, 2016), he confidently answered, "Yes, I think now for every dollar a man earns, a woman earns about 78 cents in 2016!" as the whole class burst into loud laughter.

I did not laugh, but I asked him a question, "Dear, do you think it is a big change that the increase in these thirteen years was about 2.5 cents? If you walk toward the classroom from a parking lot, if you see two to three pennies here and there on the ground, are you going to pick them up?"

"It depends if I am in a hurry or not. If I need to do something, I will not waste my time to pick them up," he answered.

His statement, "I am not going to waste my time for the pennies," was his answer to evaluate a cent in his daily life. I knew that many cents together would add up to a lot of money. However, I disagree that by increasing a female's wage by 2.5 cents for every dollar that a man earns is a "big social change" in thirteen years. Let's say that a man earns about $50,000 a year, as his income, while a woman earns 75.5 cents of this man's every dollar, bringing her salary to $37,750. Today, earning seventy-eight cents, a woman's salary only increased to $39,000. I will not deny there is an increase. However, I feel this is a slow progress because it has taken thirteen years for an increase of $1,250.

After I calculated the salary comparisons, I asked the class, "Are you going to call it a big social change?" A student continued, "It is better than nothing."

"I do not think it is a big change. I think this is not fair for females," I quickly declared, "Men and women should be equal."

A male student shouted, "Professor, are you a feminist?"

"My best answer to you is: I do not belong to any feminist organization, but that does not mean I am not going to fight for women's rights," I answered. "By the way, what is feminism?"

He paused for a moment and smugly replied, "I do not want to answer your question."

"Why is that?" I continued with my questioning.

He kept on avoiding my question, "Because you will be angry with me."

"No, I will not," I assured him. "You just need to tell us your understanding of feminism. You might be right or wrong, but I will give you the correct answer."

"I think feminism is a bunch of crazy women who want to kill all of us," he answered.

The whole class started to laugh. I think people may know the word of feminism, but may not understand the actual meaning of it. **Feminism** is an organized social activity to fight against patriarchy and sexism and battle for females' rights. Some people may have wrong ideas about feminists and the activities they partake in for their rights.

There are mainly three kinds of feminism. The first type of feminism is **liberal feminism**. They accept the patriarchy society as it is, but want to make sure that females have the same rights as males. Second, it is a group of people who belong to **socialist feminism**, which links male-dominated society to the formation of social classes and the capitalist economic system. This means in patriarchal societies, males dominate females because they are economically in control, maintaining the power and higher social statuses compared to females. The last type is **radical feminism**, which agrees with the ideas to look for social equality between males and females, but still believe it is not doing enough. Radical feminists feel that patriarchal societies will never end, even with a revolution.

Many people would think that men should earn more than women because they are more capable to do so. Some individuals hold the belief that females are considered not as strong as men and then should be under the protection of men. Within these traditions, if any females try hard and do better than men in some areas, such as attaining a higher degree of education, these women may not be able to find an ideal husband. Some men may feel that the particular woman is too intelligent and aggressive, which makes them feel intimidated.

There was a talk show in China years ago. It described how Chinese people thought about the differences between males and females. When mentioning males, people will use "big boy," "big man," and when talking about females, the words they use are "little girl," "little elderly woman," or "little married young woman." This has nothing to do with the size of the males and females, but with the social statuses men and women have in society. Obviously, when saying the words "big" or "little," people can tell different social values between men and women in a society.

In America, I have heard some strong remarks on men and women partially pertaining to "females' attractiveness due to their physical appearance" and "males' attractiveness because of their achievements in life." Based on these statements, men and women are taught that females may not receive any attention even if they work extremely hard. They might have a better life if they look pretty. Men have to achieve a higher status; otherwise, they will not receive respect. I think this social value has been accepted not only in America but also in China, as well as in many other societies as well.

According to American culture, a male or female should behave like their perceived and expected sex role. If a female behaves like a boy, she may be called a "tomboy," on the flip side, if a male has female tendencies, he may be called a "sissy." The words tomboy and sissy represent a culture that has already formed accepted limits, so people can only have certain behaviors the society allow them to have within acceptable confines. Otherwise, this behavior could be defined as unsuitable conduct.

Another example to explain cultural expectations on men and women in American society is if a father is home to take care of his children, people will say, "Are you babysitting your kids today?" However, if a wife is home to take care of the children, people would assume this is her normal job because she is a "stay-at-home mom" or a "homemaker." This is normal by social values for the man to support the family financially, while the woman offers to take care of the family. These things represent the cultural expectations, which strongly influence men and women's behavior and thinking.

Both structural-functional theory and social conflict theory analyze the gender roles and their cooresponding behaviors in human society. **Structural-functional perspective** argues that the practice of gender role in the family will create a harmonic and consensus relationship. According to traditional American family values, the father will work and the mother will stay at home to take care of the children. In fact, today, 71 percent of all mothers work outside their homes (Cohn & Caumont, 2014). This percentage is much higher than the 19 percent of working mothers in 1960. There are a multitude of reasons for both the couple to go to work, such as inflation rates, housing prices, job security, or divorce rates. Also, gender roles can be identified as each gender needing to provide their efforts to make the integration of the family work. With an increasing divorce rate, some analysis shows that 40-50 percent (American Psychological Association, 2016) and some data indicates that about one-third (Swanson, 2016) of married couples will end up separated or divorced. Based on the above either statistics, many families cannot fully practice such gender roles. Even if everyone has their designated gender role, there should not be strict limits on each other's responsibilities.

A few years ago, I was busy with a research paper and I did not have time to get the laundry finished. When I got back home after my three-hour evening class, my husband held the door between our garage and laundry room and asked me to smell. I thought that he carelessly burned something. He shook his head and said, "Can you smell something good?"

"Good? No, actually I smell nothing," I wondered. "What did you do?"

"I did your laundry," he answered, ready for a big hug.

"Did you say that you did 'my laundry'?" I asked. "So you just picked out my clothes and did not wash yours?" I was confused.

"I did mine, too," he answered.

I started to get angry with him, "I do mine and yours every week and have never asked you for appreciation."

"Because that is your job," he replied.

That was not the right answer. I quickly shot back, "What? Are you kidding me?"

Based on my personal experiences, I think when deciding to practice their gender roles, people must also help and respect others, which are are the essentials in keeping harmony in the family.

Social conflict perspective connects gender stratification with capitalist economic development, which explains why men have higher economic social status than females and dominate the society. I had explained this point earlier. Women's social status, because they work for no pay as a homemaker or with a low paying job, is devalued in many societies. For example, I received a Ph.D. and my husband earned a Master's degree. When he was working toward his Ph.D., he received a few job offers, then he decided he wanted to quit his Ph.D. program. I cannot say this is a popular situation in America that a wife has a higher level of education or earns more than her husband, but I have often heard my students say similar situations of their parents. One day, my husband and I tried to make a decision on something, but we disagreed with each other. I said, "I would like to make the decision."

"Why?" my husband asked.

Wanting to make fun of him, I smugly stated, "I have a Ph.D., therefore, I think I am smarter."

"No, you cannot make decisions, at least not in this house," he said without any hesitation.

I asked puzzled, "Why?"

"Why? It should be our decisions for most of the time instead of only yours. You need to recognize that a higher education level is nice, but it will not always allow you to make decisions by yourself only." I had no way to fight back because the decision we were making was about choosing a house to purchase.

Even though we were joking about who had more power in the family, I recognized the connection between financial status and the position to be the head of the family. However, some of my students often told me that my example only represents traditional relationships between couples. In current American families, a decision is made by the couple together. For my student, his mother was a homemaker, but she became the head of the family, and was constantly in control of everything in the house.

Not sure how true it is, but I think with social advancements and rapid social change, women's status should also be changed. Compared with history, today's women have the right to vote, have the chance to receive a higher education, can aspire and attain their career goals more easily than in previous years, as well as play an important role in politics throughout the different levels of government. Although these are all positive advancements, they are not enough. There are still very few females in the House of Representatives and in the Senate on Capitol Hill, which are prime arenas to exercise political authority and decision making. The fact is, there are more females than males in our society. A woman still only earns seventy-eight cents compare for every dollar a man acquires. Considering the gender stratification worldwide, women as well as men need to work together to improve women's social status and gain more rights, attention, and respect from society.

Chapter 10

FAMILY

Key words: family; marriage; six patterns of marriage: endogamy, exogamy, monogamy, polygamy, polygyny, and polyandry; residential patternas: neolocality, patrilocality, and matrilocality; nuclear family; extended family; structural-functional perspective (functions of family); social conflict perspective; symbolic interaction perspective

Like most Chinese people in the United States, I often watch Chinese TV shows broadcasted via satellite or Internet on different channels. A few years ago, I watched a show made by the Chinese Central Television station. In conjunction with various social organizations, they highlighted over three hundred exceptional people. These people, the Chinese society believed, represented the ideal moral standards and were regarded as an "ethical banner" or "role model" for other Chinese people to learn from. One of these heroes was a female medical doctor. She was often so busy with her job and taking care of the local residents' health issues that she frequently left her five-month-old baby girl alone at home.

One day the baby became ill and instead of staying home to take care of her child, she tied the baby to the bed and went out to visit her patients. Although this behavior resulted in the death of the child, she was honored following this incident. When I heard the story, my initial thought was that this doctor should be arrested for neglect. The burning question here is, why was this doctor so greatly admired in China and considered to have such high moral and ethical standards? First, it is important to note that this situation is rare and most Chinese parents, especially those who only have one child, do not neglect their children. Another key factor is that American and Chinese values regarding family are very different. When I was growing up

159

in China, we were often taught to sacrifice our individual and family interests in order to serve other people's needs. In Chinese culture, family is considered an extension of the individual; in other words, my family is "mine" and I can do with my children as I wish. As a result, it is considered selfish and shameful to put one's family first in China. This is the reason the above mentioned medical doctor was commended as an "ethical banner." After moving to the United States and becoming acculturated to American family values, I changed my opinion on this issue.

In the American society, family is considered very important, and much more significant than a job or money. Americans consider people who do not put their family first selfish. After years of residing in here, I believe that the above mentioned Chinese doctor's priority should have been to be a good mother and to take care of her daughter. If she could not take good care of her own daughter, how could she possibly take care of others? The Chinese society presented the "ethical banner" to her for a few reasons based on its traditions. According to the social values in China, family is considered less important than other people in the society. After watching the TV show, I checked some of the discussions about her on different Chinese Internet websites. Many young Internet users did not think that the doctor deserved the honor to be regarded as an "ethical banner." Their questions and conversations online illustrated that the traditional Chinese values are in the process of changing with younger generations and contrasting with older generations.

American society puts a lot of values on the family. Children are not only believed to be the hope to their parents, but also, the future of the society. Here in America, the Chinese doctor mentioned above would have been prosecuted for child abuse or neglect and she most certainly would not have been held up as an "ethical banner." If I had never moved to the United States, my values regarding this issue would have sided with the Chinese views. After moving, my value system regarding family has changed. Instead of holding this doctor up as a role model, I immediately questioned the Chinese point of view and favored the American family ethics. According to sociological concepts, the values regarding this issue do not have right or wrong answers because of different societies having different traditions and standards to evaluate people's behavior. My viewpoints are the results of value influences by living in a different society as well as the years of socialization from the Chinese culture that I was in and my continuous socialization experiences in America.

Throughout history, family has played a significant role in any society. **Family** is defined as a group of two or more people who are together because of their connection by blood, marriage, or adoption. A family cares for each other and shares their economic possessions. Family is the smallest unit/group of people in a society. According to historical perspectives, the major reason for people to be united was for survival. The functions of family, according to the structural-functional perspective, involved almost all of the necessary endurance aspects, including economy, socialization, as well as education. Due to the development of human society, schools, factories, and companies have gradually replaced some of the functions of the family, but it still plays an essential role in every society. Today, most people still receive early socialization from their families and parents are still the first teachers for their children. They teach them language, norms such as table manners, social values, and the skills necessary to interact with other people and to survive in life.

Adoption of a child is also an option for families. Unlike Chinese tradition, American families tend to tell their children if they were adopted. Often the adopted parents will help their children find their biological parents when they grow up. I once met an American family that had adopted a girl. I asked the mother,

"Are you going to tell your daughter that she was adopted in the future?"

"Yes, why wouldn't I?" she questioned me.

I answered, "I would not."

"Why?" she continued to ask.

"Because I would want the girl to be my daughter and take care of me when I am old. If she knows I am not her biological mother, she might leave me to go back to her biological mother. What is the purpose of me adopting her?" My answers to her were based on my traditional Chinese values.

She countered by stating, "No, I disagree. The reason for me to adopt this child is because I would like to help and give her a stable home to live in. Otherwise, she may remain in an orphanage. I can care for her and she can grow up in a loving family."

"Have you thought that she may not want to take care of you when she knows the truth?" I could not understand her point of view.

"I have never expected to depend on her when I am elderly," she answered.

I was really shocked by what she said, "So you did not have any selfish intentions for the adoption?"

"You should also know that my little girl brought happiness to my family," she said with a smile. "I truly gained my identity as a mother," she replied.

"How are you going to explain the situation of her adoption? If you tell her the truth, you may hurt her feelings." I was interested in continuing the conversation.

She replied in a calm voice, "I will tell her that for some reason her biological parents could not take care of her after she was born. They really felt sad to let her go, but we love her and are happy to have her in our family."

I had nothing further to say. In my opinion, she sounded too calm when discussing such a big issue of her daughter's adoption. Of course, I understand she loves her daughter. She believes that telling her adopted daughter the truth about how she came to the family is also showing her that her adopted parents love her. I think she serves as a mirror for me, which reflected my narrow-mindedness. I only thought about what kind of advantages this adoption could bring to me, but not what I could do for an adopted child. I thought in a different way because I had strong Chinese values about adoption. In China, people like to have their own children, and only couples that cannot have their own biological children choose to adopt. The purpose of adoption in China is mainly that couples need someone to take care of them when they are old. This is because, for thousands of years, the care of the elderly people is the responsibility of the family and children. Therefore, children have become important care sources. Most people believe that if their adopted children knew the truth when they reach their adulthood they would leave them without care in their old age. Family has different functions according to **structural-functional perspective** including care giving for the younger and older generations, emotional support, regulations of sexual behavior, and protection of the family members. Among all of the functions of family, taking care of the young and old is the most important function. In the past, Chinese families preferred to live together for five generations, which was considered the happiest family. Growing up in China, children are taught by both their parents and society that since their parents took care of them when they were young, it is their responsibility to return the favor to their parents when they are older. This kind of responsibility is particularly expected of sons. With this tradition, children in China are most likely to be considered the property of their parents.

In the Chinese society, the care for the elderly people happens at either their home or their children's homes. Children are considered the economic and respite care sources for their elderly parents. This is not only because of the traditional values, but also because China's institutionalized care facilities were not very popular and the use of a nursing home may not be accepted by both of the parents and their children. Now because of the one-child policy and lack of caretakers at home, many elderly parents started to accept nursing care facilities. However, there are a limited number of assisted living and nursing homes, which are run by either public or private organizations. These facilities are overpopulated with elderly people. In the past, these institutionalized services took care of the elderly who were childless. The traditional thought was that if elderly people had children, but lived in an institutionalized care service, they would feel ashamed. To them this meant that their children did not want to care for them. This situation has changed in recent decades, but the number and size of institutionalized care is still limited. For instance, the No. 1 Social Welfare Home in Beijing owns 1,100 beds. This is a public nursing home. However, there were 10,000 applicants waiting for a bed (Moore, 2013). It is estimated that those people are on a 100-year waiting list for a bed in this nursing home. In addition, the cost of living in an institutionalized care facility is expensive. The cost of a public care home for elderly people ranges between $110 and $550 per month (Moore, 2013). For private nursing homes, the cost can be from $1,485 to $4,545 per month. This is considered very expensive according to the Social Security payment an elderly Chinese person receives per month. This is the reason most elderly Chinese people will remain at home and obtain the care from their children (see Fig. 10.1).

When I first started graduate school, a professor showed us a short video from an international television station in a Southern Asian country. The

Figure 10.1. China's elderly population makes up the largest portion of Chinese residents. This photo shows a very expensive nursing home in Beijing. The advantage of this institutionalized facility for the elderly is that its service concepts are from the Western world. This nursing home also hires international professionals to assist in running its day-to-day services.

video displayed a conversation between a TV station representative and a young woman who graduated from the same department from which I graduated. She discussed her experiences in America by offering her opinions about living and studying there. When she was asked for her opinion about the younger generations in America, she said that young Americans did not want to take care of their elderly parents. The woman continued to explain that the younger American generations like to move out of their parents' house around the age of 18 or shortly thereafter. They would rather take care of a cat or dog, but not their elderly parents in their house.

This information was completely new to me because the tradition in China is that the care for the elderly parents depends highly on the younger people in the family. While still in China, I occasionally would hear on TV or read from the newspaper that some elderly person won a lawsuit against their children for not taking care of them. Anyone who did not offer financial help or care to their elderly parents would be criticized by others in the Chinese society. When I heard that America's younger generations did not want to take that responsibility, I felt that they were absolutely in the wrong. After watching the show, I kept asking myself over and over again: why have young Americans refused to take care of their elderly parents? Was it not their responsibility to take care of their parents if their parents had taken care of them? How could most young American people escape such obligations?

Later, elderly issues became one of my major research interests and their living arrangements became one of the topics I studied. In 1995, I did a comparison study between American and Chinese college students' attitudes toward future living arrangements for their elderly parents when 75 years and older. A survey was conducted among 119 Chinese students and 199 American college students by using the same questionnaires in Chinese or English. The purpose of this study was to compare two different cultural views of younger generations regarding the living arrangements for their elders. I have to admit that the international TV show I discussed earlier really shocked me. As a result, it greatly influenced me in seeking out the facts for myself.

Three major questions were asked about the living arrangements of their parents for when they reached old age. The answers varied according to the student's different cultures. When asked how close they wished to live to their parents' homes in the future, more Chinese students (69%) answered that they wanted to live in the same or nearby community with their parents compared to that of American students (59%). Of the American students, one-third wished to live within one to four hours from their parents while less than one-fifth of the Chinese students felt the same way. The percentage of the Chinese students (14%) who wanted to live beyond a four-hour distance from their parents was higher than the American respondents (6.5%). At the time of the survey, private cars were not popular in China and it was more difficult for Chinese people to travel more than four hours to visit their parents weekly or more often. That was likely the reason more Chinese students wanted to live in the same community with their parents (see Fig. 10.2).

When asked what type of living arrangement they felt was the best for both their parents after they reached the age of 75, the majority of the American respondents (62%) felt that their elderly parents should live in their own home. Only one in four of the Chinese students answered the same way. The majority of the Chinese students (70%) felt that their elderly parents should live with their children, but only one in six of the American respondents agreed. One in five of the American students felt that their older parents should live in retirement housing, and only one Chinese respondent answered in this category. None of the Chinese students answered that their

Figure 10.2. Beijing has more than 90 colleges and universities. The photo above shows the Capital University of Economics and Business, which was established in 1956. This university now has around 18,000 students including both undergraduate and graduate students. The Chinese survey I discussed in this chapter includes the research results from the students at this university.

parents should live in a nursing home, neither retirement houses nor nursing homes were popular in China at the time. The American student responses were not significant either, being only three people said that their parents need to be in nursing homes. The reason was that Americans could accept retirement housing, but do not like nursing homes for their elderly parents because they thought of nursing homes as a place for the elderly to go toward the end of their lives, when they could no longer handle their daily activities.

The last question asked was, "If one parent happened to be deceased, what type of living arrangement would be the best for the living parent?" About half of the American respondents felt that the elderly parent should still live in his or her own home. There were only about fifteen Chinese students who answered the same. About ninety-seven Chinese student respondents truly believed that the elderly parent should live with their children. The results contrasted with only one in three of the American students feeling that way. Around fifteen of the American students thought that the remaining parent should live in a retirement house and only one Chinese student marked this category. None of the Chinese respondents and only one American student felt that the remaining parent should live in a nursing home.

From the above percentages, it is not difficult to say that Chinese people considered the care of their elderly parents as their responsibility. More Americans felt that their elderly parents should live in their own homes in order to remain independent and have more freedom. This might be because of the traditional Chinese values emphasizing the importance of care functions offered by the younger generations to the elderly family members. In recent years, because of the rapid increase in the number of elderly people in China, the number of "Kong Chao" families, which means "empty nests," has increased dramatically. In the United States, "empty nests" are not considered a serious issue, but it is a rising problem in China. This has brought social concerns to the surface of who will take care of the elderly.

The practice of the one-child policy, which began in 1979 in China, has greatly decreased the size of urban families. This policy, in addition to the increased life expectancy, has also resulted in the rise of the elderly population. This group of elderly people, when distributed into different families, includes both the elderly parents and grandparents. This has placed a large burden on the only child in the family. This has resulted in an urgent growing need for institutionalized care for all types of elderly people. Given these recent demands, there has been an escalation of the number of elderly care institutions in the country. More than 70 percent of the Chinese elderly in urban areas do not live with their children (Timm, 2015). The percentage of the seniors with the type of living arrangement as "empty nesters" is projected to keep growing because from now until 2035 there will be an increase of 10 million seniors annually in China (Timm, 2015). This "empty nest" phenomenon is possibly because of the result of change in the family structure and caregiving values.

Now, due to industrialization and new job opportunities, many children have to work away from home and subsequently leave their elderly parents behind. Many of them, influenced by the traditional values and the feeling of obligation to their parents, feel guilty when moving away from their family. I know many Chinese natives here in America. When talking about their elderly parents in China, many sound worried and blame themselves for being away from home. I have often heard them saying, "It is a shame I am too far away from my elderly parents," or "Even though I send money home, money cannot make up for the care I should be offering."

After living in the United States for many years, I have learned the value of being independent and that children are not the property of their parents. I think all countries, especially aging societies, need to develop different programs for elderly services. This is necessary for social advancement. I also think that younger generations need to be educated to respect and take care of their elderly parents. I believe that everyone, especially the elderly, needs to learn to be more independent as well. My student and I did a research and wrote a paper on American people's values of being independent. This article discussed how elderly parents would like to depend on themselves or seek help from different social services and care facilities (Li & Smither, 2015).

Unlike China, America does not have a strong tradition of taking care of elderly parents. In the past 100 years. because of the relatively slow growth of percentage of the population that is 65 years and older, the American society is able to cope with the growing demands of these care facilities and services. The projected population growth of the elderly in America for the next fifty years will be faster than the last century, which leads to the American family structure eventually resembling or becoming similar to that of China's. That means there will be fewer young people compared to elderly in families and society. This is especially true when thinking about the baby boomers, who were born in 1946 turned 65 in 2011 (Colby & Ortman, 2014). It is estimated that every single day more than 10,000 baby boomers will reach their senior age (Fisher, 2015). This will continue until the year of 2030. Therefore, more attention should be given to elderly issues so that more facilities and services will be available. In addition, it is important to educate younger generations and to prepare them for the adjustment to the changing needs of the elderly.

Family also has other functions, such as regulations of sexual behavior. A friend of mine told me a story about a Chinese graduate student who came to the United States in the 1980s without his family. After seeing American and Western world movies, this Chinese student, along with many other Chinese people, got the impression that people from the Western societies could have sexual relationships easily with anyone they met. They felt that sex is not a serious topic in the Western world. Under such an impression, this Chinese male student decided that he would not invite his wife and child to join him here immediately. Other Chinese students joked with him about the possibility of being able to quickly find a sexual partner. After two years, he had no luck finding anyone. Later on, he finally invited his wife and child to come. After years of settling down in the United States, I have learned that many Americans do feel that marriage is a serious issue. Sometimes, I even have a feeling that most Americans are traditional. Even though there is a high divorce rate, I have found that many couples celebrate their golden marriage anniversary (50th anniversary of marriage), which means they have a successful matrimony and strong loyalty to their family.

Family also includes the function of socializing the younger generations. When I was young, I was always told by my parents that I should not waste anything, especially food. My mother often said to me, "It is a shame to waste your food. You should know that there are many kids in other countries who are starving right now." I can recite her sentence because she repeated it thousands of times.

"I cannot finish everything you put in my bowl," I told my mother, trying to find a way to stop eating the food.

My mother tried to use Chinese values and norms to socialize me, "Okay, I will eat the food for you this time. In the future, you have to tell me how much you want and you have to eat everything in your bowl before you leave the dinner table."

What my mother told me still influences my behavior on eating food. Today, whenever I see anyone throwing away any food, I will have an impulse to tell this person to pick it up and eat it. The process of socialization in the family is important for children and seems to lay a good foundation for their social values, norms, and beliefs during their developmental years. No society can be further developed without the groundwork by each family's socialization process. This is because within the family, children will not only be taught the basic social morals and behavior codes, but they also can observe what their parents do in real situations. This socialization process in childhood is crucial and will continue to influence them throughout their lives.

A few years ago, I was at an underground railway station in China, where everyone stood in a line to wait for the train. An older lady with her granddaughter, who was about six years old, stood behind me. As the young girl tried to move to the front of the line, she said, "Grandma, I want to be the first person to get into the train, then I will have a seat."

"No, we have to stand in the line and wait," her grandma answered.

When the train came, the grandma suddenly moved toward the door of the car without waiting. It did not bother me that much because she was elderly and had a young child with her. As soon as I walked into the train, I found them sitting in two seats. The girl laughed out loud and said, "Grandma, you always do that for me. I really love you."

I did not stay near them; instead I walked to the opposite side of the train because I felt uncomfortable continuing to listen to their conversation. At this point, the grandma's actions contradicted what she had said previously, which was to stand in line and follow the rules. Actions speak louder than words and I felt that this could negatively influence the child regarding her basic socialization process and normal behavior in the future as well as how she might try to socialize her children or grandchildren.

Family also provides a function of care and protection. When I was young, it was common for all the children to be outside their houses playing in the streets. I was never warned that I might be susceptible to dangerous situations such as kidnapping. One month after I came to America, I went to a shopping mall with several other Chinese friends where I saw a lovely American boy about six-months old sitting in a car seat, which was carried by his mother. The boy looked so adorable that I could not help, but touch his feet and say, "Oh, you are so lovely!" His mother looked at me, became cautious and angry, and then immediately moved the car seat in another direction. Seeing her move the car seat away, I could tell that she was obviously unhappy with my behavior and all I felt at that moment was that the boy's mother had some kind of mental disability. In reality, American parents are socialized to be wary and suspicious of strangers. Today, of course, I completely understand why the boy's mother was so angry with me.

With the rapid social changes in China, this kind of socialization is now being seen there as well. Once I visited Beijing the apartment where I was staying was close to an elementary school. I often saw many parents and grandparents standing outside of the school gate a few minutes before school ended. I first thought they might have an activity after class, but I was later told that these parents waited outside of the school every day to meet their children. Most schools do not offer school buses and many feel uncomfortable letting their young children go home by themselves and the students' families have the responsibility of providing this kind of protection.

As previously mentioned, when I was a young girl, children were not socialized the way today's young generation is. Later, when I came to the

United States, people like me had to be socialized to learn how to protect ourselves. When my husband and I moved to a state in the South, we lived in a first floor apartment. One day, I was taking a bath and I suddenly heard someone talking with my husband. After a few minutes, I walked out to the family room and asked my husband with whom he was talking. To my surprise, he said, "A couple, I do not know them. They knocked on the door and said that they had a flat tire and wanted to use our phone." At this time in the early 1990s, cell phones were not common.

"How dare you! Even American kids know that they should not talk to strangers and should not allow them to come into their home. How could you do that?" I was really angry with him.

"But they said they needed help," my husband argued, knowing that he had made a mistake.

"I know most of them are good people, but we should be careful. You have to make sure that you are safe before you help others." I was still unhappy with what he had done and kept complaining.

Then I continued, "Okay, I will borrow a safety videotape from our Chinese neighbor's children, so you can learn how to be a safe child." I was not joking, but really felt that my husband need to be socialized like a child.

The last function of family is emotional support. Because I am away from my parents, I strongly feel that the emotional support provided by my immediate family is significant. For about six months after I came to the United States, I was really homesick. One day, I felt sad so I called my husband, who was my boyfriend at that time. I did not call my mother because I did not want her to worry about me. While I was talking to my husband, I cried a lot. We spent a long time on the phone and my husband tried to persuade me to stay until he came. In the late 1980s, to my knowledge, there was only one company that offered overseas long distance telephone services to China. However, the fee to call was extremely expensive, the surcharge was also high. I later received a bill for $287 for calling home using the company mentioned above. Even today I do not regret calling my husband, or the expensive bill that I had to pay. The call to my husband really comforted me and also encouraged me to continue my education here. I did have many other Chinese friends on campus at that time, but what I needed at that moment was my family for emotional support.

To me, marriage is an important reason for people to have a family. Marriage used to be defined as a social commitment between one male and one female, approved by society, who are together to love, care for each other, and share their economic possessions. This definition is an outdated one. I clearly remember when the first edition of this book was written, there were only six states that allowed same-sex marriage. Before the Supreme Court legalized same-sex marriage in a 5–4 decisions in 2015, it was only allowed in 37 states. So **marriage** today can be defined as a social commitment between two people, approved by society, who are together to love, care for each other, and share their economic possessions. In today's society, there are many people who are divorced. I heard that for every ten married couples, six of them end in divorce or separation. The divorce rate is much higher than it was before, not only in America, but in China as well. Therefore, in class I often use divorce as an example to discuss current social issues. Whenever I ask the class if there is someone who does not know who is divorced, there are usually no raised hands because divorce is a normal social phenomenon in American society. On one occasion, to my surprise, a girl raised her hand.

"You have never met a person who has been divorced?" I asked.

"No ma'am," she answered immediately.

"Oh, is that right? You know, I ask this question every year in every class I have taught and I have never had anyone who raised their hands and told me that they have never met anyone that is divorced. Thank you for telling me that." After hearing what she said, I started feeling happy. "I also explained my points to the class."

"Wait a minute," she stopped me. "I said I have never met anyone who has been divorced. This is because the people around me do not believe in marriage."

"What do you mean?" I guess the color of my face changed and my smile froze as well.

"I meant that no one was married around me because they do not believe in marriage, even though they live together and have kids," she explained.

What she said was a shock to me. I am married and I personally believe in marriage. I registered and received my marriage license in the county courthouse after my husband came to the United States. To get married in China at that time, a couple had to carry an ID with them, permanent residence cards, and also an introduction letter from the couple's work places. The introduction letter included a statement that the person is going to obtain a marriage license. Another function of the letter was to verify that the person was single. In the United States, it is much easier; all we need is our driver's licenses and two people who can verify that the couple is single. When the judge said the vows, he informed us that if we agreed to be married, we should love each other and work together to overcome any problems. After reading the vows, the judge asked, "Are you going to say yes?"

"I beg your pardon," my husband said. He was still trying to understand every word the judge said. Everyone laughed in the room because they had never met anyone getting married who did not say yes, but instead asked to repeat the vows. I did not understand all of what the judge said either. I thought this was because the judge said the vows so frequently that he was fluent and fast and perhaps no one paid any attention to what he said.

"You just go ahead and say yes," I said.

"I did not quite catch what the judge said," my husband told me with a whisper.

"I did not catch all the words either. You just go ahead and say yes." I was a little embarrassed because everyone laughed. I did not laugh. The fact was, in my mind, I was deeply moved by his question to the judge, because he wanted to understand fully what he was promising to me before he said yes. When he was sure of what the judge was asking him, he did say yes and promised his life to me. To this day, I remember how much this promise meant to both of us.

Everyone understands that marriage is a commitment between two individuals. Unfortunately, some people feel that marriage is not as serious as it once was. There is an international grocery store in my town and once my husband and I went there to buy groceries. My husband accidentally grabbed another person's cart, which I did not figure out until I got to the checkout line. As a result, when we went to the store again, I specifically told him, "You really need to help me this time," emphasizing the word help.

"I have already helped you," he answered.

"When did you help me?" I asked with a puzzled face.

With a large grin, he replied, "I drove you here."

"Come on. You call that help?" I could not believe what he said. "Yes, ma'am. Oh, by the way, if I do not help you what will happen to me?" he asked.

Without hesitation, I warned, "I will divorce you."

"I beg your pardon," he said with astonishment. "You are going to divorce me because of this?"

"Yes, sir," I laughed. "So you have to help me if you do not want a divorce!"

"I would like to know how we would divide our money and property if you divorced me," he continued.

I thought for a minute, "If I divorce you, I think we should split everything 50/50."

"What if I divorced you?" He sounded like he wanted to know everything in detail.

"Did you say that you would divorce me? Why would you divorce me? Okay, if you divorce me, you need to take off your shirt and slacks and leave the house. You will get nothing," I suddenly heard someone's laugh. There was an older Chinese couple standing behind us who heard what we said and could not help but to laugh.

I felt embarrassed because I was only joking. I thought about this joke for a long time. I always felt that I grew up in a traditional family and society. Marriage to me is serious and important. I did not mean to make our marriage look frivolous.

The divorce rate is getting progressively higher in China now. According to statistics, there were 3.84 million of couples who divorced in 2015. It increased close to 6 percent compared to the divorce rate the year before (Chen, 2016). There were 3.6 million couples who divorced in 2014 (Yao & Yang, 2015) It seems that divorce has become the only option today for some couples and this holds true in many societies. In America, the divorce rate has shown surprisingly optimistic news. In the past, out of ten couples, four to five ended up divorced. However, it is said that the divorce rate was higher in the late 1970s and early 1980s. Nowadays, about 70 percent of marriages that began in the 1990s have celebrated their 15th anniversary The statistics also showed that the divorce rate for the couples who married is even lower in 2000s (Wong, 2014).

When discussing marriage in all human societies, there are different marriage patterns. **Endogamy** involves a married couple that belongs to the same social group. For example, a couple is from the same racial group within the same age range and also belongs to a similar social class. Opposite of endogamy, **exogamy** involves a married couple that belongs to different social groups. An example of this would be a couple that is from different racial categories, or an older person married to a younger one, or an upper class person married to someone who belongs to a lower class. There is no right or wrong, good or bad with these two different marriage patterns, as long as a couple is happy, their marriage is good.

A marriage between two people is defined as **monogamy**. A marriage between three or more people is **polygamy**. Under this term, there are two types of marriage. The first type is **polygyny**, which is defined as a type of marriage that involves one man and more than one woman. We have often heard that a man had several wives. An example is in ancient China, an emperor could marry as many wives as he wished. The second term is **polyandry**, which is defined as a type of marriage that involves one woman and more than one man. An example of this type of marriage can be found in Northwestern Nepal. I once read a book which included a photo of a young lady who was sixteen and had two fathers, who were brothers and her two fathers married one wife, who was the mother of this young lady. She had three husbands who were aged fifteen, twelve, and nine. Worldwide, the marriage form of polygamy is not popular or well known. The most accepted universal form of marriage is monogamy.

After a couple is married, where they will reside will be an important question for them. Traditionally, a Chinese couple would live with the hus-band's family. However, young American couples will likely live without their parents. In sociological terms, people's residency is divided by three types. First, **neolocality** is defined as a type of residency where a married couple lives apart from their parents on both sides. The second concept, **patrilocality**, is defined as a type of residency where a couple lives in the same house or near the husband's family. Third, **matrilocality** is a type of residency where a couple lives in the same house or near the wife's family. These three different residential patterns symbolize not only where people reside, but also represent a cultural background in a society. In both American and Chinese societies today, many newly married couples would most probably have neolocality. The values behind their residency are indepen-dence, privacy, and less family conflict.

In the past, neolocality was not possible in China. When the newly mar-ried couples moved away, it meant that they did not want to take the oblig-ation for the care of their elderly parents. The residency was most likely to be patrilocality. This is because for thousands of years, sons have been ex-pected to take the responsibility of caring for his parents, not the daughters. This tradition has been continued even today when practicing the one-child policy. In China, many couples would rather have a boy instead of a girl because of this reason and the continuity of the family name.

There is a tradition in China that the younger generations are socially expected to take care of older people. China has established this tradition as a law. The basic rule of this law is that parents have the responsibility to raise and educate their under-aged children and adult children are obligated to take care of their aging parents. By law, if the elderly parents do not have any economic resources, their adult children have to support them financially. I read an article years ago about an old Chinese couple who had a few chil-dren. When this couple could not distribute their money fairly to each child, the oldest son refused to go back home to visit his parents. Finally, this elder-ly couple took the son to court and he was forced to make several trips back home each month and also support his parents financially.

However, in the last two decades, great social changes have taken place in China. One of these changes is the alteration of the family structure be-cause of the practice of the family planning policy established in 1979. Even though this one-child policy came to an end in 2015 due to reasons such as the shortage of labor supply, the increased cost of manual labor at the mar-ket, and the need of younger generations to provide care to the rapid in-crease in the population of senior citizens. The practice of the one-child pol-icy for 36 years (1979–2015), the current family structure has changed into 4:2:1 or 2 ratio, which means that a family consists of four grandparents, two parents, and one child or two. This type of family is facing some problems in terms of caring for the elderly. There are also increased numbers of families which practice neolocality with 2:1 or 2 ratio (two young parents and one child or two). This is also called **nuclear family**. It normally involves one or two parents and the children in a family.

In recent years, the rapid social change and development of new values, such as individualism and privacy, both elderly parents and their adult children have shifted to the neolocality type of residential pattern. This type of residency has resulted in a higher rate of "empty nest" as previously discussed. This social phenomenon has never existed in Chinese history and is completely different from the traditional model of care giving for elders in China. The current family structure, because of the practice of one-child policy for years, cannot possibly maintain this honored Chinese tradition. The stress on the single child or a young couple to provide care and support for both aging parents and in some cases grandparents, may exceed their ability.

Extended family is defined as one or two parents, children, and other kinships such as relatives. I used to live with my grandma before I went to elementary school. My grandma was old and sometimes fell asleep while telling me a story. One afternoon she fell asleep and I felt bored, so I used a piece of paper and rolled it into a small stick, then I put it into her nose. When she woke up, she was mad at me. She told me to stand in the corner of the room and then she went back to sleep. I quickly walked back to her again and put another stick of paper into another part of her nose. Finally, my grandma told my mother, who was angry at me for doing this to my grandma.

"I did this because grandma did not talk to me and instead fell asleep," I argued back.

"Grandma is old. You must show respect to your elderly," my mother answered and tried to educate me.

"Why do I have to respect grandma? Do you have a reason for that?" I asked with hesitation.

"Your grandma delivered eight children, including me. Two of them died. Your grandpa passed away when grandma was young. She took care of the six of us by herself. Do you think grandma should be respected?" At that time, I could not understand how difficult it was for a widow to take care of six children, but I started to feel that my grandma was a nice mother because she raised my mother, and my mother was the best mother in the world to me.

My grandma lived in my uncle's house and he had three teenage daughters at the time. I not only learned to respect to my grandma, but I also learned how to interact with my three cousins as well, by learning to share.

In the past, I always felt that my mother was only mine. In my uncle's house, when my cousins asked my mother to help them knit or sew clothing, I first said that they should ask their mother to help them. I later learned that it was nice if you could help others do something. I did feel that by living in an extended family I would not receive as much attention as in my nuclear family; however, I learned how to interact better with others.

Structural-functional perspective was discussed earlier in this chapter when analyzing the functions of family. The other two theories are social conflict theory and symbolic interaction theory. **Social conflict theory** is defined as the family as a social group representing social inequality in terms of racial categories and social classes. This perspective basically focuses on how family reflects social inequality in a society. In other words, social inequality symbolizes a social stratification system on a macro level. This social system consists of many individual families, which are the foundational units for the development of social classes in a society. Without these basic units of families, it would be impossible to illustrate social layers/differences which are represented by the rich and poor families within the social stratification system.

Symbolic interaction perspective defines the interaction among people in the family as changing all the time based on various shifts of family members. An example is a divorce may result in the change of relationships between the formerly married couple and their children. After remarriage, they will have to readapt to the new family. Symbolic interaction perspective focuses on the internal interactions of family.

Different cultural backgrounds establish different family values. Since I was born and raised in China and have lived in the United States, for many years I have combined family values from these two different cultures. My international experience has helped me widen my views to recognize American morals and functions of family life, different types of residency, the care taking of the elderly and similarities of divorce issues in America and China. After coming to the United States, the most important family value I have learned is the moral of independence and how Americans are expected to be independent, whether young or old.

Even though I have immigrated to America from China, I still feel that the Chinese value of taking care of the elderly by their family should not only be continued in China, but should be utilized in America as well. Although nursing homes and assisted living facilities are abundant in American society, caregiving by family members can provide more personal care. Furthermore, family care should be the first resource offered and it should be the foundation of the social care services system.

Chapter 11

RELIGION

Key words: religion; totem; charisma; religiosity; ritual; experiential religiosity; ritualistic religiosity; ideological religiosity; consequential religiosity; intellectual religiosity; secularization; civil religion; structural-functional perspective; social cohesion; social control; social conflict perspective; symbolic interaction perspective

Many years ago, I had a student who majored in World Religions. One day after class, he asked me if I had some time to talk with him.

"Do you have a question about the class notes?" I asked.

"No, no. I have some questions about religions in China, especially about Buddhism," he replied.

"Oh, I am not the person to answer your questions, because I know nothing about Chinese religions." I felt embarrassed, but I actually did not know much about Chinese religions.

He continued, "If you do not have time now, I can talk to you later."

I was afraid he might have thought I did not want to talk with him, so I replied, "I would love to talk to you if I knew something about Chinese religions, but I really do not know anything about them."

"Why don't you know anything about religions in your country? Do you have a belief?" he could not comprehend what I had said.

"Oh, my goodness, I have to explain to you the way we were brought up in a socialist society," I tried to begin my long story.

I explained to him that after the establishment of socialist China, organized religious ideals were never a part of people's lives. We were told that religion was the opium of the people, an idea which was given by Karl Marx.

This means that the function of religious beliefs is to permit people to accept the suffering in their life, and to look forward to happiness after the suffering. As a child, I was educated about Marx's opinion of religion, even before I knew any detail in religious beliefs either in China or the world. At that time people in China were taught that there was no God. I learned in school that humans can conquer nature, and we are the masters of our own fate. Before coming to the United States, I traveled to quite a few temples of different Chinese religions including those of Daoism and Buddhism. These temples were open to the public primarily for tourists' purposes. In these temples, there were no monks, just empty rooms and some religious symbols (see Fig. 11.1).

People are now allowed to choose their own religious beliefs with the current rapid social changes taking place in China. I had already attended a few Catholic and Baptist churches in America before my first visit to China many years ago, but I had never visited any Chinese Buddhist temples that offered religious services. The day I visited a temple in Beijing, I saw many people on their knees praying. I was shocked because I had never seen

Figure 11.1. Buddhism was the most popular religion in China for hundreds of years, but after the establishment of the People's Republic of China in 1949, religions were not allowed to be practiced. In recent years, government policies have been more open toward religious practice.

Chinese people practicing their Buddhist religion in a temple before. With the rapid social change and economic development, the Chinese society has begun to accept people with different religious beliefs.

In a recent trip to Beijing, I went to a Catholic church on a Sunday morning (see Fig. 11.2). This was the first time I had been inside of a church in China because a visitor cannot typically enter into a church unless it is the time for Mass. The church I went to could hold up to 500 people. All of the seats were full and there were also people standing in the back. People attending the Mass were ranged by age. The church looked nice and modern with quite a few flat screen TVs, which had captions of the Bible scriptures and songs in Chinese. I observed that the people in the church were very familiar with the procedure. I was shocked and deeply moved from seeing so many people sincerely singing songs, reciting the sentences from the Bible in Chinese, and holding hands together. This was the first time I observed a Mass in a church in China. I deeply felt that China now has more

Figure 11.2. This is a Catholic church located in Beijing near Tiananmen Square. It was first built in 1655, and then rebuilt in 1905. After 1949 it became an elementary school, but more than two decades ago the school was torn down. It was renovated and remade into a church again so that people could attend mass.

freedom for personal religious beliefs (see Fig. 11.3). When I started my job as a teaching assistant in graduate school at an American university, it was a big surprise to me that an introductory book to sociology deemed Confucianism a religion in China. As I said earlier, I was not very knowledgeable about religions in China. However, personally, I had a hard time grasping the idea that Confucianism was a type of religion as opposed to just a set of beliefs. What I knew about it was that Confucius, or better known as Master Kung (551 BCE–479 BCE) was a famous Chinese thinker and philosopher. One of the books he wrote is called *Spring and Fall Annuals.* Even though I have never read any of his work, his famous quotes can be found in many Chinese books referenced by other authors in China. He was also an educator and taught many students. His values and thoughts on morality, justice, people's relationships, and sincerity among other things, as well as his viewpoints and beliefs have significantly influenced the Chinese society for thousands of years. Confucius' judgments also have deeply influenced China's neighboring countries like Japan, Vietnam, and Korea.

Figure 11.3. This is the inside of the church, where people pray on Sundays.

Even today I still wonder why this particular American sociology book I read put Confucianism as a type of Chinese religion. I discussed this question with some of my Chinese friends who were almost the same age as me; all of them were surprised. We were puzzled as to how a man who was simply a great thinker in Chinese history could ever be regarded as a religious being. The more I understood the concept of religion, the more I believed that Confucianism should not be considered a religion. **Religion** can be defined as people's beliefs and practices that are generally based on morality and supernatural power. Although I know that Confucianism is based on morality, I cannot say with certainty that Confucius had supernatural power.

It was not until I came to the United States that I began to understand Christianity and the functions of religion in society. The first year that I started my graduate school I was lonely and very homesick, so an American friend introduced me to a Chinese man who served as a Catholic Bishop in a small nearby town. I met him when he was attending a conference at a church in my area. He moved to the United States in 1949 when socialist China was founded. He left China when he was told that the Communist Party did not allow people to have religious beliefs of their own.

He was kind to me and invited me to the church that he was visiting and said, "You will meet more people in church. This particular church is big, and I believe you will feel comfortable here."

I did not know how to answer his invitation because church was an unfamiliar world and environment to me. He seemed to figure out that I did not understand what he was saying and said again,

"You do not need to worry. You do not have any obligation to come. You can visit first and if you like it, you can continue. If you do not like it, you can stop coming at any time," he said.

I immediately asked, "Really? I do not have any obligation to continue to come if I do not want to?" I felt much more comfortable accepting his invitation.

"No, definitely not," he said.

I still remember the first Sunday morning I went to a Mass; I was completely taken aback by the beauty of the church. It had stained glass windows, pictures, paintings on the high ceiling and pews, capable of holding around 500–600 people. When I arrived, I purposefully went to the second floor and sat in the first seat of the front row. That way I could see people below me and I could also turn around to see people on the second floor. When the service began, the priest asked if anyone was a newcomer. I could see about twenty people who raised their hands.

All I remember during the service was that people stood up, sat down, knelt down, and sang songs. Because of unfamiliar church proceedings and language barriers, I understood neither the actions they took nor the songs they sang. I could not comprehend the meaning of the sermon either. Finally, I heard a word that I recognized: offering. I was curious as to what context they were using this term in. Who would offer? Was it us? Was it the church? Was it God? It seemed that I immediately got an answer when I saw a group of people wearing formal clothing and walking toward us with many different baskets.

I told myself, "I see, 'offering' means the church presents gifts to the newcomers. This church is so nice."

It seemed that my assumption was correct because I saw a gentleman walking toward me, and he then gave me a brand new basket. I looked down below on the first floor and saw people passing some baskets to others in the same row. It seemed that they were passing the "gift" to the newcomers.

I thanked the gentleman and held the basket. At that moment I had already decided to come back to this church again. An elderly lady sitting beside me gestured for me to give her my basket, but I was convinced that the basket was a gift for me; so instead of passing it to her, I said, "Isn't it nice?" I was referring to the kindness and generosity of the church to newcomers. She smiled back at me. Obviously, she could not understand the meaning that I was trying to convey to her. She asked me for the basket again after about twenty seconds or so. I thought it would be mean not to show her my gift.

I told myself, "Okay, if she is really curious about this gift, I will let her have a look." After I passed the basket to her, I saw her put something into it. I almost wanted to tell her that I had already received the basket as a gift. They did not need to give me too many gifts. I also felt the urge to tell her that the people in the church were so nice and I would come back next week. Of course, the basket never came back and I soon learned the meaning of offering.

Whenever I would tell my students in class about my first experience in the church, they all could not help but laugh out loud and think how naïve I was. I certainly feel embarrassed talking about this personal experience, but I think the most important information I can pass on to my students so that they realize how a person from a different culture tried to understand a new religion, which is a part of American culture to me. Most of my students would feel it is easy to understand Christianity because they grew up within the culture. They learn other skills and language through social interaction with others, as well as learning different religious beliefs. I continued to go to this Catholic church on and off for about a year. But eventually I stopped going. The main reason I stopped attending was that I had become busy with my schoolwork, but also because of the way I was raised and the education

I received when I was a child in China. After I stopped going to church, I convinced myself that I did not have any religious beliefs, but that would soon change. A few months after I stopped attending church, as I prepared for my final statistics exam, one of my classmates was studying with me in the student coffee lounge. I wanted to get a cup of coffee, but in order to do so; I had to put twenty-five cents in the box. This coffee lounge was run by graduate students from two departments in the building. There was no one there to collect payment for the coffee. However, most people knew that they should put at least a quarter there as their payment. I searched my pocket for a little while, but could not find the change.

"Hurry up. We do not have much time left before the test," my study partner said.

"I know, but I cannot find a quarter. I need to pay for the coffee," I answered.

He said, "If you do not have the money, just do not pay for it. I am not going to tell anyone and you can pay next time. No one will know."

"No one knows but God," I answered without thinking, and then I immediately realized what I said.

Later, I kept asking myself whether I believed in God or not. I thought about this for a long time and I began going to church again. I decided to attend church for the second time after my husband and I moved to the South. In the beginning, we were invited by my husband's colleague and only went because we had been invited a few times and it was awkward to keep refusing. After attending the church activities, we began to feel that it was enjoyable to be there and meet other people. We also felt it was important to understand the Bible and then we can comprehend the American culture. We went to this church for quite a few years until we moved. Before we left, the church pastor, David, had dinner with us. This was the first time I had talked to him face to face. By listening to his personal experiences, I learned his process of understanding God and the Bible. This really gave me an incredible feeling about how extraordinarily a person could be inspired if that person had a religious belief.

After attending church activities for years and sharing many experiences with the people involved in my church, I now have a better understanding of Christianity and am willing to learn and accept it as my religion. Many people I have met in America told me that they are Christians and believe in God, but I feel they have different levels of beliefs. I have a Chinese friend who came to the United States for her graduate degree. One day she called me and asked,

"Do you go to church?"

I replied, "Yes, I do."

"How serious are you?" she continued.

"What do you mean, how serious am I?" I did not understand her question.

"I mean; do you really believe in your religion or just go to church to be social?" Her questions began to upset me.

"I am in the process of learning about the Bible, religious beliefs, and the American culture. You know I have to understand it to believe it." I tried to explain my learning process.

"You mean that you still have questions about your religion?" She was unsure about what I had said.

"Yes, I think that going to church is a learning process," I answered.

"Although I came to the United States much later than you did, when I went to church, I immediately believed in God. You should not have any questions; you should just believe it," she said.

I replied, "Yes, but I still feel that the process of learning is very important for me because we did not grow up with a religion."

She continued, "Just go ahead and have a belief. God will help you no matter what."

I asked, "Can you give me an example of what you mean?"

Then she said, "Yes, I was very sick for about two weeks, and then I had to take a test, but I could not put much time in for the review. The night before, I prayed and hoped that God would help me. The next day, when I took the exam, I felt the test questions were fairly easy."

"Do you think that after you prayed, you felt you had more confidence? Do you think you are a good student anyway and you studied very hard for this course, which laid a good foundation for your test?" I asked.

"No, I believe that God helped me," she answered with confidence.

When I told my class what my friend said to me, different students had different opinions about this experience. Some of them said they believed that if people helped themselves, then God would help them. The students who offered this idea said that the test questions would not have changed, but the level of confidence could have changed. Obviously, after my friend prayed to God, she had gained more confidence to deal with the forthcoming test. Therefore, her religious beliefs in God helped her have more self-assurance. Some of my students argued that it did not matter what a person was doing, that God would help anyway. The students with this idea felt that God would have supernatural powers to help anyone who believes. I was strongly influenced by both of the ideas offered by my students. Compared to most of my students, I do not have much personal religious experiences. I am still in the process of learning and understanding my religious beliefs, even though I do not attend any particular church. This is a new experience for me, because I was not taught or influenced by any religious beliefs when I was young. The comprehension of the meaning of religion is especially important to me.

There are also objects people may think have been filled with sacred implications according to religious beliefs. In sociological terms, a **totem** is defined as an object from the natural world that has been imbued with sacred power. I first heard of the word "totem" in China. The term was used as part of the phrase "totem pole." A cross can be seen as a totem. More often than not, when people in America see a cross on a building, they know that structure is a church. When driving on highways, people occasionally will see one cross or a few crosses with flowers on the side of the highway and know that this is the site of a car accident that took lives. The Bible is a book for Christians to study as well as a connection to their religion. This can also be considered a totem.

I also believe a national flag could be regarded as a totem. Many years ago, I did my co-op as a tour guide in China International Travel Service, Beijing Branch. And, I once accompanied a group of American tourists and we had lunch near the United States Embassy. I had forgotten to tell them that we would pass the embassy on our way to another tourist destination. So after lunch, when we had been traveling a short distance from the restaurant, suddenly I heard a loud voice, "Look! It is an American flag!" everyone strained their eyes to find the flag and asked, "Where is it?"

"It is there." An American man pointed to his right side. Then everyone stood up and looked in that direction.

"Why is there an American flag here?" another American woman asked me.

I apologized, "I am sorry. I forgot to tell you that we just passed the U.S. Embassy."

"Stop, please stop the bus. We would like to get off the bus and take pictures," quite a few people said. So the bus pulled over in front of the Embassy.

I noticed that many of them, when seeing the flag, put their right hand over their heart. The expression on their faces was solemn, respectful, and sincere. I leaned on the door of the bus and watched what they did, it was extremely shocking to me at the time. While growing up, I was always taught that the United States of America was an imperialist country and that American people had miserable lives. The only way they could liberate themselves was to have a revolution and end the capitalist system in order to have a better life. On the contrary, what I saw that day was that Americans sincerely loved their country.

When the tourists again sat down on the bus, I heard a person's voice, "How about we sing our National Anthem?"

"Yes!" People began to applaud.

I did not know who started singing. It was a beautiful male voice at first, then two people, then the whole group.

> Oh, say, can you see, by the dawn's early light, what so proudly we hailed
> at the twilight's last gleaming? Whose broad stripes and bright stars, through
> the perilous fight. O'er the ramparts we watched, were so gallantly stream-
> ing? . . .

At that moment, my heart was deeply touched and I suddenly had an impulse to cry for their patriotism. Later, I was sworn in as an American citizen. And, after taking the Oath of Allegiance at a naturalization ceremony, I received my Certificate of Naturalization. At the ceremony, people started to sing the National Anthem. I suddenly remembered my experience at the United States Embassy that day. These two important dates were about seventeen years apart; I could never have imagined that I would experience such an amazing life.

From my point of view, all national flags have the same meaning. They are momentous totems: patriotic symbols of a country for the people who will unite under it. An example of this is, on Independence Day, the tradition in my neighborhood is to have a bike and scooter parade. Parents and their children decorate their bicycles with the colors of red, white, and blue. They also wear clothing with these three colors. Parents, children, and even their dogs meet at the swimming pool and start the parade with scooters and bicycles both large and small. They walk and bike around the roads in the subdivision for about an hour. During the parade, children will learn the true meaning behind the flag, the history of America, and the meaning of the three different colors of the flag. The most important thing is that the practice of decorating and also the parade itself are processes of patriotic education from which American children learn to love and be proud of their own country.

When I was growing up, I was taught the meaning of the Chinese national flag, which is called "Five Star Red Flag." I remember my elementary school teacher said that the Chinese national flag is red with five yellow stars. The red color of the flag represents revolution. The yellow stars are in the upper left corner, with one star bigger than the other four. The four stars represent the unity of the Chinese people, surrounding the larger star, which represents the leadership of the Chinese Communist Party. When I visited China in recent years I heard from a taxi driver that people could go to Tiananmen Square to see the Honor Guards of the Chinese Liberate Army raising the flag in the morning.

He said, "You have to be there early if you want to stand very close to the flag pole. I know that there will be so many people there and it will be very crowded."

"I never realized that this has become a tourist attraction now in Beijing." I said surprised.

He replied, "Oh, yes. This is a good chance for the patriotic education of the people. Many people there are not only from Beijing, but also other cities."

I did not go because it was winter time. For one thing, it was too cold to wait outside for a few hours but I had also watched similar ceremonies on TV a few times. I found exactly the same solemnity, respect, and sincerity from these people's faces when they looked at the Chinese national flag, that I had seen on the faces of the Americans outside the Embassy years ago.

While the concept totem defines a symbolic structure, **charisma**, is another term defined as a quality that certain individuals own and use to attract people as followers. Many people have charisma and others are attracted to them, such as fans' attraction to their favorite singers, football players, or movie stars. To many Americans, Martin Luther King Jr. had charisma. His famous avocations for civil rights influenced thousands of Americans and brought about revolutionary changes.

When charisma is connected to religious beliefs, it is clear to see there are also many famous religious people with such magnetism. In June of 2002, my husband and I passed a church in our local area. We saw the church congregation was offering drinks to people passing by on the street and one of them came up and asked if I would like to have a drink.

"There will be an event later this month in this area," she began to talk to me, "Billy Graham will be in town for a wide assortment of interfaith activities. Would you like to attend?"

"Yes, I really want to get two tickets and go. Thanks a lot," I replied.

I know Dr. Billy Graham is a famous religious leader because I have seen him on TV before. I wanted to go to experience people's reactions to his speech.

Unfortunately, in the summer of 2002, my husband's company announced that they would be closing in two months. So we were got very so busy revising his resume in order to apply for other jobs that I completely forgot about Billy Graham. Later, I watched TV and saw that many people were emotional and crying, while listening to his speech. I realized that Dr. Graham has a significant personal charisma. I really regretted missing such an important event. It would have been a wonderful opportunity for me to learn more about religion because I have never had another chance to see him since 2002.

When people discuss how important religious beliefs are in their lives, they are referring to **religiosity**. People are more likely to say they have strong religiosity if they often go to church for ritual activities. The ceremonial forms of conduction, which are rules that govern people's behavior when practicing their religious belief are defined as **rituals**. This concept can be used to show that people have a religious belief, but this is not the only measurement of the importance in religion in people's lives. Years ago, when discussing the term of religiosity in the class, a student asked me a question. "I do believe in God and I have strong religious beliefs. I come from another city and my church is in my hometown, so I do not attend church here. Are you suggesting that I do not have a strong religious belief?"

I answered, "No. I am not going to say that you do not have a strong religious belief because religiosity is measured by five dimensions. So the ritual activity is only one of the five."

The first dimension is **experiential religiosity**, which can be understood as an individual's emotional connection with a religious belief. People, without a doubt, have their own internal private emotional connections to their religion. Some people's connections to their religious beliefs are much stronger than others. This is not only limited to Christianity but many other religions. I used to go to a small Chinese grocery store when I lived in a Southern state and the owners were a couple who practiced Buddhism. One day while I was there purchasing food, a man came into the store who was familiar with the owners. He obviously had something to do with a Buddhist temple, or was the organizer of a ritual ceremony because I overheard the owner's wife say to this customer, "We are sorry that we have not gone to the temple for a long time, but we pray at home. We also always remember that Buddha is in our minds, in our words, and in our acts."

The man answered. "Yes, it is absolutely correct, as long as you continue to keep your emotional tie to Buddha. I don't think you have to attend the ceremony all the time if you are busy."

The sentiment that "Buddha is in our minds, in our words, and in our acts" represents the personal emotional connections between the couple and their religious beliefs.

The next dimension, **ritualistic religiosity**, is measured by whether an individual person will practice the ritual behavior, such as how often they attend religious services as well as how often they pray. My husband and I started to go to a church three years after we moved to the South. The original reason we started going was because we were invited and we also wanted to study the American culture and to be social with others. We did not think we would gain any revelation about religious beliefs because we did not think we could understand Christianity because of our upbringing in

China. During the process of going to the church we learned a lot about religious beliefs and we also got to know many people within the church (see Fig. 11.4).

The third term, **ideological religiosity,** is defined as the extent to which an individual obeys the religious doctrine of their beliefs. If a person believes in a certain religion, he or she needs to confirm all the doctrine of that religion. In Buddhism, monks and believers are asked not to eat any meat, not to kill any creatures and so on. If they eat meat, they would be considered nonbelievers. Many religions ask people to be honest and treat other people as brothers and sisters. Many followers practice these doctrines, because they believe that adhering to these rules is important for them in their religious life.

Consequential religiosity is the fourth measurement, which is defined as the connection between religious beliefs and an individual's daily activity. I used to have a friend named David. And when I started my Masters' degree, he was about to graduate. He introduced me to a Chinese bishop and a Catholic church, where I began my understanding of religion. Every time I asked him a question, he would recite long paragraphs from the Bible.

Figure 11.4. This is another Catholic church located in Beijing. It began service in 1703.

During our conversations, he always ended with the sentence, "I will pray for you and God bless you."

At that time, I had never been in a church and I knew nothing about the Bible. One day, after David cited a long paragraph from the Bible, I asked another graduate student in my office, "Maureen, do you think what David cited is from the Bible?"

"I do not know because I do not go to church," Maureen answered, "but I will tell you how you could figure it out."

"How? I really want to know," I said to her.

"Go to his office and take the Bible from his desk and let him recite a paragraph. We will see if what David said is from the Bible or not," Maureen suggested.

"Okay, I will do it," I was very excited.

After I took the Bible from David's office, I gave it to Maureen and we decided to let David recite a paragraph from a section. Maureen sat in our office with the open Bible to check if David would make any mistakes. I was outside the office and I left the door open so Maureen could hear my conversation with David.

"Hello, David, every time I ask you a question you tell me what the Bible says. Are you sure your words are from the Bible?" I asked.

"Yes, of course, they are from the Bible," David replied with a tone implying he could not believe I questioned him.

I challenged him, "Then, can you recite a paragraph from Chapter 3 at the beginning?"

"Yes, certainly," David answered with great confidence. Then he started to recite a few paragraphs of a verse.

"Good, that is enough. I really appreciate it." I made a gesture to stop and then he left.

"Maureen, were there any mistakes?" I asked.

She said, "No, there is no mistake at all, but I think you are pretty silly."

"Hey, you asked me to do that. How dare you say that I was silly?" I was not excited anymore.

Maureen laughed, "I meant that you should ask David to recite the passage and also the grammar, such as comma, period, and question mark and he might have made mistakes."

After graduation, David started to serve in a small local church, according to what he said, to become a priest was his dream ever since he was a child. David had a great impact on my religious beliefs and now, many years later, I still remember the time I questioned him about the Bible. The ability to recite passages from the Bible represented his knowledge about his religion, which also demonstrates the next measure of religiosity: **intellectual**

religiosity. This concept describes an individual's knowledge about their particular religious' beliefs. Many students in my class graduated from private Catholic junior or senior high schools, from which they learned a great deal of religious knowledge, such as the history of their faith and the Bible. I think this is an important step for young people to learn and understand why they believe what they believe.

Today, with rapid social change, there is a phenomenon which is called **secularization**. This concept describes how the importance of religious beliefs has had a tendency to decline. As a professor, I have often heard from my students about their reasons for attending or not attending churches when starting their college career. Some said that they could not go to church with their parents because they are in school and away from home. They did not want to go to an unfamiliar church, they had to work and had no time to go, or after entering college, their parents want them to make a decision if they wanted to continue to attend church. Many students have to work on weekends, and one student in particular told me that he felt that money was more important than church because he has to pay for his rent, food, and car insurance. He also said that when he was young, his parents asked him to go all the time, and now his parents have no control over his church attendance. Therefore, he felt that he did not need to go.

Another important concept is **civil religion**, which is defined as a kind of religious allegiance that ties people together with the country they live in and the land they love. When former President Obama announced his new immigration policy in 2015, his closing statement was, "God bless this country we love."

What these words represent is civil religion, rather than a real religious belief. I believe what former President Obama meant was, let's pray for the God we believe in, the land we live on, and the country we love. American Christians go to different churches with their specific religious beliefs, although overall it is called Christianity. There are also other religious beliefs in this country, such as Judaism, Islam, Sikhism, and Buddhism. American Christians believe that there is a God and hope that God will help them and their country. Therefore, this big arrangement of beliefs in this country is no longer just Christianity's religious beliefs, but has become civil religion.

To understand religion, the impact of religious beliefs on a society, and the functions of religious beliefs in coping with other social affairs, we again use three sociological theories to guide our discussion. Émile Durkheim (1965; orig. 1915), using the **structural-functional perspective**, argued that religion has been used as a tool by society to enhance the social power over individuals. Durkheim specified that religion has three functions: social cohesion, social control, and providing meaning and purpose to life. **Social co-**

hesion is defined as religion used to unite people with identical social values and norms. Every religion will have certain values and norms like being honest or helping others whenever you can. Therefore, all these values will be shared by people who have the same religious beliefs, which will instruct them on how to think and behave when doing things.

Social control is defined as religion used to manipulate society through shared values and norms. Social control is exercised by the people with power, and religion will help them influence the public by using socially accepted values and norms. The last function of religion, given by Durkheim, is providing meaning and purpose to life, which means that religion is used to help people explain things that happen to them in their daily lives, either good or bad. This enables people to better understand their life circumstances, which otherwise may not make sense to them.

Using the **social conflict perspective**, Karl Marx (1964; orig. 1848) pointed out that religion supports patterns of social inequality. What Marx did not recognize was how religious ideals have motivated many people to seek greater equality within society. When I lived in a small apartment in graduate school, I needed a bookcase for my textbooks, I first checked a furniture store, but it was so expensive and I did not really want to spend the money on a brand new one. After school one day, I passed a church that was about a block away from my apartment, where they were having a basement sale in the church. This is because it was winter and there was snow and the sale had to be in a warm basement. I went there and found a bookcase for only five dollars. The church people also asked me if I would like a delivery service for free. I said I lived only one block away and they could help others who had to move something heavy and a longer distance. After that, I went to quite a few basement sales there because everything was so affordable and many college students also went there to look for things they needed. After moving to different places for a few times, I did not keep the bookcase, but I still have a small stool that I got from that church. Whenever I see it I remember the church and their generosity in helping those people in need.

According to Karl Marx (1964; orig. 1848), religion is the opium of the people. Opium is a kind of drug, which numbs or stupefies people's nerves. Once I saw an American television had a commercial about illegal drug use; A person held an egg and said "this is your brain" and then the egg was badly scrambled and cooked, and a voice said "this is your brain on drugs." The obvious meaning of the commercial was to tell people not to use drugs because it would damage a person's brain and health. Karl Marx described religion as a kind of drug that would numb people's nerves and stop them from looking for a solution to certain questions. These questions included why individuals are not equal in a society and why certain individuals exploited others' economic resources. According to Marx, religion permits people to admit the misery in their life and hope for happiness in the future. Therefore, Marx indicated that there was no God and people should depend on themselves to fight for a good life.

According to **symbolic interaction perspective**, people acquire religious beliefs through the process of social interaction. When people are born, they have no religious beliefs, but by interacting with others, people will generate certain values and knowledge about religion. The more they talk with others, the more they will understand, and the more they may believe or comprehend a religion. I discussed earlier that I had no religious beliefs when I came to this country, but later, I went to a Baptist church in the South. The more often I went to the church and interacted with others and the pastor at this church, the more I wanted to know about the religion, and the more I felt that I had a certain kind of attachment and sentiment with the church and my belief. Symbolic interaction perspective also emphasizes the significance of religious beliefs and the ability of these beliefs to bring people the feeling of security.

Religion is important for many people and essential for the formation of the culture in any society. It provides meaning, security, and purpose for their everyday lives. Religion is also an important topic studied by many sociologists. For me, religion is a part of a culture in any society, which directly influences people's values and norms in their daily lives. As a sociologist and coming from China, I had never experienced religion before. Even though Buddhism was a very popular and strong religion for more than 2,000 years prior to socialist China, which was founded in 1949. During the time I grew up, Buddhism was forbidden, However, it has never stopped influencing Chinese people's values as well as its culture. Today, China allows people to have their own religious beliefs. At the same time, I really feel that without understanding the Bible and many American peoples' religious beliefs, especially Christianity; it would be hard to understand the American culture. American society involves many different people from all over the world. It is also comprised of many religious groups and allows people to have freedom to choose their beliefs. I have seen Chinese Buddhist monks as well as Islam Mosques in the town I live in now. It becomes important to have other religious beliefs in this country, which can coexist to help shape and influence American culture.

Chapter 12

POPULATION

Key words: demography; zero population growth; migration; net migration; push factors; pull factors; sex ratio; crude birth rate; fertility; life expectancy; mortality; crude death rate; infant mortality rate; dependency ratio; Malthusian theory: geometric progression, arithmetic progression, positive checks, and preventive checks; demographic transition theory

As human, we have lived on this planet for thousands of years. The world population growth was increased very slowly in 99 percent of human history and then rapidly growing in the past century to today's size. As of 2007, the world population was estimated to be 6.6 billion people (Central Intelligence Agency, 2007). Seven years later, in 2014, the population increased to an estimated 7.32 billion people (Central Intelligence Agency, 2016). By 2050, the estimated global population will reach 9.6 billion (Kochhar, 2014). From 6.6 billion in 2007 to 9.6 billion in 2050, the increase is over 45 percent in 43 years.

Currently, China has the largest population in the world accounting for 1.367 billion, and the second largest population belongs to India with an estimated 1.23 billion people. The United States has the third largest population in the world, with close to 324 million people (Central Intelligence Agency 2016). It is projected that India's population will increase by 400 million by 2050, making the total population 1.6 billion, which is greater than the projected populations of China and the United States combined. China's projected population by 2050 will increase by 25 million (Kochhar, 2014). The world population growth trend has happened much faster from the last century than ever before in human history. Looking back at the world population in 1804, there were only one billion people. However, by the year 1960, it had reached 3 billion. It is clear that this population growth is staggering and one major point of concern that we face today and will continue to face in the future, is the lack of food and natural resources.

Demography is defined as the scientific study of human population. There are three major factors which influence the number of people in a population. These factors are birth rate, death rate, and migration rate. Many countries in the world have a higher birth rate than a death rate. The birth rate in the United States in 2016 was 12.5 per 1,000, the death rate was 8.2 per 1,000, and the population growth rate was 0.81 percent (Central Intelligence Agency, 2016). In contrast, the world birth rate in 2016 was 18.6 per 1,000, the death rate was 7.8 per 1,000, and the population growth rate was 1.08 percent (Central Intelligence Agency, 2016). Those statistics indicate that the world population is increasing because of a higher birth rate than death rate.

Since the rapidly growing ratio of birth is over death, scholars suggest that the goal of worldwide population growth should be **zero population growth**. Zero population growth is defined as demographic growth to the point where population size does not change as a consequence of the mixture of births, deaths, and in-and-out migration. People who advocate this concept believe that it would benefit the best if the current world population keep the size as it is today. This idea states that the population should not continue to increase or decrease, but remain stable and stay where it is today.

When discussing zero population growth, most people will focus on birth and death rates in a society or a specific region. The increase of international migration has also become an important issue, because it significantly impacts the population size in a country as well. **Migration** is defined as people who move in or out of a particular area. This affects the number of people in a given society. The net migration rate in the United States, according to the 2016 data, was 3.9 per 1,000. **Net migration** is the variation in the number of people who move in and out of a particular area, such as within a state or a country, or from one state or one country to another.

When people move out of one country, the nation they move from is called the "donor country" and the international destination that people are moving to is labeled the "host country." I moved from China to America; China is my donor country and America is my host country. To China, I am considered an emigrant, but to the United States, I am an immigrant. The words emigration and immigration can only be used for an international move.

There are many reasons for people to move, either domestically or internationally. This can be basically explained by push and pull factors. **Push factors** are the situations which persuade people to move out, such as bad living standards or lack of job opportunities. **Pull factors** are the situations that persuade people to move into an area, such as a better climate, better living standards, or more educational opportunities. The reason I came to the United States was for opportunities to attend graduate school. Therefore, I feel that the pull factors affected more than the push factors for my situation of migration.

My international migration story started after I finished my four years of college education in China, where I was offered a teaching position in the same school I graduated from. At that time, China did not require a Ph.D. or a Master's degree to teach in college. During the process of teaching, I felt that I had a desire to further my education in order to be competent to teach well at a college level. If individuals wanted to attend graduate school during this time in China, they needed to take an entrance examination, which required a written permission from their employer. If their work place did not agree with the applicant applying for graduate school, the person had no way to further his or her studies. With rapid social changes in China today, people have a lot more freedom to seek their dreams for further education. However, at that time, after weighing the advantages and disadvantages, I realized that going to the United States for graduate school was my best option. I wrote in my prologue that:

> I can still remember the night before I left home; my mother told me that after I received my Master's degree, I should come back to China immediately. I asked why. She said, 'You are an unwed girl, and you do not want to get a Ph.D. It will be very difficult for you to find an ideal husband with the same level of education.' I remember I raised my right hand and swore to her that I would be home after two years. Ultimately, I failed to keep my promise to my mother because I received a Ph.D. and I also decided to settle down in America permanently.

There were many reasons I did not go back to China because of both push and pull factors. A higher paying job in America is one of the pull factors, but it was not the only one for me. The main reason was that my husband majored in advanced technology in the United States. At the time he completed graduate school, his field of expertise was not needed in China. In the late 1980s, China was not as developed as it is today (push factors). He applied for a job in the United States and was immediately hired (pull factor). Many Chinese people, after receiving their various degrees, preferred to stay and seek their careers in the United States during that time (pull factors). They chose to settle in America for many different reasons. The main reason for most of my friends, was the higher living standards and pay rates (pull factors) compared to China at that time. Also, there were more opportunities for self-development due to the population size in the United States, which is much smaller than that of China. However, today the situation has changed. Many Chinese students, after finishing their American education return to China, where there are more opportunities as a result of the economic development of the past more than two decades.

As previously discussed, China is the most populous nation in the world. In 1979, China started to practice a family planning policy, which allowed each couple in urban areas to have only one child and in rural areas to have no more than two children. This policy is also known as the one-child policy, which was put in place to stabilize the population growth in order to accelerate economic development. This is also because by the year that the Chinese government began to practice the one-child policy, the population had increased from 541 million in 1949 (the year the People's Republic of China was founded) to 975 million in 1979 (China today.com, 2011). Many of my American students could not understand how the Chinese government could make this kind of decision and limit the number of births. A majority of them believed that the limitation meant legalized abortion. I always tried to explain the situation by telling them the experiences I had before (see Fig. 12.1).

When I was a young girl, I often heard that China had 800 million people. I was so young at the time I could not grasp the meaning of 800 million. Later, my school teachers started to talk about 900 million people. This figure still meant nothing to me, but I understood that the number had become larger. By the time I realized that there was a massive population in Beijing, the city where I lived before, China had already reached one billion people. Even with such a large population, I never had any questions, such as why there were so many people, why they were living in small spaces, and why the Chinese government started the family planning policy. Instead, I thought that this was a normal way of life for people living all over the world, not just in China.

Also during this time in Beijing, there were not many high-rise residential buildings and many people lived in one-story houses. They shared public bathrooms with communal showerheads and water faucets, and they cooked their food outside their rooms in public areas. Most families did not have a family room or a living room, because it was likely, they used all the rooms as bedrooms. With the issues of rapid population growth, limited job opportunities, and housing problems, China began to think seriously about limiting the birth rate. As a result, the family planning policy was put into practice in 1979. Initially, this policy was relatively easier to accept in urban areas than rural areas. This was due to Chinese traditional values. These morals are still relevant in rural areas today. The traditional culture includes the desire to have a son who can continue the family name and ensure that there is a caregiver available when the parents age. Therefore, the practice of the

Figure 12.1. In Beijing, many families, especially young people, would like to have a car; however, due to issues such as Beijing's large population, air pollution, traffic jams, limited parking spaces, and the fact that it is difficult to maintain roads to keep up with increased automobile production, people's ability to purchase new vehicles has been restricted. People still use different forms of transportation such as private cars, motorcycles, public buses, taxis, underground trains, and recently, Uber.

policy was challenged by the people in rural areas. The following is a conversation between Xiao Lin and I, while visiting China.

Xiao Lin was eighteen years old when I first met her at my in-laws' house. She came from a small rural village, which was about 1,000 miles from Beijing. She was hired as a caregiver for my in-laws. She also lived with my in-laws in their home.

I was surprised to learn that Xiao Lin was the third child in her family among five children. All of them were born after 1979, the year China started the family planning policy.

"Having four daughters, my dad really expected the fifth one to be a boy," said Xiao Lin.

"Only in this way would my dad not feel sorry for his parents, my grandparents, because he is the oldest son in the family and he has the responsibility to have a son to continue the family name," she tried to explain the tradition in her hometown.

Her points were very familiar to me. Growing up in China, I received almost the same traditional values as Xiao Lin received, but because I have lived in the United States for so long, I had nearly forgotten these values. In contrast to Xiao Lin, I lived in urban areas of China. The social solidarity in cities is not as strong as it is in rural areas, where Xiao Lin grew up. This weak social solidarity is caused by many social factors, such as higher levels of education, more senior social services, and a better financial status as well as health insurance for the elderly in urban areas. In addition, many young urban couples no longer feel that having a son for the husband's family is a responsibility.

From sociological viewpoints, I personally believed that the Chinese government only practices the family planning policy temporarily. This is because if the one-child policy is kept in practice, it will reach a point where the *first* generation of Chinese with this policy may have no idea about brothers and sisters because they are the only child at home. The *second* generation may not know anything about siblings, or uncles, aunts, nephews and nieces because their parents do not have siblings. This kind of society will be abnormal without family blood relatives.

I have personally seen this happen with a relative who lived in the United States and went back to China because her husband was assigned to work as a director in his American branch company in China. At that time, her daughter was 7 years old and her son was about 2. These two children were both born in the United States. My relative was asked incessantly while in China why she had two children: "Are they biologically brother and sister?" and "How can you have two kids?" From those questions, it is obvious that everyone knew and practiced the family planning policy in urban areas of China.

Traditionally, Chinese couples preferred to have a son. But, because the policy only allowed each couple to only have one child, some couples, even though it was unusual and likely to occur in the countryside, abandoned their female infant in order to be legally to have another child and hopefully it would be a boy. This behavior has directly impacted a population concept, **sex ratio**, which is defined as the number of males compared with every 100 females in a given population. Many countries have fewer males than females. For example, the United States had an estimated 97 males per 100 females in 2016, and the average of the world sex ratio was 101.581 per 100 females (Central Intelligence Agency 2016).

China had 106 males per 100 females in 2016 and the sex ratio in China is becoming imbalanced. The number of males has increased since 1980

(Chen, 2015), soon after starting the practice of the family planning policy. Chen (2015) indicates that China now has the most serious gender imbalance issue in the world. There are many reasons for this imbalanced sex ratio, such as abandoning female infants in order to have a boy for another pregnancy or sex selected abortion of female fetuses. In the past, I met many young Chinese girls who were adopted by American families and most of them are probably from Chinese orphanages. In recent years, it has become rare that Chinese parents abandoned their female infants. I believe this has related to the rapid economic development in China, as well as the weakening of the traditional Chinese values on having sons.

The Chinese family planning policy has been altered twice in recent years. The first change was if a young couple who both come from a one-child family, were allowed to have two children. Less than two years after the first change, the Chinese government announced another change at the end of 2015. The new policy stated that any couples who want to have a second child will be allowed and encouraged to do so. The reasons behind the modification of the family planning policy within a few years are that Chinese population structure changed, which is so tremendous that the one-child policy can no longer fit into the current needs of the society, such as demands for labor supply and employment volatility. This is because since 1979, the Chinese government has strongly encouraged people to delay having a child and to have sterilizations or abortions after their first child is born. The policy has slowed down the population growth in China from 6.3 children per woman in 1970 to 1.6 children per woman in 2015 (Clarke, 2015). As of 2016 the birth rate was 12.4 per 1,000 (Central Intelligence Agency, 2016). The meaning of 12.4 per 1,000 is a concept called **crude birth rate**, which is defined as the number of babies born in a year in proportion with every 1,000 people.

The calculation of this formula will be the same when applied to a country that has a large population or a small region with a relatively small amount of people. This is because the equation is based on every 1,000 people. The crude birth rate in the United States in 2016 was 12.5 per 1,000; China's was 12.4 per 1,000, and Afghanistan's was 38.3 per 1,000. This means that in 2016, in the United States, for every 1,000 Americans, there were 12.5 newly born babies (Central Intelligence Agency, 2016). It is called crude because these 1,000 people involve all different individuals, old and young, male and female. We know that only females can deliver babies. In addition, these females are also divided into two groups: childbearing age and non-childbearing age. So only those females in the period of childbearing period can have children. Therefore, crude birth rate is a rough calculation based on the total population, which can only represent a fertility level in a nation.

Birth is also called **fertility**, which is defined as the number of babies born in a population.

After the Chinese government announced the termination of the one-child policy in 2015, there have been different surveys which asked those childbearing couples if they would like to have a second child. Many of them were concerned that it would be very expensive in urban areas to raise a child until he or she is eighteen years old (Phillips, 2015). The cost of raising a child is one reason but not the only reason. Some people were concerned that China has already had a large population; it is very difficult for those children to grow up in a competitive environment for a life-long process. This is shown with the way the Chinese children have to compete to go to a better kindergarten, a superior elementary, junior, and senior high schools in order to find a better paying job. Many childbearing-aged parents have gone or are going through the competitive process with their current child. They may think it would be too much and/or too hard to go through that process an additional time with another child. According to an Internet survey, about 41 percent of people, out of 140,000 respondents, said that they would not choose to have a second child even though they were able to do so. About 29 percent were undecided and 30 percent said that they would (Bergman, 2015).

Generally, we can find that countries with a lower birth rate will have a higher elderly population and the average age of the population tends to be higher. An example is the median age (calculated by the 50th percentile) in the United States has reached 37.9 years old. Those 65 and older make up 15.25 percent of the total population (Central Intelligence Agency, 2016). We will find that this trend will continue as baby boomers enter into senior citizen status. By 2050 about 20.9 percent of American population are projected to be senior citizens (Casselman, 2014). In China, the decrease in birth rates, resulting in fewer babies, plus the longer life expectancy, and the fact that more people are able to live until a much older age (Copeland, 2014) will accelerate the aging process in a society. Therefore, given the slow down in the fertility rate and the steadily increasing life expectancy of the Chinese, a serious issue has arisen: the growth of the older population.

In China, the definition of a senior citizen is someone aged sixty and older. As with the aging issue, another serious concern is that the 8:4:2:1 or 2 family structure is occurring in China. This means that a couple (2) with one child (1 or 2) has four parents (4: mother, father, mother-in-law, and father-in-law) and eight grandparents (8: two sets for each parent). In this situation, it is hard for this young couple to offer care for both the elderly grandparents, parents, as well as their children.

People can live much longer than ever before. The definition for this measure is called **life expectancy**. It is defined as how long, on average, a person is expected to live. My neighbor's grandma passed away at the age of 83 in Beijing and was considered a person with longevity about fifty years ago. Today, eighty-three years old would be considered relatively young. However, life expectancy in the United States is close to eighty years of age (Central Intelligence Agency, 2016).

Once, a female student of mine called me before class one morning because I was giving an exam that day. She cried and said, "Professor, I will not be able to come to school today."

"Why? Can you give me a reason because we have a test today?" I asked.

"I know, but my grandpa passed away last night," she answered very upset.

"Oh. I am sorry to hear that," I replied. "It is not a problem; I can postpone your exam. Please contact me when you can do the makeup test."

Three weeks later, she came back to school. After class I talked to her and asked when she could do the makeup test. She started to cry and said that she did not study for the test because she was sad, since her grandpa passed away.

"I really feel sorry that your grandpa passed away, but you have to go on with your own life." I tried to comfort and persuade her.

I could see the tears run down her face, "I know. But I really miss my grandpa."

"I understand. Dear, you need to know this is a natural law that older people will die before the younger generation."

"My grandpa was not old when he passed away," she cried loudly.

"I am sorry." At that moment I could not find any words to calm her down or to make her feel better.

Later, I agreed to give her another week to prepare for the makeup. Then, she said, "I will try to study hard. My dad said that time will help me forget my sadness."

"Yes, what your dad said is definitely right. By the way, how old was your grandpa when he passed away?" The reason I asked this question was because I also teach the topic of population and wanted to understand more about birth and death in America. Therefore, I was curious.

"He was only eighty-seven years old." Tears ran down her face again.

I understood that she really loved her grandpa. And, she felt that eighty-seven years of age was still young. As a matter of fact, if a person died at eighty-seven years of age, he would not be considered young. When compared to a person who has lived for one hundred and five years, eighty-seven years old is young. The data of 2016 showed that the average age of life expectancy was 77.5 for a man and 82.1 for a woman in America (Central Intelligence Agency, 2016).

Life expectancy depends highly on different countries with different living standards. The life expectancy in China was 75.5 years and in Afghanistan it was just 51.3 years (Central Intelligence Agency, 2016). The different average death rates in a country also highly rely on advances in medicine, sanitation, nutrition, and other factors. In sociological terms, death is also called **mortality**, defined as the number of people who died in a year in a given population. There is also **crude death rate** which is defined as the number of people who died compared with every 1,000 people in a given population. Like different crude birth rate, crude death rate varies from society to society too. According to Central Intelligence Agency (2016) the estimated crude death rate in the United States in 2016 was 8.2 per 1,000, in China was 7.7, and in Afghanistan was 13.7 per 1,000. These different rates show that in 2016 the estimated figure for China was that for every 1,000 Chinese, roughly 7.5 people died. It is called crude because the measure includes difference ages within every 1,000 people, yet we know that the death rate is not even between young people and the older generations.

When discussing death rate, the infant mortality rate also needs to be addressed. **Infant mortality rate** is the number of babies who died in the first year of life with every 1,000 live births in a given year. An illustration is the estimated infant mortality rate in the United States in 2016 was 5.8 per 1,000 live births, in China it was 12.2 per 1,000, and in Afghanistan it was 112.8 as of 2016, which has decreased from 157.43 in 2007 (Central Intelligence Agency, 2007, 2016). The numbers indicate that in the year 2007, in Afghanistan, for every 1,000 live births, about 157 infants died within the first year of life.

Infant mortality rate is a general measure of the overall quality of life in any society. That means with a high infant death rate, a country would be more likely to have lower living standards. In other words, a more developed country would have a low infant mortality rate because of a better quality of life. Crude death rate, infant mortality rate, and life expectancy are indicators of the overall health standards of a society's population health. If a country, such as Japan has a high life expectancy, a low crude death rate, and a low infant mortality rate, the people in that society would have better health standards than in a country that had a low life expectancy, and high rates of crude death, and infant mortality, such as Afghanistan (see Fig. 12.2 and 12.3).

Even though America has the third largest population in the world, many people from other countries with high population densities, when first coming to the United States, were not used to seeing so few people around. America has almost the same territory size as China, but had close to 324 million people in 2016, while China had a population of more than 4.2 times of the American total population. When I first came to America, I did not see as many people as I saw in China, I felt very uncomfortable. In the spring

Figure 12.2. This photo shows a public hospital, which is one of the best hospitals in Beijing. In the past, China only had public hospitals and there were no private hospitals or family doctors available in clinics. The public hospitals are very crowded, and have a limited number of doctors.

of 1993 my in-laws visited my husband and I while we were living in Alabama. They also felt uncomfortable and complained about the quiet environment. They said that they missed their neighbors in China because they could meet and talk to them every day.

I said, "You do not speak English. It is hard to find a Chinese person to talk to you in the neighborhood here."

"No, it is not because we do not understand English. It is because there is nobody outside walking around," they tried to explain. "You both can speak English, but how many of your neighbors have you talked with?"

I answered, "This is true. This is because American society does not have a large population and everyone is busy."

My father-in-law told me, "Your mom felt so lonely here that she counted the number of street cats that ate at the back door of one of the neighbors' homes."

Figure 12.3. Now, the Chinese government has allowed the establishment of private hospitals. However, private hospitals may charge more, which may not be reimbursed by medical insurance services. Therefore, the majority of patients still go to public hospitals. The photo shows a famous private hospital in Beijing.

I have heard similar experiences from many Chinese and their elderly parents who have visited the United States.

The study of demography includes three major essentials: birth, death, and migration. These three elements play a major function for the change of the population in any country. When I first started graduate school here in the United States, I was interested in birth and women's attitudes towards having children. And the reason I was very interested in these topics was apparent: I came from a country with the largest population in the world. Later, in the process of doing research, I began to feel that birth rate could be managed or controlled by individuals or even a policy, but aging in a society cannot be manipulated by anyone or any policies, which can be only implemented to help the elderly maintain a higher quality of life. People will become old, which is a natural process for humans. As previously discussed, the relationship between birth and aging is that the slowing down of the fertility in a society will inevitably result in the growth of aging.

A society is considered young when the population has at least 15 percent of the people aged fifteen years old and younger. A society is considered old, if it contains 10 percent of population when people are aged sixty-five years and older. The increase in the number of the elderly people in America is largely due to the gradual decrease in the birth rate and number of the baby boomers who are going to be senior citizens. This trend is happening now and will continue for years to come. Since 2011, the baby boomers who were born in 1946 (the beginning of the baby boomer era) turned sixty-five. In the future, many of them, in millions, are rushing towards their retirement age. This is because it is estimated that each day from now on, there will be more than 10,000 American baby boomers who will enter into their senior age (Cohn & Taylor, 2010). This situation may last until 2030 (Geiger, 2011).

The increase in the number of elderly people will create many other issues, such as the society needing to establish more senior services, institutionalized facilities, and additional people in the pool for Social Security and Medicare benefits. Also during this time, the dependency ratio has become more lopsided. **Dependency ratio** is defined as an index calculated to indicate the economic load on workers. It calculates the ratio of people of dependent age (0–14 and 65+) to people of economically active ages (15–64) in a society. If there are fewer workers with many retirees depending on them, it is believed that the dependency ratio is heavy and the economic development will become hindered. According to statistics offered by the United States Social Security Administration (2016), in 2015, the number of workers per beneficiary was 2.8:1, but by the year 2037, it is projected to be only 2.1:1. These figures indicate that in the future, for every two workers who have to be responsible within the society for either a child under fourteen or an elderly person sixty-five or older. There are also additional issues to consider such as not all people between the ages of fifteen to sixty-four will be working and some people who are sixty-five and older who will still be working. This will create a different dependency ratio.

The improvement of the quality of senior services is also needed with the rapid growth in the elderly population. One semester, I gave an assignment, which asked each student in my Sociology of Aging class to visit a senior citizen in an institutionalized facility to see the resident's levels of satisfaction with the quality of services that were provided to them. One of my students went to visit his grandmother, but she was sick on the day of the visit, so instead he talked to another older woman who was in the same institution. The estimated time for the survey was about twenty to twenty-five minutes, but my student was with her for about two hours. My student received many in-depth responses and felt he learned a lot from the conversation. At the end, my student apologized for using too much of her time.

"I am sorry. You know that I am currently in a class studying aging processes and issues. Everything you said is interesting. I think I have learned a lot from our conversation. I am sorry I took too much of your time," my student said with a grin.

"No, no, you are absolutely fine. I think I have to thank you," the lady said with excitement in her voice."

Thank me? Why?" my student said, confused.

"Yes, I would like to thank you for the time you spent with me. I had a good time talking with you. You know I am old and not many people like to share ideas with me," she told him, feeling a bit dismal.

After hearing this story in the class, all the students kept quiet for a moment. I almost wanted to cry because at that time I began missing my mother back in China. Is she feeling lonely? Loneliness is one of the major issues that elderly people face. If a country is becoming an aging society, not only will the dependent ratio create an issue, but also the quality of senior's life will need to be improved. This is a serious subject within the American society and also in many other countries. Such as China, for example, which currently has the largest elderly population in the world, because it has the largest population.

Due to the rapid growth of baby boomers entering into the senior citizen age, American society has to establish new strategies and policies to meet these challenges in order to help the elderly population remain healthy, both physically and mentally. At this time, with 14.5 percent of the elderly, America have already become an aging society. Those people who were born between 1946 and 1964 are baby boomers (Rosenberg, 2014). During this period (19 years), approximately 79 million babies were born, which consists of 26.1percent of the total American population (Hellmich, 2010). In 1940, the average birth per woman was 2.19 and in 1957, the peak time of the baby boomers, it increased to 3.58, which made 4.3 million babies born in that year alone (Rosenberg, 2014). When baby boomers who were born in 1964 finally reach the age of sixty-five, the oldest born in 1946 will be eighty-four years old. It is estimated that in 2050, the elderly population will increase to 83.7 million, which almost double the elderly population of 43.1 million in 2012 (Ortman, Velkoff, & Hogan, 2014). In 2000, the elderly was only 12.7 percent of the total American population, and in 2050 it will reach 20.9 percent (Ortman, Velkoff, & Hogan, 2014). This means that for every five Americans there will be one elderly person.

One of the two summer graduate classes I took was population studies after arriving in the United States. Before that, I only knew by my personal experience in China that if a country had a big population, then the government would need to implement policies to solve the problem. I neither understood why the country decided to manipulate the population growth nor any other demographical theory for population growth. When I first learned the detailed Malthusian theory, I found that it was absolutely true in real life. Malthus (1926; orig. 1798) indicated that with the rapid population growth, the world faces an increasing shortage of food, which could ultimately lead to widespread starvation. This is because population growth is with **geometric progression**. The numbers of the population will increase like so: 1, 2, 4, 8, 16, 32, 64, 128, and so on. At the same time, there will be a shortage of food because the food production is an **arithmetic progression**. The numbers increase like so: 1, 2, 3, 4, 5, 6, 7, 8, and so on. I lectured to my students about this in class.

My students asked, "Wait a minute, what do these numbers mean?"

"Okay, let's say for a Thanksgiving meal, if you buy one turkey for a married couple, will it be enough?"

"Oh, yes, it's plenty," one student answered.

I continued, "Will two turkeys be enough for four people?"

"It is good enough," another replied.

Then a student said, "I think three turkeys can provide enough food for their eight grandchildren?"

"Then, how about five turkeys for their thirty-two great grandchildren?" I asked.

"Well, you have to add some other dishes," a student said.

"How about six turkeys supplied to this couple's fifth generation of sixty-four people?" I continued.

One student responded, "I think it will be a problem."

"What will happen to the sixth generation? There will be one hundred and twenty-eight people who share seven turkeys?" I tried to let them think in depth.

"You would probably have to eat all the turkey bones," a student snickered.

Another student shouted, "Can you tell me why turkeys cannot grow as rapidly as the population? I mean if population can grow geometrically, why can't turkeys?"

"That is a good question," I replied. "Turkeys are in the food chain, but humans are not."

Another student questioned, "Then how can we solve this problem? I do not want my future great-grandchildren to have to fight for food."

According to Malthus, there are two checks: **positive checks**, which include disease and war to reduce the number of people, and **preventive checks**, which use artificial means of birth control, sexual abstinence, and delaying marriage to control the increase in the number of population. The major point is that Malthus lived a long time ago, at the beginning of the Industrial Revolution. His viewpoints were influenced by the historical era in which he lived and thus, limited his ability to anticipate how industrialization and technology would make the revolutionary changes in food production for human society. So therefore, the situation of world starvation as Malthus predicted has not emerged yet, even though some people in certain regions and areas have suffered hunger. But also, human beings have to watch the demographic growth to avoid any possible population problems in the future.

Besides Malthusian theory, there are also other population theories. Since this is an entry level of Introduction to Sociology, only two main population theories will be discussed in this chapter. The second theory is **demographic transition theory**, which is defined as a pattern of population growth that relates to different levels of technological development. This theory basically divides human history into three stages: preindustrial society, early industrialized society, and mature industrialized society. These three stages are distinguished based on their rank/level of development. In preindustrial societies, because of the low quality of living standards, lack of nutrition and medication, and no methods of birth control, the fertility rate and mortality rate were both high. Therefore, the population growth is slow. During the second stage, because of the development of technology, early industrialized societies had improved the living standards, nutrition, and medication; but birth control methods were not very popular. Therefore, the fertility rate remained high, but the mortality rate began to decline. With the introduction of advanced technology, the population growth at the third stage grew slowly again because of the low fertility rate and the mortality rate dropped from high to low. This is not only because of the higher standards of living, but also because the usage of birth control methods became popular.

I posed the following question to the class: "This decline in population growth is also because many people delay having a child due to other priorities. This has indirectly influenced the birth rate in a society. Can you tell me what they are?"

"We do not have a family planning policy to limit the number of children in each family. How can we slow down the population growth?" a student asked.

"I said the word 'indirect influence'," I replied.

"I see. I am here for a college education, so I am not going to have a baby because my education is my first priority. Am I right?" the same student answered.

"BINGO. This is exactly one of the indirect policies that helps decrease the population in a society," I answered.

There are many ways humans can help slow the population growth down, and eventually reach the goal of zero population growth. Currently, the most important is educating individuals in order to gain more knowledge on the issues of the increase or decrease in the future population and the consequences of that increase or decrease. As a sociology professor teaching the subject of population studies and also coming from the most populous country, I feel that demography is an important field for everyone to gain knowledge in and to do research. I personally believe that different societies with different population pressures should have different methodologies to work out different solutions.

For human society, the issue of controlling the population size should be a vital issue. I would like to make clear that controlling the population growth and reaching the goal of zero population growth worldwide does not mean abortion. As previously discussed, there are many other methods that could function to control the size of the population indirectly, such as education, offering more opportunities for women to work, and the spread of information about the consequences of population growth. It is believed that if any societies have accumulated adequate knowledge, and are well prepared for any possible future population problems, then there will be effective ways to prevent any extreme methods, such as forced abortion or any other population policies.

Chapter 13

SOCIAL CHANGE

Key words: social change; discovery; invention; diffusion; collective behavior; social movement; modernization; urbanization; industrialization; modernization theory; world system theory; urban; urbanism; community; structural-functional perspective; social conflict perspective

In the late 1980s, very few American families had a home computer. At that time, a computer consisted of a mainframe system and an operating system. The mainframe system could not be found in any family homes but was seen in large institutes, such as companies or schools to deal with bulky data processing. Technology then was not as developed the way as it is today. Computers at that time were made heavy combining the screen and keyboard as one. I learned how to use a computer in graduate school after I came to the United States because I had never seen one in China. We purchased my first home computer in the early 1990s, along with many other families. Today, most people take having a desktop or laptop for granted and feel that it is a tool for everyday use. According to statistics (Rainie & Cohn, 2014), 84 percent of American families had a home computer in the year of 2014. Compared to China, in 2012, there were about 56 computers for every one hundred households (Zhang, 2014)

Another fast advanced technology is the development of cell phones. I started to use a cell phone in 1995, when they were about the size of cordless handset phones. After paying the monthly phone bill, I would receive an additional ten minutes for free. Today, almost everyone has a cell phone. Some of them get thousands of free minutes, paying less than what I paid in the 1990s. According to Robbins and Turner (2002), AT&T developed cellular technology in the early 1980s and expected that in the United States there would be about one million users by the year 2000. As a matter of fact, there were 97 million users in 2000 and by mid-2001, that figure reached 118 million. According to Pew Research Center (2014), as of January, 2014, 90 percent of American adults had a mobile phone and as of October, the same year, 64 percent of adults in the United States own a smartphone.

Chinese telecommunication services experienced an even more rapid communication development. When the People's Republic of China was founded in 1949, telecommunication services were limited to authorized offices, and to the homes of certain officials with higher social statuses. Most Chinese people had to write letters to communicate with their family and friends. In the early 1990s, Chinese people were introduced to home telephone services, and later landline phones became increasingly popular in urban areas.

Chinese people immediately accepted cell phones when they were introduced because the devices were mobile, accessible, convenient, and interactive. Cell phones are more popular than the Internet and email simply because of their mobility. According to statistics (Statista, 2016), there were over 1.28 billion Chinese people who used cell phones as of February, 2016. It can be assumed that there is nearly one cell phone per person statistically. The Chinese telecommunication service charge system uses phone cards. People purchase the cards with different amounts of money and then are charged while using the phone, like a GoPhone here. This method allows individuals to have two or three phones in operation. This is especially true for the younger Chinese generations, who also frequently abandon their used cell phones to look for better ones with extra functions. According to statistics (McEwen, 2011), by the year 2008, 80 percent of adults had a cell phone in China and in 2010, the percentage had rocketed to 89, which means that in two years between 2008 and 2010, more than 90 million Chinese people obtained a cell phone. Cell phone users have outnumbered landline phone users. Now, every one hundred households in urban areas own 212 mobile phones (Zhang, 2014) (see Fig. 13.1).

Technological changes discussed above are only one representative part of **social change**, which is defined as a transformation of people's behavior, attitudes, and thoughts over time in a society. For instance, one topic that continues to be affected by social changes is that of parents teaching their children about sexual intercourse. A female student told me the conversation between her and her mother on this topic when she was about thirteen years old in the 1990s.

"What did your mom say to you?" I asked, curious about her upbringing. "Did she say that a sexual relationship with boys was forbidden?"

"Basically it was," she said.

Figure 13.1. As of July 2016, there were about 1.28 billion mobile phones in use in China.

I questioned her further, "Did she say you could use condoms?"

"That was not an option," she answered.

"Why?" I continued. "What are you going to tell your kids when they are thirteen?"

"I will definitely tell them that there are options to protect them from becoming pregnant. I think parents need to realize that their kids are living in a real world, not in a cradle and under their control," she explained.

Today, when I asked my eighteen-year-old students the same question, most of their parents would tell them that they should not have sexual intercourse because they are too young. However, their parents also discuss with them that if they will have sexual intercourse, they must know how to protect themselves. This is a type of social change that has gradually modified people's attitudes and behavior on sexual relationships. This conversation also reminded me of when I was sixteen years old. At that time, schools never taught students about the human body or sexual intercourse in their biology courses. This is because it was deemed taboo, not only among children, but also in the Chinese society as a whole. According to the data from World Bank (2014), the adolescent fertility rate per 1,000 women aged 15–19 in China in 1960 and 2014 changed from 68 to 7. However, the fertility rate of 68 is not because of school teenagers' sexual relationships in 1960 but likely because of early legal marriage and pregnancy after their marriage at that time, especially in rural areas. The fertility rate of 7 is mainly because of teenager's sexual relationships now because the age of marriage has increased to their late 20s. In America, the rate was 85 per 1,000 adolescent women in 1960 and 24 per 1,000 in 2014. It is believed at the fertility rate of 85 also represents some early legal marriage and pregnancy after their marriage in 1960. The above figures in both the United States and China have shown a rapid decrease in adolescent pregnancies. At the same time, we can also see social changes in people's ideas about marriage age.

When I was 16 years old, I had never really heard of a teenager becoming pregnant except for a girl who was one year older than me. The baby's father was later discovered, he was a middle-aged man, and was arrested. The girl had an abortion and her family moved out of my neighborhood. After hearing the news, almost all my girlfriends went back home to ask their mothers the same question: How can a girl get pregnant? All the mothers gave nearly the same answer: You will know when you get married someday. Because they did not give honest responses, many girls started to use their own imagination; for example, they refused to sit on chairs if a boy had sat there before. They were afraid that if they sat in the same spot it would cause them to become pregnant.

Figure 13.2. Chanel No. 5 is a well-known perfume in China. Chanel stores are always located in very expensive malls. In a 2016 market research survey, which included people who were post-95 (referring to the 1995-2000-born population), it was revealed that more than 20 percent of the respondents have purchased luxury products, and nearly 60 percent stated that their favorite brand is Chanel. Gucci and Hermes were ranked second and third, respectively (Sina.com 2016).

Today, the younger generations in China are different from my own. They know a lot more and receive a variety of information from different sources. Parents' attitudes have also changed; they would like to provide more information about sexual intercourse to their children. Rapid social changes in the past twenty years have resulted in the change of behavior and attitudes throughout Chinese people's lives (see Fig. 13.2).

Social change has different characteristics. an example of this would be that social change happens all over the world, but regions and societies are affected in different ways. For instance, in 2012, Americans' lives were significantly affected by the increased price of gasoline. This resulted in higher prices on food, milk, and other daily necessities. Therefore, one of the social changes needed was to invent a substitute for gasoline in the United States. In some other countries at the same period, the shortage of food, such as in

Venezuela in 2016 (BBC News, 2016), caused people to suffer hunger. The most important social change for these countries would be to figure out how to increase the food production.

The impacts of these gasoline shortages and food deficiencies have resulted in different social changes, such as, many Americans carpooling when gas prices are high. This happened in 2012, when the nationwide average price for a gallon of gas hit $3.60. People would also reduce their expenses for the things they did not need to have immediately. The higher gas prices resulted in individuals' self-responses to adjust their social behavior in order to compromise the change. The actions may in the long run influence a society to develop new technology and solve the issues of the gasoline shortages. Countries with insufficient resources, such as food supplies may see riots in some regions, encouraging their government and/or law enforcement to take actions to solve the issues immediately. The riots may threaten the social stability and damage the social integration/harmony of a society.

Overall, social changes can be divided into two dimensions: changes that are planned and changes that are spontaneous. One example of a change that was designed or planned by people was the invention of computers. Computers can help people restore documents and data, as well as create communication channels, such as social media and email. The unplanned changes that occurred influenced job qualifications by requiring the necessity of computer use. Due to the advancement of high technology, many people lost their jobs. This was especially the case in the early 1990s. Another illustration of planned and unintended changes is the introduction of birth control pills. The planned change was to help people prevent unwanted pregnancy. The unplanned change was that many young people started to have sex, believing it to be consequence free, as they were presumably protected by birth control pills.

Obviously, people always have different attitudes toward certain social changes. An example of this is, when former President Bill Clinton was elected in 1993 (presidential term: 1993-2001), one of his early policies was to legally permit gays and lesbians to serve in the military. This policy resulted in both agreements and disagreements among Americans. Later, former President Clinton offered an alternative plan, which was the "Don't ask, don't tell" policy (DADT). The basic idea of this policy was "do not ask, do not tell, do not pursue, and do not harass gays and lesbians because of their sexual orientation while in the military." This policy (DADT) was officially repealed in September 20, 2011 as a further example of social change. Now, gays and lesbians serving in the military have the freedom to come out as well as be honest about who they truly are. People honored this day, September 20, 2011, as a historical day in America.

For every change in a society, people have diverse attitudes either supporting or opposing the adjustments. People understand the outcomes of change differently. The result of each change may not follow whatever was planned or designed, which means that the consequences of changes may not be predictable. A planned change in my school district was to build a new elementary school for the increasing population of children. After the first raise in property tax was passed, the Board of Education proposed another one in order to add facilities for classrooms. Later, the board created a third proposal which would hire new teachers. The majority of the residents in the community got tired of having their property tax raised every year and began rejecting the board's proposals. The new school finally had to cut different programs because of the failure that planned change caused. Another characteristic of social change includes the duration needed for the change to take effect. An illustration of this is that American Revolutionary War was fought from 1775 to 1783 for the independence of the country. However, compared to the time some changes are very short, such as an introduction of a smartphone to the people in a society.

There are many aspects that contribute to originate social changes, including: cultural processes, changes in social structure, ideas, natural environment, population, and technology, as well as human actions. The first aspect causing social changes includes cultural transformations/processes. These transformations/processes can be further broken down into three different concepts: discovery, invention, and diffusion. Cultural transformations may be attributed to **discovery**, which is defined as recognizing something that previously existed. An example of it is, the Curiosity Rover was launched to Mars on November 26, 2011 and landed on Mars on August 6, 2012. Since the landing, the Curiosity Rover has brought many surprises to our human society by sending back photos every day. The purpose of this advanced technology device was to discover if life currently exists or had formerly existed on Mars. With Curiosity Rover's landing, and the subsequent discovery of Mars' terrain/geography, we are able to find a reality we were not aware of before. The second type of cultural transformation is **invention**. It can be understood as using prior knowledge to develop something new. I often find that I am falling behind due to rapid technological development. A few years ago, I bought a MP3 player. I really liked it because the size was suitable for my needs, and I could listen to the radio as well. Two years later, I bought an iPod because I saw almost every student of mine had one. I never used it because I did not know how to use the radio function on the device. Before I even learned how to use the new radio feature on the iPod to broadcast the radio news, I found that my students had, at this point, purchased the latest iPod, which could be used to watch movies. Due to rapid technological advancement, we always see new technology coming out. Most of these technologies are based on the preceding information. Since we are all living in a rapidly growing society with more advanced technology, we often have to work with inventions.

The last type of cultural transformation is **diffusion**, which is defined as spreading different cultural factors from one country to other regions or societies. Many people in China, born after 1992, may feel that hamburgers are a part of Chinese culture instead of solely an American food staple. This is because in 1992 the first McDonald's fast-food restaurant opened in Shenzhen, China. Since then, McDonald's has spread throughout the country. There were about 2,000 McDonald's in China in 2013. The Chinese chief executive of McDonald's indicated that "China has been the fastest-growing market for McDonald's worldwide with regard to new restaurant opening," (Yan & Jones, 2010). It took McDonald's 19 years to open 1,000 restaurants in China. However, from 2011 to 2013, the number had been doubled. The fast-food industry has significantly influenced the younger generations' way of life.

When I visited China in 1995, I met my friend's son, who was about 5 years old. He knew that hamburgers were American food and a discussion occurred one evening when trying to decide where to dine.

"Where should we go for dinner tonight with my best friend?" the mother asked her son.

"I want to go to McDonald's," her son answered.

"No, I would love to go to a Chinese restaurant," I stopped him and gave my suggestion.

He tried to persuade me to agree with him, "I like McDonald's better."

"I live in America, so I eat hamburgers every day. I do not want to eat them today," I said.

He was surprised, and with wide eyes, asked, "Did you say that you have a hamburger and fries every day?"

"Yes," I told him.

I persuaded the little boy to eat at a traditional Chinese restaurant, but at the end of dinner, he whispered to me that he would like to come with me to America.

I could not understand his request but felt pleased that he might have really liked me, "Why do you want to leave your mom and dad and come with me?"

"So I can have hamburgers and fries every day. I cannot go to McDonald's every day in China," he explained. McDonald's, Starbucks Coffee, and Pizza Hut becoming so popular in China are examples of the process of diffusion (see Fig. 13.3).

Figure 13.3. Beijing now has a Sam's Club and seven Wal-Mart stores. In China, there are 408 Wal-Mart stores, which are in 21 provinces. The first Wal-Mart Store was established in Guangdong province in 1996. In Beijing, there are also 264 Starbucks Coffee stores as of 2014. Starbucks established the first coffee shop in 1999 in China, and it now has more than 2,100 shops in more than 100 Chinese cities.

Another illustration of diffusion is when Chinese food entered American society. Many people learned how to use chopsticks. Some dishes became familiar to Americans, such as egg rolls and chow mein, which is cooked as fried noodles. Today, everywhere in America, in big cities and small towns, we can usually find Chinese restaurants. To Chinese people in the United States, some types of food are Americanized. An example is that many Chinese do not order egg rolls in Chinese restaurants in the United States. This is because we do not cook egg rolls the same way American Chinese restaurants do. I learned how to make chow mein from American Chinese restaurants, but they are not prepared the way authentic Chinese cuisine is made. However, Chinese restaurants in the United States do spread Chinese cultural essentials to American society.

The second aspect that causes social change is people's ideas, which include great and small ideas, scientific and moral, or realistic and fantastic ideas. Many people have created new technology based on their work-related experiences or from their daily lives. Many new developments began from people's ideas. For example, when Joseph Swan, a British inventor, first officially invented the light bulb one year prior to Edison's patent date, his idea was meant to find a substitute for candles.

Many new technological developments begin with an idea in order to find a better way of life, such as solving some problems that humans are facing. One Thanksgiving, I was with a long-time family friend and I asked her son, who was in his second year of college, what he finally decided on as his major. "I want to be a chemical engineer," he said.

Impressed with his answer, I questioned, "Why do you want to be a chemical engineer?"

"Since oil reserves are very limited and the prices are high, I think it is time for our society to develop a substitute for gasoline," he answered.

"That is a great idea! I have always dreamed that we could use tap water to make my car run!" I jokingly responded. "What do you think of my idea?"

"That is not a bad idea. You know that everything starts with an idea first," he smiled and encouraged me to dream.

Our natural environment is another aspect of changes reflecting people's behavior, attitudes, and thoughts over time in any society. An example of it is that many people want to move to California or Florida because they are both sunshine states. Another example is to further illustrate how our environment influences people's thinking and behavior. When I first started to work in the early 1990s, my students asked me where I was from. Of course, I answered that I was from China originally and worked in the South prior to the city that my current university is located.

After class, a female student came to me and said that I should not tell people I came from the South.

"My advice is that you do not tell your students you come from the South." I guess she still had the idea that the northern part of America was more developed than the southern part because she also grew up in a southern state. For a while, I always kept what she said in my mind when people asked me where I came from in the United States, but I disagreed with her ideas about the South. I think her opinion is out of date. However, her views had been influenced by stereotypes about the regions, and thus her behavior/attitude changed because of it.

A society's increasing or decreasing population will also be an aspect that causes social changes. Since 1975, the population size in the Sun Belt region of America has outnumbered the population in the Snow Belt region. Some cities found in the Sun Belt include, Dallas, Phoenix, and San Diego, which are called sun belt areas due to warm weather, The Snow Belt areas, of course, where snow can be found because of the cold weather, include cities such as Baltimore, Cleveland, Indianapolis, and Detroit. I have visited Florida many times since the 1990s. I believe more than ever seniors are living there today, because of Florida's warm weather. Now many relevant services have been established and new residential houses have been built in order to meet the needs of the increasing number of the senior population.

On the other end of the aspect, over population also stimulates social change. The introduction of the Chinese one-child policy was based on the concern and the fear that population growth would deter economic development in China. The practice of the policy resulted in many other changes. Some of these changes include the implementation of new policies, an alteration of values on family size, sex of the children, greater acceptance of birth control facilities, and also other relevant changes.

Another example of population change, which causes social change is American policies on undocumented immigrants. Due to an increase of many immigrant workers coming from Latin American countries, the American government began to realize the safety issues at the borders and the importance of keeping records on immigrants. American society has also been greatly impacted because of both legal and illegal immigration. The changes include the increased need for those who are bilingual, the introduction of new food, and the acceptance of other cultures.

Technological development is also an aspect, which results in social changes. The advent of the computer, as we discussed earlier, caused great changes worldwide. Social media, such as Twitter, Facebook, as well as Instagram and email have made the world a "global village," and because of this, information can spread anywhere in the world to anyone in a very short period of time. The cell phone produced amazing mobile communication for individuals to use anywhere at any time. All of these technological advancements have created even further social changes. I used to teach classes using a blackboard with chalk, and later started to use an overhead projector, where all I needed to do was print the class notes on transparency sheets. Now I teach in smart classrooms, which have computers connected to projectors. I can use PowerPoint and Microsoft Word to save all the files and present them in class. I can also use a computer program, blackboard on the Internet to teach classes. So students can read the class notes, announcements, and submit their assignments to blackboard, which in turn help make a paperless class, which was not even imagined throughout history of education. Technological development really accelerates social changes, which can also provide more opportunities for further technological advancements.

In real life, social changes can also be caused by the tension or the conflict of a social structure. This is also an aspect of social change, which influences/causes the adjustment of people's behavior and thoughts in a society. Conflicts may arise between labor unions and management of companies on workers' benefits, retirement pensions, healthcare coverage, or hourly wages. After the workers' union starts a conversation with the management for changes, the union may set up a date and time limit. If the management cannot reach the level of satisfaction set by the workers, a strike may occur. Tensions or conflicts in this situation may result in changes.

The last aspect that causes social change is human social activities. A famous human social activity/movement in American history was the anti-Vietnam War efforts made by many college student activists. They demonstrated their opposition to the war in 1963. Their protest continued until the end of the war on April 30, 1975, when the capital of South Vietnam, Saigon, fell into the control of the communist North Vietnam. Another example is the American Civil Rights Movement between 1955 and 1968. The goal of this movement was to eliminate racial discrimination against African-American people and bring back suffrage in some states in the South.

Human activities can be divided into two different forms: collective behavior and social movement. **Collective behavior** is a type of human action that is defined as an unplanned action that people have when facing or having to work out uncertain circumstances. A well-known collective behavior was displayed in Ferguson, Missouri, on August 9, 2014. Michael Brown, an eighteen-year-old African American male, was shot to death by a police officer. The shooting of the unarmed young man resulted in civil unrest not only in Ferguson, but also drew attention from the whole country. Collective behavior is composed of different forms, such as riots, rumors, and rallies, because they are most likely spontaneous actions. This means disorganized human activities or unrest due to some events, which are not expected to happen. The major purpose of these activities often tries to work out unclear situations.

The other type of human action is **social movement**, which is defined as a group of people joining together to support or defend against certain social changes. An example of this is, the American Women's Rights Movement, originating in 1848 and continuing today, resulted in a social movement. This movement was organized to make sure that females have equal rights and opportunities in American society. As a result, the state of Colorado adopted an amendment granting women the right to vote in 1893.

There are also other aspects that can cause social changes in a society. For instance, different ideologies, which are held by different people with their own systems of beliefs, will result in changes or even revolutions in a society. Competitions or conflicts will produce changes, as well as economic recessions or rapid economic growth. Globalization is also an important aspect that generates social changes. This phenomenon, although only gaining popularity in the last two decades, has greatly impacted the entire world by unifying people in different societies. People would most likely connect globalization with economics, such as international trading, foreign investment, and technological development. However, this process has a lot to do with global influences on social, cultural, or political changes in a society.

A good illustration of globalization is outsourcing from more developed countries to less developed nations. I once saw a cartoon where a young American girl was unhappy because her dad said to her, "No, you cannot outsource your homework to a foreign country." The interesting point is that those less developed countries have become world factories to produce most of the goods and services for more developed countries. My students often discuss this phenomenon in class. Some argue that it would result in limited job opportunities in our nation, but others fire back that the goods would be more affordable because of outsourcing.

In the last two decades, great changes have taken place in China, where many American companies have outsourced part of their products. I had never thought this outsourcing had anything to do with my life, even though I realized that I could buy some affordable products in America. When I visited China, I would normally buy gifts in America and bring them to friends and family. One year, without noticing the tags "Made in China," I carried some gifts back to Beijing. A friend of mine asked me if I bought the gifts in China.

"No, I bought them in America and I carried them back here," I said.

From her face I could tell that she did not believe me, "But the tag said it was made in China."

After I came back from the trip, I went to a department store for an investigation. I checked many tags on clothes, toys, mugs, and electronic devices. I found that most of them were "Made in China." Now if I buy gifts for my family and friends who live in China, I carefully check the tag first. I know in order to avoid confusion I have to buy things that are "Made in USA" or elsewhere. Frankly, it is not easy to find a gift with a price that I am willing to pay and also say "Made in USA." Since I am living in America, I would like to take things made in the United States back to China as a gift. I really do not want to take back something that was originally made in China. Through globalization, outsourcing has become popular due to the lower cost of the labor and materials. Outsourcing helps less developed countries by providing job opportunities, but most importantly, it helps them learn the standard requests for a product and allow them to stay current with the most advanced technology.

Any social change, although these events or changes happen at a macro-level, have undoubtedly impacted an individual's life directly. Many of our

grandparents never went to college, but a majority of the younger generations have graduated or will attend college. This is because of social changes
affecting the requirements of higher levels of education necessary in order to
find better jobs. Furthermore, with technology spreading worldwide, computer software and hardware has become a popular major for college students because it is easier for them to find higher paying jobs. Finally, high
birth rates or low death rates in a society have influenced individuals' decisions on the time they are going to marry and the number of children they
decide to have or even not have. This is due to less pressure from family on
young individuals to choose if pregnancy is their priority or not when they
reach the childbearing age.

An illustration of how I was influenced by the advanced technological
development is that I teach a summer class every year in May for three
weeks. The university requires a minimum of twenty students to be enrolled
in the class; yet, I always had a full thirty-five students. Sometimes, I would
even have to specially sign in extra students who really needed to have this
general study course completed. In the summers of 2007 and 2008, I had
only twenty-one and twenty-two students in the two classes, partially due to
the increased popularity of web courses. I personally like to teach a course
in an actual classroom because I believe students will learn more from face-
to-face interaction.

I did a research project to test if my above thinking was correct. I surveyed my students by asking them whether they would like to learn in a
classroom or through a web course. More than 90 percent of my students
chose classroom learning, but all the web courses were filled immediately for
the year of 2008 summer classes at my university. Later, I also surveyed my
students who took my online class that summer to understand why they
would rather take a web course instead of face-to-face learning. I found that
it was due to the concern of high gasoline prices and the freedom of controlling learning time. For these reasons, many nontraditional students preferred learning via web courses. This is possible because of the increase in
technological advancement; students have more choices to decide their
learning platform. An example of one conversation I had with a few students
that discussed the above topic went something like this:

"Who knows if web courses are good or bad? We will see," one female
student said.

"It is only one course in the summer time. I would not do online in a reg-
ular semester with four or five courses," another female student told me.

"I want to take a summer face-to-face class, but gas prices are too high. I
think a web course will help me save money on gas. Since the technology of
online class is available, I think I should completely use the advanced com-

puter technology," a male student replied after I asked why he chose a web course instead of coming to school.

The popularity of computer technology means that, classroom learning is no longer limited to classrooms; instead, as long as one has access to Internet, anyone can learn at home and receive a degree. This phenomenon represents how social change at the societal level impacts an individual's daily life, behavior, attitudes, or decision making. It will also change my way of teaching. I have to reexamine my attitudes toward web courses and classroom learning in order to meet the challenges and needs of my students.

The purpose of social changes at a societal level is to improve or enhance people's quality of life, or social development, in order to make the country modernized. **Modernization** is defined as the process in which countries are transformed from agricultural to industrialized societies. Major characteristics of modernization include urbanization and industrialization. **Urbanization** is a process through which the number of people living in urban areas increases. An example of this is before 1990 in China, there were 188 cities. In 2006, that number increased to 661 cities (Hartzell, 2015). The phenomenon of urbanization is often accompanied by **industrialization**, which is where manual labor is replaced by technological advancements. This development is symbolized by specialized divisions of labor in a society and changes in the functions of family as well as the development in other areas, like education in schools. The process of modernization includes the adaptation of advanced technology and new ideas or methods to make a country more developed. The spread of smart phones in China has made a new pattern of communication behavior, which helps people send and receive information in a quick way that has changed their personal relationships with others. Recent data shows that smartphone users in China accounted for 913 million (Perez 2015) or more than 71 percent of the 1.28 billion mobile connections, which was more than the United States, Brazil, and Indonesia combined.

The question remains, how can a country become modernized? Well, there are two theories to answer this. The first theory that addresses how a country becomes modernized is known as the **modernization theory**. This theory involves less developed countries changing/developing through industrialization and becoming similar to more developed countries. So, is it true that industrialization is the key for modernization?

I once had a student from a country in Northern Africa. He kept telling the class that he would definitely go back home after he received his bachelor's degree. Other students asked him why. "With a bachelor's degree here, you just find a job. But with an American degree in my country, I will find a fantastic job with a higher salary," he replied.

"Why?" the class was confused.

"Because there are not many well-educated people there and also foreign companies in my country are reluctant to hire people without foreign higher education. I will be guaranteed to have a decent job with a higher salary because I have an American college degree."

With the several reasons that were listed above, he concluded that he would definitely go home to work. According to the student, although his country is in the process of development, and many foreign companies have established their branch offices there, it will not help the country quickly become modernized. There are only a few people who are able to afford a higher level of education from foreign countries, and only those people would be able to find a high paying job. Most local people will not be hired or receive benefits from this kind of industrialization. Therefore, the quality of ordinary people's lives will not be changed that much. As previously asked, do you still think the establishment of 1,000 companies in Afghanistan will help this country become modernized and result in women's status to change significantly? The answer is "probably not." Therefore, the process of modernization will be the result of more than the impact of industrialization; it should also include other aspects.

The second theory of how a country becomes modernized is known as the **world system theory**. The world system theory views industrialization as not just being a key in the process of modernization, but that it is necessary to evaluate a country's economic position in the world system. That means if a less developed country wanted to become modernized, this country's basic economic situation has to be examined. If this country is too poor in the world's economic system, it would be difficult to develop it into a rich country such as the United States. This theory exemplifies that it is almost impossible for a homeless person to become a millionaire because the starting economic point is too low for this person to become rich. To become modernized, a country needs to satisfy many aspects, such as raising the national level of education, accelerating industrialization and urbanization, advancing technological development, and many other factors. Among the basics, I think that education is the most essential. Without emphasizing education in a country, it is difficult for a society to be advanced or become developed. The root cause of the rapid economic growth and development in China during the past two decades has become a societal emphasis on education in the past three decades. This is the foundation for a country to become modernized.

Urbanization is an important factor in studying the level of modernization in a country or region and also a symbol of how advanced a country can become. Essentially, the more people who live in urban areas in a country, the more that society will become developed. Areas in which people live with little to no agricultural activities are known as **urban** areas. Urbanization is a process, and at the beginning of the nineteenth century, less than 3 percent of the world population lived in cities. In the early 1990s, about 45 percent of people worldwide lived in urban areas. There were more than three-quarters of the American population living in cities. Large cities have unique characteristics, such as large populations with different cultures and racial groups that are most likely densely settled. **Urbanism** is the term that is used to explain the urban lifestyle that accompanies living in urban areas. Another term, **community**, is used to describe people who live in an area as a group with a sense of belonging.

Important reasons for people to move to urban areas include higher wages and more job opportunities. Young generations tend to move from rural to urban areas. I remember more than thirty years ago in Beijing, when a few American movies played in cinemas, such as *On Golden Pond, Coal Miner's Daughter,* and *Singing in the Rain.* Many young people wanted to see these movies because were eager to know about the outside world and, to practice their English. These movies were not dubbed in Chinese yet, but some of them had Chinese subtitles at the bottom of the screen translations underneath the film. As a college student with a major in English, I saw all of these movies. I cannot recall from which movie I heard it, but I clearly remember a line which mentioned "going to New York for better opportunities." This sentence seems like common sense today because the world now assumes that America is seen as the land of opportunity. At that time, I had never thought that one day I would see Times Square or Fifth Avenue, however, I realized that a large city like New York was attractive to people from all over the world because of its better opportunities. In the 1950s, New York was the most populous city in the world; Tokyo, Japan became the largest city in the 1990s. Recently, reports are that Tokyo, Japan, with 33.2 million people still remains the largest city in 2016, followed by New York, with about 17.8 million people.

My home city of Beijing is the country's capital, which means that this city is the center of economy, politics, and culture. Beijing is the twenty-third largest city in the world. Many famous universities, the central government and all the departments, most renowned museums, art galleries, department stores, and artists can all be found in Beijing. The reason that the capital is often the center of the country is because in the majority of the less developed societies, the process of urbanization is relatively slow and more people are in rural areas (see Fig. 13.4).

I visited cities such as Houston, Seattle, Atlanta, New York, Los Angeles, and Miami before I traveled to Washington, D.C., and because of my familiarity with Beijing as a capital city, I had high expectations of Washington,

Figure 13.4. The increasing economic development of China in recent years, the subsequent use and popularity of vehicles and air conditioners, and pollution from nearby heavy industrial regions have made Beijing a very polluted city. In the photo above you can see the toll this pollution has taken on the air. As a result, many Chinese wear a mask over their nose and mouth to protect their lungs from this dangerous pollution.

D.C. Much to my surprise, other than the city's special characteristics, such as monuments and government department buildings, Washington, D.C. is not drastically different from other large American cities. Now, I no longer have such high expectations for capital cities because with the rapid development in China, many other cities have also accelerated their process of urbanization. I feel some cities, such as Shanghai and Guangzhou, are even better than Beijing, where is no longer the center of economy and culture of the country.

Opportunities for education and high paying jobs are the characteristics of cities, but there are also other benefits by residing in cities. The benefits include advanced hospital facilities in urban areas, such as many specialists and experienced physicians and surgeons, people's lives can be saved. I had a car accident in 1997 near the entrance of my university when a student ran into my car and created a pile-up involving five cars. My legs were bleeding, and my shoulders were sore, and I could not move because my left knee was injured.

A few minutes later, I was rushed to a hospital emergency room that was a short distance away. Doctors made sure that I had no serious injuries before they released me. However, if I had indeed been injured or had any major problems because of the accident, my life would have been saved because I was close to the hospital. Because of an easy access to medical facilities and different lifestyles compared to people living in rural areas and farmland jobs, cities have both lower birth rate and lower death rate than rural areas. The low birth rate is influenced by many social factors. The factors include higher levels of education, more information on sexual relationships, and methods of birth control which can help lead people in urban areas to have fewer children compared to rural areas. This is because women are not confronting to the demands of family life. Some of the freedoms they enjoy include their work, social interactions, opportunities to change their social status, vacation time, and other factors that may strongly influence them to have a different lifestyle. This kind of lifestyle exemplifies all the qualities of urbanism.

There are two major sociological theories which discuss the causes and consequences of social change. **Structural-functional perspective** views social change as an evolutionary change that happens gradually. The changes result in specified divisions of labor, highly interdependent relationships between people and rapid social, cultural, and technological development, which all lead to social integration. According to this theory, social change is a continuous transformation from one stage to another.

When I was young, I recall that many people had a bicycle in my neighborhood, which was considered an important mode of transportation in

China. People utilized bicycles to carry heavy objects. At that time, no one owned a private car and only some government officials were provided a car and a driver because of their high status and power. Today in China, most of the cars are privately owned. More people can afford to buy a car, and bicycles are no longer thought of as important property of the family. The transition from a bicycle to a car represents gradual social development and changes in China.

These changes have resulted in division of labor in the Chinese society, which means people have different jobs with different responsibilities. The more specified division of jobs that are created, the more people have to depend on each other, which is believed to make the society more cooperative and integrated. In sociology, there are many specified topics and each professor concentrates on limited topics, such as marriage and family, aging issues, methodology, as well as other topics. This is the reason we need and depend on each other to make our program run because we all contribute in unique ways. Society is also similar to our sociology program, but with even more complicated divisions of labor to make people rely on each other to survive and to keep society going.

Social conflict perspective does not discuss different types of social change, but examines how social changes occur. Opposing the structural-functional theory's evolutionary changes, conflict theory indicates that social changes are the consequences of significant events that happened in human history and continue to happen in current society. According to conflict theory, social changes in America are based on big events, such as the American Revolution, Civil War, or the Civil Rights Movement. It is because of those historical and significant events in the United States, which have moved forward and progressed socially.

Another example is the 9/11 attack on the World Trade Center and also other locations, which has significantly changed the American society and people's thoughts and actions. The American political system did not previously have a Homeland Security Department, but it has now been established as a result of 9/11. Terrorism and antiterrorism have become significant issues everywhere, such as mass media, public opinions, presidential elections, and international affairs.

Both theories are important when discussing social changes. These two theories, among all other theories, are used to study and analyze social changes from different angles. People from different positions will have different solutions. It does not matter how people study the phenomenon of a social change; changes will inevitably happen. From a sociological perspective, we need to study how it happened, why it happened at a certain time, how the equilibrium of relationships within the society and internationally is broken, how the new relationships are established, how the procedure of change occurs, what influences the results of the change, negative and positive factors, and the impacts on human society in the short term and long run. Social change happens every single day in our life; it does not matter if people like the changes or not. The purpose for most of the changes is to make our life easier and better, like technological developments. The invention of cell phones has drastically improved our quality of life in the past two to three decades. At the same time, it has seriously changed the patterns on how humans interact with each other. This has also resulted in value changes or debates because some people accept cyber relationships and network marketing. However, some others like to emphasize face-to-face communications and interactions. There are also some other social changes, such as social cultural processes. An example of this is when McDonald's was first introduced to the Chinese society, it was not only burgers and fries, but McDonaldization, which I discussed in Chapter 4. The McDonaldization phenomenon represents the social changes from traditional to rational thoughts, and also the acceptance of advanced methods of management. The adaptation of McDonald's by traditional societies further indicates their efforts to be influenced by the Western world as well as willingness to let social changes take place in their society.

REFERENCES

American Foundation of Suicide Prevention. (2014). Understanding suicide–Facts and figure. *American Foundation of Suicide Prevention.* Retrieved October 7, 2016, from: http://li526-53.members.linode.com/understanding-suicide/facts-and -figures

American Psychological Association. (2016). Marriage and divorce. *American Psychological Association.* Retrieved November 12, 2016, from: http://www.apa .org/topics/divorce/

BBC News. (2016). Going hungry in Venezuela. *BBC News.* Retrieved December 2, 2016, from: http://www.bbc.com/news/magazine-36913991

Becker, H. S. (1966). *Outside: Studies in the sociology of deviance.* New York: Free Press.

Bergman, J. (2015). China ending its one-child policy won't change the sad reality for parents. *Mashable.* Retrieved October 12, 2016, from: http://mashable.com /2015/10/30/china-one-child-parents/#yng05ZiTGkqd

Casselman, B. (2014). What baby boomers' retirement means for the U.S. economy. *Our Changing Economy.* Retrieved October 7, 2016, from: http://fivethirty eight.com/features/what-baby-boomers-retirement-means-for-the-u-s-economy/

Central Intelligence Agency. (2007). The World Factbook. *Central Intelligence Agency.* Retrieved December 1, 2007, from: https://www.cia.gov/library/publications /the-world-factbook/ geos/us.html

Central Intelligence Agency. (2015). The World Factbook. *Central Intelligence Agency.* Retrieved May 15, 2016, from: https://www.cia.gov/library/publications/the - world-factbook/geos/ch.html

Central Intelligence Agency. (2016). The World Factbook. *Central Intelligence Agency.* Retrieved October 10, 2016, from: https://www.cia.gov/library/publications /the-world-factbook/geos/ch.html

Chen, M. W. (2016). Divorces up 63% in past decade. *China Daily.* Retrieved October 8, 2016, from: http://www.chinadaily.com.cn/china/2016-07/13/content _26067806.htm

Chen, X. L. (2015). China has the most serious gender imbalance in the world. *Sina Finance.* Retrieved November 28, 2016, from: http://finance.sina.com.cn/china /20150211/081121526750.shtml

China Daily. (2013). Chinese buyers pay more for Audi, BMW, Mercedes. *China Daily.* Retrieved November 27, 2016, from: http://www.chinadaily.com.cn /busi-ness/motoring/2013-08/28/content_16927605_2.htm

China Highlights. (2014). An introduction to China's largest cities. *China Highlights.* Retrieved October 30, 2016, from: http://www.chinahighlights.com/travel guide/top-large-cities.htm

China today.com. (2011). China Population Statistics and Related Information. *Chinatoday.com.* Retrieved December 2, 2016, from: http://www.chinatoday .com/data/china.population.htm

Clarke, A. (2015). See How the One-Child Policy Changed China. *National Geographic.com.* Retrieved November 27, 2016, from: http://news.national geo-graphic.com/2015/11/151113- datapoints-china-one-child-policy/

Cohn, D., & Caumont, A. (2014). 7 key findings about stay-at-home moms. *Pew Research Center.* Retrieved March 18, 2016, from: http://www.pewresearch .org/fact-tank/2014/04/08/7-key-findings-about-stay-at-home-moms/

Cohn, D., & Taylor, P. (2010). Baby Boomers Approach 65 – Glumly. *Pew Research Center.* Retrieved October 5, 2016, from: http://www.pewsocialtrends.org/2010 /12/20/baby-boomers-approach-65-glumly/

Colby, S. L., & Ortman, J. (2014). The baby boom cohort in the United States: 2012 to 2060. *U.S. Census Bureau.* Retrieved October 7, 2016, from: https://www.census .gov/prod/2014pubs/p25-1141.pdf

Cooley, C. H. (1964; orig. 1902). *Human nature and the social order.* New York: Schochen Books.

Cooley, C. H. (1909). *Social organization.* New York: Schochen Books.

Copeland, L. (2014). Life expectancy in the USA hits a record high. *USA Today.* Retrieved October 8, 2016, from: http://www.usatoday.com/story/news/nation /2014/10/08/us-life-expectancy-hits-record-high/16874039/

Durkheim, E. (1965; orig. 1915). *The elementary forms of religious life.* New York: The Free Press.

Durkheim, E. (1964; orig. 1893). *The division of labor in society.* New York: The Free Press.

Fisher, A. (2015). "Baby Boomers slowly growing more comfortable with retire-ment." *Fortune.* Retrieved October 1, 2016, from: http://fortune.com/2015/02 /18/baby-boomers-retirement

Fu, J. (2015). China's population to peak in 2025. *China Daily.* Retrieved March 18, 2016, from: http://www.thejakartapost.com/news/2015/10/07/chinas-population - peak-2025.html

Geiger, J. (2011). Rep. Eric Cantor says 10,000 baby boomers a day are becoming eligible for benefits. Politufact Virginia. Received March 23, 1017, from www .politifact.com/virginia/statements/2011/may/04/eric-cantor/rep-eric-cantor-says-10000-baby-boomers-day-are-be/

Gillespie, P. (2015). Dow plunges 531 points. *CNN Money.* Retrieved September 29, 2016, from: http://money.cnn.com/2015/08/21/investing/stocks-market-lookahead -august-21/

Goffman, E. H. (1959). *The presentation of self in everyday life.* Garden City, New York: Anchor Books.

Hartzell, M. (2015). How many cities are there in China? *Quora.* Retrieved October 18, 2016, from: https://www.quora.com/How-many-cities-are-there-in-China

Hellmich, N. (2010). Baby boomers by the numbers: Census reveals trends. *US Today*. Retrieved September 20, 2016, from: http://usatoday30.usatoday.com /news/nation/census/2009-11-10- topblline10_ST_N.htm

Hiirschi, T. (1969). *Causes of delinquency*. Berkeley: University of California Press.

Huang, Y. Z. (2013), Population aging in China: A mixed blessing. *The Diplomar*. Retrieved March 20, 2016, from: http://thediplomat.com/2013/11/population-aging-in-china-a-mixed-blessing/

Infoplease. (2014). Top 50 cities in the U.S. by population and rank. *Inforplease*. Retrieved March 20, 2016, from: http://www.infoplease.com/ipa/a0763098 .html

Infoplease. (2014). Women's earnings as a percentage of men's, 1951–2013. *Inforplease*. Retrieved November 4, 2016, from: http://www.infoplease.com /ipa/A0193820.html

Kiersz, A., & Kane, L. (2015). Here's what you have to earn to be considered middle class in the 50 biggest US cities. *Business Insider*. Retrieved October 30, 2016, from: http://www.businessinsider.com/what-middle-class-means-in-50-major-us-cities-2015-4

Kochhar, R. (2014). 10 projections for the global population in 2050. *Pew Research Center*. Retrieved October 23, 2016, from: http://www.pewresearch.org/fact-tank /2014/02/03/10-projections-for-the-global-population-in-2050/

Lemert, E. (1972). *Human deviance, social problems, and social control* (2nd ed.). Englewood Cliffs, NJ: Prentice Hall.

Li, Y. & Smither, L. (2015). As baby boomers age, fewer families have children under 18 at home. *Journal of Healthy Aging, 4*(2): 1–7. Retrieved March 26, 2016, from: http://www.har-journal.com/wp-content/uploads/2015/02/HAR11-0630 .pdf

Long, H. (2015). The stock market drop...by the numbers. *CNN Money*. Retrieved October 13, 2016, from: http://money.cnn.com/2015/08/24/investing/stocks-market-crash-by-the-numbers/

Malthus, T. R. (1926; orig. 1798). *First essay on population 1798*. London: Macmillan.

Marx, K. (1964; orig. 1848). *Karl Marx: Selected writing in sociology and social philosophy*. T.B. Bottomore Trans. New York: McGraw-Hill.

McEwen, W. (2011). The People's Republic of wireless. *Gallup*. Retrieved November 23, 2016, from: http://www.gallup.com/businessjournal/145520 /article-2011.aspx

Mead, G. H. (1962; orig. 1934). *Mind, self, and society*. Charles W. Morris, ed. Chicago: University of Chicago Press.

Mead, G. H. (C. W. Morris ed.), (1934). *Mind, self, and society from the standpoint of a social behaviorist*. University of Chicago Press, Chicago.

Merton, R. K. (1967). Manifest and latent functions. In *On theoretical sociology*. New York: Free Press.

Merton, R. K. (1968). *Social theory and social structure*. New York: Free Press.

Mills, W. (1959). *Sociological imagination*. Oxford University press. Retrieved December 2, 2016, from: http://www2.widener.edu/~spe0001/105Web /105WebRead/105webreadings/Sociological-Imagination.pdf

Moore, M. (2013). China's ageing population: 100-year waiting list for Beijing nursing home. *The Telegraph.* Retrieved October 29, 2016, from: http://www.telegraph .co.uk/news/worldnews/asia/china/9805834/Chinas-ageing-population-100-year-waiting-list-for-Beijing-nursing-home.html

National Bureau of Statistics of the People's Republic of China. (2009). Report No. 5: a modest increase in the total population structure significantly improved. *National Bureau of Statistics of the People's Republic of China.* Retrieved December 1, 2016, from: http://www.stats.gov.cn/ztjc/ztfx/qzxzgcl60zn/200909/t2009 0911_68637.html

Newsique. (2007). Officers faulted in Iraq mission that left 3 troops dead. *Newsique.* Retrieved May 17, 2007, from: http://www.newsique.com/conflicts/officers-faulted-in-iraq-mission/

Nugent, H. (2012). Suicide on the rise among older men. *The Guardian.* Retrieved October 27, 2016, from: https://www.theguardian.com/society/2012/jul/15 /suicide-rise-older-men

O'Brien, S. A. (2015). 78 cents on the dollar: The facts about the gender wage gap. *CNN Money.* Retrieved November 5, 2016, from: http://money.cnn.com /2015/04/13/news/economy/equal-pay-day-2015/

Ortman, J. M., Velkoff, V. A., & Hogan, H. (2014). An aging nation: The older population in the United States. *U.S. Census Bureau.* Retrieved March 18, 2016, from: https://www.census.gov/prod/2014pubs/p25-1140.pdf

Perez, B, (2015). China has more smartphone users than US, Braizil, and Indonesia combined, *Business Insider.* Retrieved October 9, 2016, from: http://www .businessinsider.com/china-has-more-smartphone-users-than-us-brazil-and-indonesia-combined-2015-7

Pew Research Center. (2014). Mobile Technology Fact Sheet. *Pew Research Center.* Retrieved October 29, 2016, from: http://www.pewinternet.org/fact-sheets /mobile-technology-fact-sheet/

Phillips, T. (2015). China ends one-child policy after 35 years. *The Guardian.* Retrieved October 20, 2016, from: https://www.theguardian.com/world/2015 /oct/29/china-abandons-one-child-policy

Piaget, J. (1954). *The construction of reality in the child.* New York: Basic Books.

Potts, M. (2006), China's one-child policy. *British Medical Journal, 333*(7564): 361–362. Retrieved October 2, 2016, from: https://www.ncbi.nlm.nih.gov/pmc /articles/PMC1550444/

Rainie, L. & Cohn, D. (2014). Census: Computer ownership, internet connection varies widely across U.S. *Pew Research Center.* Retrieved October 23, 2016, from: http://www.pewresearch.org/fact-tank/2014/09/19/census-computer-ownership -internet-connection-varies-widely-across-u-s/

Rizer, G. (1993). The "McDonaldization" of Society. *The Journal of American Culture, 6,* 100–107.

Robbins, K., & Turner, M. (2002). United States: Popular, pragmatic and problematic. In J. Katz & M. Aakus (Eds.), *Perpetual contact: Mobile communication, private talk, public performance.* Cambridge, England: Cambridge University Press.

Retrieved May 17, 2007, from: https://www.questia.com/library/105066057/perpetual-contact-mobile-communication-private

Rosenberg, M. (2014). Baby boom: The population baby boom of 1946–1964 in the United States. *About education.* Retrieved October 17, 2016, from: http://geography.about.com/od/populationgeography/a/babyboom.htm

Schwartländer, B., & Fong, G. T. (2015). 1.34 billion reasons to say 'No smoking'. *World Health Organization.* Retrieved December 14, 2016, from: http://www.wpro.who.int/china/mediacentre/releases/2015/2015101902/en/

Shaw, C. & McKay, H. (1942). *Juvenile delinquency and urban areas.* Chicago: University of Chicago Press.

Sina.com. (2016). The people of post-95's favorite luxury brand is . . . *Sina.com.* Retrieved December 10, 2016, from: http://finance.sina.com.cn/roll/2016-11-07/doc-ifxxnffr6983417.shtml

Social Security Administration. (2016). Fast facts & figures about Social Security, 2016. *Social Security Administration.* Retrieved October 20, 2016, from: https://www.ssa.gov/policy/docs/chartbooks/fast_facts/2016/fast_facts16.pdf

Statista. (2016). Number of mobile cell phone subscriptions in China from August 2015 to August 2016. *Statista.* Retrieved October 18, 2016, from: https://www.statista.com/statistics/278204/china-mobile-users-by-month/

Swanson, A. (2016). Who gets divorced in America, in 7 charts. *The Washington Post.* Retrieved November 6, 2016., from: https://www.washingtonpost.com/news/wonk/wp/2016/04/06/who-gets-divorced-in-america-in-7-charts/

Timm, L. (2015). 'Empty Nesters': China's Graying Population Up Close. *Epoch Times.* Retrieved September 18, 2016, from; http://www.theepochtimes.com/n3/1895515-empty-nesters-chinas-greying-population-up-close/

Tönnies, F. (1963; orig. 1887). *Community and society (Gemeinschaft und Gesellschaft).* New York: Harper & Row.

U. S. Census Bureau. (2014). Facts for Features: Hispanic Heritage Month 2014: Sept. 15–Oct. 15. *U.S. Census Bureau.* Retrieved October 7, 2016, from: http://www.census.gov/newsroom/facts-for-features/2014/cb14-ff22.html

The United Sates Department of Commerce. (2013). New Census Bureau Interactive Map Shows Languages Spoken in America. *The United Sates Department of Commerce.* Retrieved October 23, 2016, from: http://2010-2014.commerce.gov/blog/2013/08/06/new-census-bureau-interactive-map-shows-languages-spoken-america.html

Wang, X. D. (2016). Elder care seen as a key concern in a graying nation. *China Daily Asia.* Retrieved November 2, 2016, from: http://www.chinadailyasia.com/chinafocus/2016-03/02/content_15393019.html

Welitzkin, P. (2015). China adds one million new millionaires: Report. *China Daily USA.* Retrieved October 23, 2016, from: http://www.chinadaily.com.cn/world/2015-06/16/content_21016323.htm

World Bank. (2014). Adolescent fertility rate (births per 1,000 women ages 15–19). *United Nations Population Division.* Retrieved October 20, 2016, from: http://data.worldbank.org/indicator/SP.ADO.TFRT

Wong, B. (2014). The truth about the divorce rate is surprisingly optimistic. *The Huffington Post.* Retrieved October 10, 2016, from: http://www.huffingtonpost .com/2014/12/02/divorce-rate-declining-_n_6256956.html

Yan, F., & Jones, T. (2010). McDonald's to double China restaurants by 2013. *Business News.* Retrieved October 23, 2016, from: http://www.reuters.com/article/ us-mcdonalds-china-idUSTRE6BE0VJ20101215

Yao, Y., & Yang, J. (2015). Divorce rate in China increases by 3.9 per cent. *The Telegraph.* Retrieved October 7, 2016, from: http://www.telegraph.co.uk/news /world/china-watch/society/divorce-rate-in-china/

Zhang, P. X. (2014). China's digital usage report 2013. *State Information Center.* Retrieved October 23, 2016, from: http://www.sic.gov.cn/index.htm

GLOSSARY OF KEY CONCEPTS

A

achieved status: a social standing that a person has to voluntarily work for and that represents the per-son's capability.

amalgamation: the intermarrying or interbreeding of different racial groups.

annihilation: exterminating another racial group by using violent behavior.

anticipatory socialization: the advanced education people receive, in order to prepare for a future desired position in their careers.

arithmetic progression: the numbers increase like so: 1, 2, 3, 4, 5, 6, 7, 8...

ascribed status: an involuntary social standing, that is given at birth or later in life.

assimilation: the procedure of a minority group increasingly changing their way of life in order to conform to the dominant culture.

C

caste system: a system of social stratification where people must remain in the social strata into which they are born.

charisma: a quality that certain individuals own and use to attract people as followers.

civil religion: a kind of religious allegiance that ties people together with the country they live in and the land they love.

class system: a system in which a person's hard work and success are emphasized.

closed stratification system: a social stratification system that does not permit a person to move between social strata.

community: people who live in an area as a group with a sense of belonging.

the concrete operational stage: the stage of child development where children will begin to use logic, but remain focused only on what they see in their daily lives.

conformity: people follow the rules of the society

collective behavior: a type of human action that is an unplanned action that people have when facing or having to work out uncertain circumstances.

control theory: deviance occurs because society does not have strong social control over people's abnormal behavior.

consequential religiosity: the connection between religious beliefs and an individual's daily activity.

correlation: those variables that are associated with each other and show meaningful relationships.

counterculture: a group of people who may share some aspects of the lifestyle but reject or disagree with part of the dominant culture in a society.

crime: a violation of social norms that has a connection to criminal laws.

crude birth rate: the number of babies born in a year in proportion with every 1,000 people.

crude death rate: the number of people who died compared with every 1,000 people in a given population.

cultural integration: the compatibility between different social elements in the process of cultural development.

cultural lag: an inconsistency between different social components due to different rates of cultural development.

cultural relativism: respecting other cultures and not using one's own culture as a reference when judging other cultures.

cultural transmission theory: people have deviant behavior because they have learned it from other people through social interaction.

culture: people's values, norms, beliefs, social activities, and material life.

culture shock: the shock and confusion that accompanies a person's experiences in new surroundings.

D

demography: the scientific study of human population.

demographic transition theory: a pattern of population growth that relates to different levels of technological development.

dependency ratio: an index calculated to indicate the economic load on workers.

dependent variable: the variable that is affected and then changed.

deterrence: the effort to detect or reduce criminal activities through punishment.

deviance: some kind of behavior or attitude that differs from the social norms and values in a society.

diffusion: spreading different cultural factors from one country to other regions or societies.

discovery: recognizing something that previously existed.

discrimination: treating distinctive racial groups differently.

dramaturgical analysis: how people change their behavior based on the situation they are in and that they try to exhibit certain behaviors to make a positive impression.

E

endogamy: a married couple that belongs to the same social group.

ethnicity: a cultural inheritance, which is distributed by a group of people.

ethnocentrism: thinking that one's own culture is better than other's.

exogamy: a married couple that belongs to different social groups.

experiential religiosity: an individual's emotional connection with a religious belief.

experiment: a research method that tests the logic or correlations between cause and effect variables.

expressive leadership: a leadership that focuses on the interests and benefits of the collective group.

extended family: one or two parents, children, and other kinships such as relatives.

F

family: a group of two or more people who are together because of their connection by blood, marriage, or adoption.

feminism: an organized social activity to fight against patriarchy and sexism and battle for females' rights.

fertility: the number of babies born in a population.

folkways: norms that may be considered abnormal, but may be accepted.

the formal operational stage: the stage of child development where children start to use conceptual thinking and alternatives to imagine issues surrounding them.

G

Gemeinschaft: a community characterized by a well-built social cohesion and common identity, where people's interaction is based upon personal relationships and traditions.

gender: a cultural definition of behaviors or attitudes attached to each sex.

gender identity: how people think of themselves based on their expected attitudes and behaviors according to the cultural definitions of each sex in a society.

gender roles: the cultural definition when people in each sex are expected to have different attitudes and roles.

gender stratification: the unequal social statuses between men and women in the social stratification system.

generalized other: keeping social cultural values and norms within the mind.

geometric progression: the numbers will increase like so: 2, 4, 8, 16, 32, 64, 128 . . .

Gesellschaft: an association characterized by a fragile social cohesion, with people's interactions based upon impersonal relationships that result from different cultures and a detachment from traditional concerns.

H

hypothesis: the relationships between independent and dependent variables.

I

incapacitation: restrictions on the freedom of the lawbreakers in order to prevent them from participating in any further criminal activity.

ideological religiosity: the extent to which an individual obeys the religious doctrine of their beliefs.

independent variable: the variable that causes any changes.

industrialization: a process where an increase in technology is used instead of manual labor.

infant mortality rate: the number of babies who died in the first year of life with every 1,000 live births in a given year.

innovation: the goal is socially acceptable, but the means to reach the goal is undesirable.

instrumental leadership: a leadership of the group that focuses on getting the job completed.

intergenerational mobility: a change in social positions that took place over generations within the family.

intellectual religiosity: an individual's knowledge about their particular religious' beliefs.

intra-generational mobility: a change in social position within an individual's own lifetime.

invention: using prior knowledge to develop something new.

L

labeling theory: deviant behavior, like conformity, is labeled by other people and society.

language: a group of symbols, which allows the members of a society to communicate.

latent functions: the consequences that are not planned or intended by people in the society.

liberal feminism: people accept the patriarchy society as it is, but want to make sure that females have the same rights as males.

life expectancy: how long, on average, a person is expected to live.

looking-glass self: a conception of self that is obtained from the response of others.

M

macro level: an analysis of society on large-scale societal levels.

manifest functions: as the consequences that are intended for people to carry out within the society.

marriage: a social commitment between two people, approved by society, who are together to love, care for each other, and share their economic possessions.

mass media: channels of communication that can reach a large number of people.

master status: a status that significantly influences a person's life.

material culture: the substantial objects that people may use for daily life.

matriarchy: a form of a social association where females govern males.

matrilocality: a type of residency where a couple lives in the same house or near the wife's family.

mechanical solidarity: social cohesion in preindustrial societies based upon shared social activities, beliefs, and traditional values.

micro level: an analysis of society from small-scale social patterns.

migration: people who move in or out of a particular area.

minority group: people are categorized by their physical being and sometimes, cultural characteristics, which put these individuals at a social disadvantage.

modernization: the process in which countries are transformed from agricultural to industrialized societies.

modernization theory: less developed countries changing/developing through industrialization and becoming similar to developed countries.

monogamy: a marriage between two people.

mores: norms that will be considered abnormal and cannot be accepted.

mortality: the number of people who died in a year in a given population.

N

nature: a human being's biological instinct.

neolocality: a type of residency where a married couple lives apart from their parents on both sides.

net migration: the variation in the number of people who move in and out of a particular area, such as from one state, or a county, or one country to another.

network: people who have different interdependent relationships but may not have any direct social interaction.

nonmaterial culture: comprised of beliefs, values, and behavior.

norms: guidelines that govern people's actions within a given culture.

nuclear family: normally involves one or two parents and the children in a family.

nurture: people's behavior as a result of learning within a social environment.

O

open stratification system: a social stratification system that allows people to move between social strata.

organic solidarity: social cohesion of industrialized societies based upon interdependence among people with a specialized division of labor.

P

participant observation: a relatively long-term, planned, intensive observation of a particular group of people, an individual person, or event that happened in the natural world.

patriarchy: a form of a social association where males govern females.

patrilocality: a type of residency where a couple lives in the same house or near the husband's family.

peer group: a group of people with the same interests or who share some characteristics, such as age.

pluralism: a situation in which different racial and ethnic groups will maintain their own traditions, beliefs, values, and identities.

positive checks: disease and war to reduce the number of people.

polyandry: a type of marriage that involves one woman and more than one man.

polygamy: a marriage between three or more people.

polygyny: a type of marriage that involves one man and more than one woman.

population: the entire population which shares the same research interests.

prejudice: a speculative overview of people who are categorized, based upon their physical and cultural characteristics.

preventive checks: the use of artificial means of birth control, sexual abstinence, and delaying marriage to control the increase in the number of population.

the preoperational stage: the stage of child development in which language is starting to be used.

primary deviance: temporary or minor deviant behavior and can be withdrawn.

primary group: the interaction of a group of people that is intimate, personal, and leads to long-lasting relationships.

public opinion: people's different attitudes toward social issues.

pull factors: the situations that persuade people to move into an area: better climate, better living standards, or more educational opportunities.

push factors: the situations which persuade people to move out; for example, bad living standards or lack of job opportunities.

R

race: a group of people who have the same biological characteristics from one generation to another.

racism: beliefs that attempt to justify different racial groups in a socially disadvantaged status.

radical feminism: agrees with the ideas to look for social equality between males and females, but still believe it is not doing enough.

rebellion: people in this group are called rebels, who may have the ability to reach a goal, such as to become rich. People in the category oppose the social system in their society and the goal to become wealthy, the existing social norms, as well as to use the means to achieve the goal.

reference group: a group that serves as the guiding principle for individuals to make decisions.

rehabilitation: to reeducate lawbreakers and avoid criminal activities.

religion: people's beliefs and practices that are generally based on morality and supernatural power.

religiosity: how important religious beliefs are in their lives.

retreatism: people who belong to this category tend to have various personal problems, such as drugs or alcohol.

retribution: punishment is given in repayment.

ritual: the ceremonial forms of conduction, which are rules that govern people's behavior when practicing their religious belief.

ritualism: people who have no ability to achieve their goal. So after questioning themselves, they simply abandon it.

ritualistic religiosity: measured by whether an individual person will practice the ritual behavior. such as how often they attend religious services as well as how often they pray.

role: an expected behavioral pattern related to a person's socially defined status.

role conflict: an inconsistency between roles with two or more statuses.

role set: a person's single social status, associated with several roles.

role strain: the conflict between roles with a single status.

S

sample: a small proportion selected to represent the population of the study.

secondary analysis: uses existing sources for the data collection, which means that the data was collected by other people.

secondary deviance: continual or persistent deviant behavior as a career or a lifestyle.

secondary group: the interaction of a group of people that is transitory, less personal, and leads to distant relationships.

secularization: how the importance of religious beliefs has had a tendency to decline.

segregation: the separation, either physically or socially, of different categories of people.

the sensorimotor stage: the stage of child development in which children through physical contact with others to experience the world.

sex: categorizing people as male and female, based on biology.

sex ratio: the number of males compared with every 100 females in a given population.

sexism: the belief that one sex is innately superior or inferior to another.

sexual orientation: a method that people practice to attain sexual satisfaction.

social change: a transformation of people's behavior, attitudes, and thoughts over time in a society.

social conflict perspective: the unequal relationships between social groups that cause tension or conflict between the groups and eventually leads to a social change.

social cohesion: religion used to unite people with identical social values and norms.

social control: religion used to manipulate society through shared values and norms.

social dysfunctions: the negative consequences that affect society as a whole.

social function: the result of the usage of the social system.

social group: two or more people sharing some bond or relations or common identity.

social inequality: the uneven distribution of wealth, status, and power in a society.

social mobility: the movement of an individual's social position within a stratification system.

social movement: a group of people joining together to support or defend against certain social changes.

social stratification: a social system in which people are divided into different social strata (layers) or classes.

social structure: the framework of a social system.

socialist feminism: links male-ruled society to the formation of social classes and the capitalist economic system.

socialization: a lifelong process based on the learning of social values, beliefs, norms, and other patterns of social behavior through individual interactions with others.

society: a group of people who interact with one another and create a culture within a defined territory.

socioeconomic status: a combination of variables used to measure different dimensions of social inequality, such as education, occupation, income, and other social factors.

sociology: the logical study of human society and people's social activities, their interactions, and relationships with others.

status: an individual's social standing in a society.

status set: the statuses a person has in a given period of time.

stereotype: a generalization on a category of people that persists even in the face of opposing facts.

stigma: an influential mark, which may negatively change a person's ego.
structural-functional perspective: society is viewed as a system of many different parts that work together to generate stability.
structural social mobility: social mobility that is not based on individual effort or achievement; but instead, a result of social changes in society as a whole.
structural strain theory: people exhibit deviant behavior because of social pressure.
subculture: a group of people, whom even though they may have different lifestyles, all follow aspects of the dominant culture in a society.
survey: a research method designed to collect data from individual respondents by using questionnaires.
symbolic interaction perspective: the view of society stemming from individuals' everyday interactions with other people in various environments.
symbols: gestures, words, or signs that have had meaning attached to them by members of a society.

T

theory: a statement describing the relationships among different concepts.
theoretical perspectives: a basic rationalization of society and what should be emphasized and used to explain a certain social phenomenon.
totem: an object from the natural world that has been imbued with sacred power.

U

urban: Areas in which people live with little to no agricultural activities.
urbanism: the urban lifestyle that accompanies living in urban areas.
urbanization: a process through which the number of people living in urban areas increases.

V

value free: the nonappearance of any personal values while doing research.
values: social standards which members of a society use as a framework for their daily lives.
variable: any concept that is valued differently in different situations.

W

world system theory: industrialization as not just being a key in the process of modernization, but that it is necessary to evaluate a country's economic position in the world system.

Z

zero population growth: demographic growth to the point where population size does not change as a consequence of the mixture of births, deaths, and in-and-out migration.

INDEX

CHARLES C THOMAS · PUBLISHER,